The European Union and British Democracy

The European Union and British Democracy

Towards Convergence

Janet Mather
Lecturer
Department of Politics and Philosophy
The Manchester Metropolitan University

First published in Great Britain 2000 by
MACMILLAN PRESS LTD
Houndmills, Basingstoke, Hampshire RG21 6XS and London
Companies and representatives throughout the world

A catalogue record for this book is available from the British Library.

ISBN 0–333–77648–8

First published in the United States of America 2000 by
ST. MARTIN'S PRESS, LLC,
Scholarly and Reference Division,
175 Fifth Avenue, New York, N.Y. 10010

ISBN 0–312–23577–1

Library of Congress Cataloging-in-Publication Data
Mather, Janet, 1949–
    The European Union and British democracy : towards convergence / Janet
Mather.
        p.   cm.
    Includes bibliographical references and index.
    ISBN 0–312–23577–1 (cloth)
    1. Democracy—Great Britain. 2. European Union. 3. European Union—Great
Britain. I. Title.

JN900 .M37 2000
320.94—dc21
                                                                    00–033347

This book is printed on paper suitable for recycling and made from fully managed and sustained
forest sources.

10   9   8   7   6   5   4   3   2   1
09   08   07   06   05   04   03   02   01   00

Printed and bound in Great Britain by
Antony Rowe Ltd, Chippenham, Wiltshire

To my parents
and to Bob, Lisa, Annabel and Steve
– three-dimensional beings in a multi-level Union.

Also in memory of Mark
who added his own dimension during
the short time he was with us.

CONTENTS

ACKNOWLEDGEMENTS

I wish to put on record my appreciation of the support I have received from the academic staff of Manchester Metropolitan University's Department of Politics and Philosophy, who have allowed me to present work at different stages, and whose constructive comments have been both encouraging and useful. In particular I am grateful to Clive Archer, Peter Barberis, John Gibbons and Neill Nugent.

The areas covered by this book are numerous, and it is impossible to acknowledge the assistance given by everyone. However, I should like to thank those members of the Committee of the Regions and members and officers of Congleton Borough Council and Vale Royal Borough Council who assisted my research. Thanks are due in particular to Bob Birchenough of Congleton Borough Council and David Owen of Vale Royal Borough Council, Cllr Mrs Helen Scholey, Leader of the Labour Group of Congleton Borough Council, and Cllr Arthur Neil, Leader of Vale Royal Borough Council. I am also indebted to those MEPs who granted me an interview. Brian Simpson, MEP and Lord Harrison of Chester (previously MEP for Cheshire West and Merseyside) have also generously acted as informal consultants in relation to the European Parliament.

Finally, I want to express my gratitude towards my family – my husband, Bob Mather, and my daughters, Lisa Mather and Annabel Roberts. Lisa has given me practical assistance with my research, acting as technician, information officer and interpreter. All of my family have had to put up with a lot of soul searching and occasional despair from me, as well as having to endure listening to arguments concerning a field which was of only limited interest to them. I have to record that I have only ever received support and encouragement from each of them.

LIST OF FIGURES

LIST OF ABBREVIATIONS

ACC	Association of County Councils
ADC	Association of District Councils
AER	Assembly of European Regions
AMA	Association of Metropolitan Authorities
CAP	Common Agricultural Policy
CBC	Congleton Borough Council
CCC	Cheshire County Council
CEMR	Conference of European Municipalities and Regions
COPA	Committee of Professional Agricultural Associations of the European Community
CoR	Committee of the Regions
COREPER	Committee of Permanent Representatives
CSF	Community Support Framework
DETR	Department of the Environment, Transport and the Regions
DfEE	Department for Employment and Education
DG	Directorate General
DTI	Department of Trade and Industry
EAGGF	European Agricultural Guidance and Guarantee Fund
EC	European Community
ECB	European Central Bank
ECJ	European Court of Justice
ECOSOC	Economic and Social Committee
EEC	European Economic Community
E/EDO	European and Economic Development Officer
EIB	European Investment Bank
EIC	European Information Centre
EICNW	Euro Information Centre North West
ELDR	European Liberal Democratic and Reformist Party
EMU	Economic and Monetary Union
EP	European Parliament
EPP	European Peoples' Party
EPP/ED	European Peoples' Party/European Democrats
ERDF	European Regional Development Fund
ESF	European Social Fund
EU	European Union
GMLC	Greater Manchester, Lancashire and Cheshire (designated area with Objective Two status)
IAC	Institutional Affairs Committee

IGC	Inter Governmental Conference
IRI	International Research Institute
LGA	Local Government Association
LGIB	Local Government International Bureau
LIPAM	Liverpool Institute of Public Administration and Management
MAFF	Ministry of Agriculture, Fisheries and Food
MEP	Member of the European Parliament
MORI	Market and Opinion Research Institute
MP	Member of Parliament
NFU	National Farmers' Union
NEC	National Executive Committee of the Labour Party
NWRA	North West Regional Association
PAC	Political Affairs Committee (of the EP)
PES	Party of European Socialists
PR	Proportional Representation
QMV	Qualified Majority Voting
RDA	Regional Development Agency
RPA	Representation of the People Act
RPC	Regional Policy and Relations with Local Authorities Committee (of the EP)
SCEALA	Standing Conference of East Anglian Local Authorities
SDLP	Social Democratic and Labour Party
SEA	Single European Act [1987]
SERPLAN	South East Regional Planning Conference
SRB	Single Regeneration Budget
SMSP	Single member, simple plurality (electoral system)
SPD	Single Programming Document
STV	Single transferable vote (electoral system)
TEC	Treaties establishing the European Communities
TECs	Training and Enterprise Councils
TEU	Treaty on European Union [1992]
ToA	Treaty of Amsterdam [1997]
TTWA	Travel To Work Area
TUPE	Transfer of Undertakings for Public Employees
UK	United Kingdom of Great Britain and Northern Ireland
UKREP	UK Permanent Representation (in Brussels)
VRBC	Vale Royal Borough Council

INTRODUCTION

The second half of the twentieth century has been significant for developments in governance. Nation states have never existed in isolation, especially in the western world, but the principal institutionalised groupings of nations have been largely post-1930s Depression and post-world war two phenomena. Most of these groupings have been formed and function among governments only. The International Monetary Fund [IMF] (1946); North Atlantic Treaty Alliance [NATO] (1949); the Council of Europe (1949); the Western European Union [WEU] (1955); European Free Trade Association [EFTA] (1960), the Organisation for Economic Co-operation & Development [OECD] (1961) and the World Trade Organisation [WTO] (1995), for example, involve no direct popular input[1]. Yet the decisions made within these organisations impinge upon the economic and/or social activities of the citizens of all participating nations. It is often noted that the globalisation of political and economic practices has reduced governmental autonomy. It is less frequently pointed out that it has diminished *popular* control within western "democracies" even more dramatically.

There is, however, an exception. The European Union [EU], whose forerunners were formed in 1951 (European Coal and Steel Community) and 1957 (European Economic Community and European Atomic Energy Community), has never been solely an *intergovernmental* grouping. From the beginning it has possessed *supranationalist* characteristics, which means that its members' obedience to its rules is obligatory, not optional. This was indicated by the establishment of a Court of Justice [ECJ] with the power to interpret Community law and to enforce its judgements. The supranationalist element also meant that from the start Community participants were uneasy about allowing governments alone and unsupervised to make decisions that were binding upon all member states. In practical terms it meant that a European Assembly, at first in a consultative capacity alone, joined the Council of Ministers and the High Authority (under the 1957 Treaty of Rome renamed the "European Commission") as one of the original three main institutions.

This overt supranationalism led to increasing "democracy" within the (then) European Community [EC] in form, if not necessarily in substance. Elected representation was procured when the European Assembly became

---

1   NATO, the Council of Europe and the WEU have consultative assemblies composed of appointed members of national parliaments.

officially reconstituted as a European Parliament[2] [EP] with fairly extensive and latterly almost decisive powers over both Council decision-making and Commission activities. Virtual (unelected) representation was also a feature of the evolving Community. There had been an Economic and Social Committee [ECOSOC] since the Treaty of Rome to represent corporatist interests. In 1995, this was joined by a Committee of the Regions [CoR], whose role was to represent sub-national government within the Union.

None of these developments have particularly impressed the people of the EU, however, and the most sceptical inhabitants of its fifteen member states appear to reside in the United Kingdom. One of the paradoxes resulting from the institution of the mechanisms intended to secure representation and some form of accountability is that they have increased popular demands for the traditional trappings of liberal democracy. For example, the relative openness of the EU's decision making processes (that is when compared to the way in which policies are formulated within the intergovernmental groupings of states), has attracted comment about a loss rather than a gain of popular control. The present EU is ill suited to conform to the popular notion of a modern democracy. It is too large and its organisation and policy processes are too complex for it to accord with general notions of liberal and accountable government. The outcome of this position is that in most people's minds, "Brussels" epitomises unpopular EU bureaucrats rather than unelected and largely unaccountable NATO personnel – although the capital of Belgium houses both institutions.

This book adopts a new perspective on the EU. Instead of judging the EU in accordance with liberal democratic *theory*, it examines how the EU has affected democratic *practice* in one of its member states. It does this by analysing what people, and in particular the people of Britain, derive from EU governance in terms of democratic participation. This involves taking a critical look at liberal democracy itself and also at the way in which it is manifested in the UK political system. It argues that a centralised state like the UK is not a particularly effective vehicle for liberal democracy and questions whether liberal democracy itself is necessarily synonymous with popular power.

To carry out this multi-faceted task, the book first considers democratic theory, and then moves to an empirical examination of the ways in which governance is practised in the UK and the EU. It demonstrates that no political developments occur in a straightforward fashion and changes sometimes result from intricate interactions among EU and member state

---

2   The first set of direct elections took place in 1979, although the Assembly had adopted the *name* "European Parliament" for itself in 1962.

participants. These can occur even when politicians and officials make decisions or institute policies without any intention of affecting constitutional practices.

Among EU academics the mass of macro-integration theories such as neo-functionalism, federalism and intergovernmentalism are giving way to micro-theories that attempt to interpret the way in which different policy areas are harmonising. This book assumes that understanding the integration of democratic practices requires the same kind of analysis, and that it cannot be understood as a single process.

The question that is implied throughout is: "may the UK's democratic practice be *enhanced* by means of its membership the European Union?" The EU is a factor, and likely to continue to be a factor, in the lives of the UK's subjects (the only "citizenship" from which the UK's population benefits is that derived from membership of the EU). It is arguably the most important single influence. Decisions made at the supranational level concerning harmonisation of trade, agricultural subsidies, the allocation of structural funds and the protection of the environment have wide implications for all EU residents. Large sections of the people are affected by EU policies such as working time directives, consumer protection or equality of opportunity. These measures are sometimes seen as confining, sometimes as liberating. They are more rarely viewed in the context of enhancing opportunities for democratic participation. The way in which the EU's decision makers formulate legislation in these areas may enable the UK's people and its sub- and non-governmental institutions, like those of the rest of the EU, to take part in framing policies of direct concern to them. On the face of it, this should represent a net gain in democratic practice.

The chapters that follow examine – and question – this supposition. Chapter One looks at the nature of democracy itself. It suggests that what is important about democracy is its *output* – what people gain from democracy – rather than what participants put into it (although the point is made that there are connections between input and outcomes). It argues that there are different kinds of benefits to be gained from democratic practice and that liberal representative democracy does not guarantee that all of them will be delivered. This enables the focus of attention to move from the assumption that democracy exists wherever government is directly elected by the people. The chapter then examines forms of representative democracy – arguing that whether or not people get what they want or need from elected government depends more upon how elected persons view the nature of their role than upon the system which put them into power. The last part of the chapter considers direct *participation* in government, including the participation of virtual, but impermanent and non-governmental, representatives. The main point is that direct democracy is a viable alternative to electing members of parliaments, and can improve prospects for acquiring better quality Sartori's [1987] "demo-benefits".

Chapter Two looks at the British state as it operated before 1997 and the election of a "New" Labour government. The anachronistic and sometimes irrational characteristics of the UK's institutions are examined. In particular the form of representation practised in the sovereign parliament is exposed as being essentially pre-democratic in character, depending upon the Burkeian notion of the representative as one who exercises his [*sic*] judgement on behalf of rather than in obedience to his constituents. It is argued, therefore, that the "unmodernised" constitution failed to meet the criteria for democracy set out in Chapter One. To add weight to this contention, the centralised nature of the UK state is demonstrated by means of a case study of pre-1997 local government. This examination demonstrates that no effective devolution of power was achieved or even contemplated by the central state during this century – and therefore options for effective sub-national participation in decision-making were not institutionalised. A flexible uncoded constitution is shown to be a poor vehicle for ensuring popular input.

Moving away from a study of the UK's governmental practices, Chapter Three focuses upon the EU. It notes that the main problem that the EU faces is the popular perception of illegitimacy. This is an issue for democracy. If people dislike and slight the EU, then the EU fails at the first democratic hurdle. Various answers to this dilemma are suggested in the chapter. The main response, which is provided by EU participants, member states' governments and some academics alike, depends upon the Parliament's role. If, the argument goes, the EP had enhanced powers, it would solve the problem. The next two Chapters examine this assertion in more detail, but Chapter Three suggests that to require the EP to carry the banner for democracy is rather a lot to demand from an institution that has not so far established itself within the hearts of the people – as demonstrated by increasingly low electoral turnouts. A second idea is introduced, to be developed in subsequent chapters: the EU may become popular inasmuch as it opens up opportunities for citizen participation. This could occur in several ways. The EU's principle of subsidiarity (decision-making at the lowest practicable level) may be applied to their home governments by the EU's member states. Or it may be that "multi-level" or "multi-sector" governance will provide a *de facto* democratic enhancement to national decision-making. It may also be that because the EU consists of many states, best democratic practices from each will become the norm for them all. People will become familiar with Scandinavian traditions of transparency, for example, and will demand the same from their own governments (as well as from the EU). Or a backward government (perhaps the UK's) will realise that to become or to remain a significant player in EU affairs, it will need to sharpen up its own governmental and constitutional practices.

The remainder of the book analyses these prospects. Chapters Four and Five consider the EU's version of representative democracy. The EP's evolving capacity is looked at in Chapter Four. An examination of the formal powers of the EP is followed by three case-studies which demonstrate that the EP is becoming increasingly able to exercise its powers over decision-making and over the EU's other policy-making institutions. The EP, at the end of the century, remains a junior partner, but its competence is not negligible. Chapter Five addresses the question of democracy, asking whether the empowered EP is a deliverer of popular ends and wishes. It subjects the EP to a similar examination as that conducted on the UK parliament and draws similar conclusions. The EP is shown to function as a representative institution in much the same way as the UK parliament, relying upon the pre-democratic Burkeian notion of "judgmental representation".

If the EP offers no immediate prospects for democratic enhancements, the second set of ideas – of the EU enabling extended popular participation – may have outcomes that are more positive. Chapter Six looks at options for increased popular participation. The first part of the chapter is devoted to an analysis of the meaning of "subsidiarity" as it applies to the EU. The conclusion here is that it has no practical legal implications for devolution *within* the EU's member states, because the principle itself is interpreted only in accordance with states' rights. To require a member state to apply the standard within its home government would itself be a violation of the principle. The second part of the chapter examines the CoR to see whether it is a means of empowering sub-national government within the EU. The argument here is that a CoR with enhanced competence and close links with sub-national authorities could achieve *de facto* subsidiarity. If the outcome were that at least some decisions were made "as closely as possible to the citizen" [Article A, TEU], this would represent a gain for democracy. The conclusion is a hung verdict. The CoR is not sufficiently powerful itself at present, and it may never become so. Yet the institution of a regional and local government committee at EU level suggests that the EU's primary decision makers are concerned about the views of sub-national government, and are ready to take an open and pragmatic approach to policy making. The European Commission, which apparently enjoys a positive relationship with the CoR, has a higher regard for sub-national government than the UK government had, at least prior to the election of the 1997 Labour administration.

The notion of an open approach to decision-making procedures is examined and expanded in Chapter Seven. Means of engaging non-national government participants through the EU are looked at in general terms, applying the types of popular involvement originally set out in Chapter One. This approach is followed by a brief study of the effect of interest group participation at EU level, as instanced by the experience of the UK's environmental lobby. The chapter concludes that there is some evidence of "multi-sector" governance within the EU, and that this, by means of involving "only the people affected", offers an enhancement of one form of popular participation.

"Multi-*sector*" governance has been deliberately distinguished from "multi-*level*" governance on the grounds that the first is extra-governmental (interest groups do not normally seek governmental office), whilst the second involves the participation of governmental (albeit at a lower tier) participants. The implementation of multi-level governance, which forms the basis for Chapter Eight, equates to the experience of government "closer to" the people. This kind of government, it is argued, may also represent specific interests of territorial diversity as opposed to those of a centralised government. Here the activities of the EU can be shown to have had a positive effect upon local democracy, although the amount of control that has descended to the UK's regional and local levels by means of the EU's practices is not, as yet, remarkable. The chapter demonstrates this by looking at examples of finance-related EU policy practices in a case study of processing EU Objective Two funding in north west Cheshire. Finally, the Chapter considers the non-financial impact that the EU has had upon local government. The experience of two Cheshire district councils' interactions with the EU shows that options for increased standing and involvement for the least significant of British local governments are available through the Union, although they are not always used to the best advantage.

Chapter Nine expands the focus of the impact of the EU by providing what is in part a case study of recent developments within the UK state. It is not claimed that the constitutional initiatives introduced by the 1997 Labour government led by Tony Blair are entirely dependent upon the examples set by the EU. Yet Blair himself claims that he wants to set Britain "at the heart of Europe", and it is pointed out that he needs to do more than play lip service to the EU's constitutional culture before this can be achieved successfully. It is also shown that the majority of the constitutional reforms set in motion have tended to bring the UK into line with the rest of Europe. They have also had a tendency to enhance democratic rights (although many of the reforms have fallen short of expectations). Hence the UK embraces the European Charter of Human Rights; there will be a Freedom of Information Act; there will not be a hereditary upper parliamentary chamber and there have been movements towards electoral reform involving proportional representation. Devolution has also assumed some prominence, although there are few signs that the government wishes to empower local government. For this, local councils may need to continue to depend upon the EU.

The conclusion of this book is that however the EU is popularly perceived at present, it presents opportunities for enhancement to democratic practices in the UK. The constitutional and governmental agenda has opened out, and, because the UK is now governed alongside and *in tandem* with another fourteen western European states, it is impossible to operate without taking this into account. Integration is generally thought to be a process mainly involving political and economic issues, but the EU's *acquis communautaire* is more wide reaching than that[3]. The EU requires its member states to conform to the general ethos of constitutional practices. Applicant states need to adapt their laws to enable their institutions to accord with EU principles of liberal democracy[4]. In reality, it is unsurprising that a more deeply entrenched conformity is evolving as the member states form "ever closer union" with each other. Democratic enhancement is likely to be one of the benefits gained in the long run.

3 This was demonstrated by the EU's initial reaction to the involvement of the far right in Austrian government

4 for example, see the Commission Communication *Com Docs* (97)2001 final (15.7.97) to (97)2010 final (15.7.97) published in 1997 that examine the progress towards EU membership made by the ten applicant states.

CHAPTER ONE

WHY DEMOCRACY?

This chapter tries to establish what democracy is *for*. To do this, it first looks at forms of democracy and its manifestations and relates the question of participation to the basis of democracy itself. It is argued that whilst democratic input is important for its own sake, democracy is as much about the *outcomes* of democratic practice – but outcomes and inputs are related to each other. Hence, this chapter takes a utilitarian approach to the practice of democracy.

1. The origins of democracy

An examination of the emergence and development of both participatory and representative democracy shows that it was not democracy that was intended by the originators of the governmental systems. It also indicates that, despite this, widespread input into government, once constituted, has been sufficiently popular in the common sense of the term to make it difficult for élites to re-establish control.

1.1. *Participatory democracy*

The best known of the earliest democracies [but see Hornblower 1992, p 1] was the most participatory, in the sense that general popular input into decision making was conceived as both a right and a duty for every citizen. Although "citizen" had a restricted application, being limited to free Athenian born men, those who took part participated fully to the extent of each having an equal opportunity to hold one of the (majority of) offices that were selected by lot.

The birth of democracy in ancient Athens did not spring from a well of popular sentiment. It was the result of the attempt of the beleaguered Kleisthenes (508-507 BC) to hold on to power by extending Solon's elected Council to a complex artificial construct of tribes to select its members [Hornblower 1992; Held 1987]. The (arguably) unexpected and unintended consequence was democracy. However by the time Pericles is said to have delivered his funeral oration, democratic *theory* had developed alongside the practical organisational details, and Pericles was able to extol the virtues of democracy as a societal as well as a governmental form

[Thucydides 1954 p 145].

Athenian democracy lasted about a hundred and eighty five years, during which time its quality deteriorated sharply. It was to be about two and a half millennia before democracy made its reappearance in the western hemisphere, and then in a form which was very different from the highly participatory Athenian practice.

1.2.   Representative democracy

- Development of representative thought

The emergence of representative democracy took much longer than the participatory form, but its evolution to its present form is equally coincidental. It is rooted in notions of government by consent, manifestations of which were found in mediaeval Europe [van Caenegem 1999]. Feudal society functioned by means of the law of contract between the lord and vassal [Ullman 1975 p147] and there was a notion of contractual government in the political thought of the later middle ages [Gough 1957]. Developing this theory, Hobbes' version of a social contract binds the people to obey the sovereign in return for security. The first stirring of the notion of utilitarian representation makes its appearance because the sovereign epitomises the unity of the people [Hobbes 1988 p 220] and their mutual interest in safety.

Hobbes' theories did not have an overwhelming influence over those who were in a position to introduce new forms of government. The liberal thinker, John Locke, however, is important both because his theories of the social contract develop the process of political thought further and because of their influence upon political practice. It is in Locke's thought that the notion of the social contract becomes noticeably linked to the theory of representation.

Locke's doctrine of popular consent is based on the idea that governmental legitimacy is rooted in the people. Like Hobbes, Locke sees man in a state of nature discovering that organised society would serve his fundamental interests better. In Locke's case this is because, although the state of nature offers perfect freedom [Locke 1986 p 118], it does not offer the *individual* protection for the "life, liberty and estates" – his "property". It is therefore a rational act to forgo just enough personal freedom to allow a ruler sufficient power to enforce a law which will provide this protection on her/his behalf [*ibid* pp 183-184]. Locke's government represents its recipients' assumed interests in protection and in freedom. It is therefore by nature a limited government.

Locke's thinking takes another step towards representative democracy in his notion of "tacit consent". The means of expressing this consent are vague, and there appears to be no means of withdrawing it. Locke also assumes rather than tests the popular will for maximum freedom from interference, and his philosophy does not include any of the mechanisms which could allow the expression of the additional popular demands.

Thereafter, however, in both the US and the UK, the idea of representation, allied to the demand for representation to fulfil requirements that were initially economic, gave rise to an ultimately irresistible movement towards democratic representation.

In the UK, the economic liberalism practised in Britain during the nineteenth century demanded freedom from tariffs and trading controls imposed by government and from the old "moral economy" supervised by local parish boards, thus allowing individual economic freedom to prevail. The prevalence and financial success of the new capitalists made the form of representation offered by a Parliament composed largely of and chosen by land interests look outdated and inappropriate. A natural consequence was an effective demand for political representation in the British Parliament.

- Development of representative democracy

Whilst it might have been assumed that "representative democracy" was a unitary term (in that the existence of the one implies the presence of the other) this short survey of the "history" of representative democracy has shown that the two do not even share a common ancestry. The principle of representation has a long pedigree in political thought; the notion of representative *democracy* has a much shorter and more mixed lineage. The effects of the *practice* of liberalism provided the link between them, as Fig 1.1 below demonstrates:

Fig 1.1.: Derivation of British representative democracy

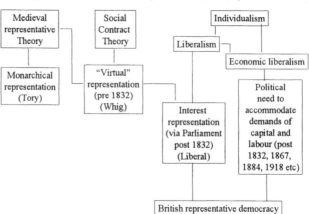

These brief histories of democracy indicate that there is no one commodity called "democracy" whose origins have determined the form which it assumed. Thus the concept can be interpreted in accordance with the views of its practitioners. The main participants in "democracy" are, however, representatives, and it is therefore their views, rather than those of the *demos* as a whole, which have tended to prevail. Nevertheless, the etymology of the term "democracy" (to which *kratos* meaning "power" is added to *demos*) suggests that it is legitimate to explore what "democracy" could mean for all of those who experience it.

2. Democratic benefits

Once established, democracy tends to survive unless it is forcibly uprooted, and there are few examples of polities electing to *stop* being democracies.

An examination of democratic systems shows that there are understandable reasons for this. A democratic system, of whatever kind, offers basic benefits for both rulers and ruled. Certain democratic systems offer different beneficial outcomes for *some* individuals or groups of individuals. This chapter looks at these outcomes in order to establish first what kind of "demo-benefits" [Sartori] enable democratic systems to endure and second what kind of additional benefits an enhancement of democracy may offer.

Democratic outcomes may be separated into three main categories:

- the *minimalist* liberal or negative democratic outcomes, which serve only to prevent power abuse[1]
- the *instrumentalist* or practical democratic outcomes – that is those which serve certain popular ends
- the *organic* or positive democratic outcomes, which are those involved with generating the democratic personality, and are therefore expected to revolutionise means of decision-making within societies.

There is some connection between the extent of democratic input and expectations for democratic outcomes. A representative *system* (in which popular input is mainly limited to elections of representatives free to exercise their judgement) is primarily designed to deliver the first category. A representative *democracy* (wherein elections are regarded as a vehicle for expressing the political preferences of the people) will include the second also. A *participatory* democracy (where the people involve themselves directly with policy making) will involve itself with the third.

---

1 For a fuller discussion see Sartori [1987 p 271]

2.1.   Minimalist democratic outcomes

Theorists who prescribe these as the fulfilment of the ends of democratic practice divide again into two categories. Those falling into the first category are the *liberal* theorists who regard restraint of power as being the primary requirement of any society and look upon democratic input merely as a means of delivering this essential end [Locke, Popper]. The second category include the *democratic* élite theorists and the *Classical* Élite theorists who regard the restraint of leaders' power as the only possible outcome of democratic practice, given the shortcomings of the *demos* (Schumpeter; Weber) or given the general nature of human society (Mosca; Pareto; Michels).

- Consent and power constraint

As shown above, the idea of popular constraint on power was not is not originally a democratic concept. Locke argues that if popular consent is withdrawn a government must fall but he does not accept that people have the right to limit abuse of power. He argues first [1986 p 227] that it is a failure of *authority* rather than power violation *per se* which may bring about the downfall of government and second [ibid p 229] that abuse of power is the equivalent of breach of contract. Locke's aim is to maximise freedom for individuals and his only use for collective power is as a vehicle to achieve this.

- Democratic élitism and power constraint

Schumpeter [1976 p 285] believes that people are unsuited to rule or even to defend their democracy, but that they are capable of refereeing between competing claimants for power. He is more concerned with the potential for power misuse at the hands of the people than with power abuse by the leaders, but as a democrat he retains for the *demos* the final choice of leaders.

- Classical élitism and power constraint

Only Michels of the Classical Élite theorists could accurately be described as a democratic thinker[2]. Michels at the time of writing *Political Parties* was a member of the German Social Democratic Party, and his relatively pessimistic prophecy for the future of democracy [1962 p 371] has been

---

2 Mosca is lukewarm about democracy *per se*, whilst Pareto, who notes and deplores the ephemeral qualities of aristocracies, is primarily a liberal.

reached reluctantly[3]. His study of German Social Democratic parties indicates to him that the masses are "perennially incompetent" [*ibid* p 370] and that their leaders are both politically astute and politically corruptible [*ibid* p 109 and p 122]. This forms the "iron law of oligarchy" which turns radical leaders into bureaucrats and bureaucrats into unreconstructed defenders of the *status quo*. It is radicalism, and by extension democracy, which is doomed in the process, although Michels [*ibid* p 371] also points out that the process is inevitably and continually renewed and that it therefore acts as a brake on the ambitions of those who lead.

- Minimalism and leaders

Whilst the sort of limited democratic input envisaged by Schumpeter delivers a minimal output – of restraining the power of leaders – which is presumably a popular benefit, at the same time this minimalist concept has several advantages for leaders.

Weber [1967, pp 78-79] set out three concepts of legitimate government: those which rely upon "the authority of the 'eternal yesterday'"; those based on "the authority of the extraordinary and personal 'gift of grace'" ("charisma"), and those which enjoy "the authority of 'legality'" (based on the rule of law). Most modern societies have governments that belong to the last category [Arblaster 1991, p 9], and it is now assumed that "legality" is derived from popular consent expressed through the medium of legally-constituted elections. This means that so long as elections are the main constitutional means of doing this, elected leaders acquire the democratically-derived benefit of the legitimate right to exercise power [Sartori 1987 p 34].

Popular consent also obviates the need to use force. It is generally accepted that force is not an effective means of retaining control [Burke 1961 p 89; Finer 1988 p 15]. Governments may prove to be unpopular with the people, but so long as the people perceive a means of holding them to account they will support the *régime* and it is unlikely that there will be civil war or revolution. Where there is unrest, elections may act as a safety valve.

There are other ways in which leaders can reap the benefits of operating in a system where democratic outcomes are restricted to power constraint. Although individual political programmes may be unpopular, they are, in theory, endorsed by the electorate and this can – and does – enable leaders to claim a popular mandate for their actions. In other words, their activities as well as their institution are assumed to be legitimate.

Even if policies are adjusted in accordance with perceived popular

---

3 but see Beetham 1975 p 4; Nye 1977

wishes, there will always be uncertainty that a particular government will continue to be re-elected indefinitely, but this too may be an advantage for leaders. As Mosca remarked, there is a need for members of ruling bodies to be constantly replaced because people who are in power too long become tired and stale. Political competition can act as a stimulus, a disincentive to dullness.

The minimal popular outcome of power restraint on rulers provided by representative systems thus has some advantages for the leaders themselves.

- Minimalist democratic outcomes reviewed

The question that remains is how those who are incompetent to make decisions for themselves about the laws which govern their day-to-day lives can be trusted to restrain the power of those who govern merely by being able to choose between them [Held 1987 p 180]. Schumpeter [1976 p 289] attempts to meet this challenge by suggesting that it is leaders – more politically competent, more self aware – who can be better entrusted not just with government but with democracy itself than the *demos* [*ibid* p 285].

However, it is arguable that the paraphernalia of elections is insufficient to restrain the power of leaders. An elected government usually has plenty of time to make decisions that have far reaching consequences. If these prove to be poor decisions, removing it from office at the end of the period satisfy the requirements of democratic constraint only in the abstract.

2.2.   *Instrumentalist democratic outcomes*

More extensive potential benefits of democracy include *popular* ends such as a reduction in inequality; a maximisation of freedom; satisfying majority interests; protecting minorities, etc. Achieving these more substantial benefits is problematic, mainly because popular democratic benefits conflict with each other.

- Sources of instrumentalist outcomes

The prospect of democracy delivering popular democratic outcomes is a relatively recent development. It has taken place alongside the evolution of individualism which has embraced other forms than democracy such as liberalism, Whig (but not Tory) radicalism, Utilitarianism, or economic capitalism. This doctrine is a long way removed from the notion of service to the state that was the primary function of Greek democratic practice [Sartori 1987 p 284].

Fig 1.2 below indicates some of the relationships between philosophical, political and economic theories and practices since the eighteenth century. For example, it is the linking of individualism with industrialisation which enables the practice of capitalism, but it is also individualism which leads to liberalism (freedom of the individual from interference) which in turn gives rise to *economic* liberalism (freedom of the market) which also enables the practice of capitalism. At the same time, individualism leads to concepts of *political* equality embraced in Whig Radicalism, which, from the evolution of the idea of universal franchise, leads to the more developed theory of democracy itself. Similarly, Utilitarianism ("greatest happiness of greatest *number*") shares a common ancestor with Whig Radicalism, but leads to a democratic principle of popular input. Liberal democracy is an enabling and legitimising factor for the practice of economic capitalism. On the other hand, the theory of political equality expounded in some theories of democracy is a precursor of economic and social equality that is an underlying principle of some forms of socialism, and is inherited via the egalitarian tradition.   None of these linkages embrace the concept of the individual's duty to the *state*.

Fig 1.2: Relationships among philosophical, political and economic
theories and practices from the seventeenth century onwards

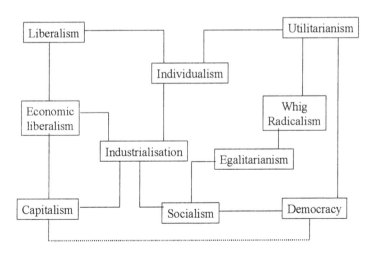

Key: ——————————   Direct link
....   Indirect link

▪   Conflicts in instrumentalist outcomes

With this varied ancestry, it is not surprising that political theorists as well as practising politicians have different ideas about the benefits to be gained from democracy.   Many have emphasised equality but this creates problems of definition.   There are many types of equality, including two forms of political equality: the simple equality of all citizens before the law (as characterised in the British notion of the Rule of Law) and political equality in the sense that all citizens have (or should have) an equal share in ruling.   In addition, some modern theories of democracy include the achievement of economic and social equalities from the practice of political equality echoing the Whig Radicals.

Tocqueville [1980 p 353] considers that the pursuit of equality distinguishes democratic communities from liberal polities.   He does not fear a conflict between the pursuit of equality and the pursuit of liberty. Yet other political theorists and political actors have expressed doubts about this.

Sartori points out [1987 p 309] that the idea of equality may be interpreted as "no-one may command us".   It is this that leads to the liberal idea of "freedom *from* interference".   Sartori suggests that the positive and negative forms of freedom may conflict because whilst the first is related to political equality, the second may be threatened by it.   These threats were clearly felt by Madison [1965] in his anxiety about "majority tyranny". They led him to advocate a representative republic (rather than a democracy) in which the people were to participate to a limited extent for much the same reasons as Schumpeter's.

Arblaster, however, does not believe that political equality constitutes the main threat to liberty.   He admits that it does not logically imply respect for personal liberty, but points out [1991, p 93-94] that it is not liberal democracy which has characterised totalitarian societies past or present and that in practice the same people who have fought for democracy have also fought for basic freedoms.   Hence, the threat which equality poses to liberty may be more perceived than real.

▪   Achieving instrumentalist democratic ends

Achieving instrumentalist democratic outcomes requires the input of something more than the application of negative liberal forms of democracy.   A society cannot achieve equality for its citizens, for example, simply by "leaving people alone", which is what a liberal democracy does best [Barber 1991 p 91].   Elected representatives need to promote their constituents' interests.   There are difficulties.   A given electorate would need to have clearly defined priorities in the first place; it would require sufficient numbers of sufficiently varied representatives to represent them; and these representatives would have to be bound by their electoral mandate. These are substantial obstacles. Modern polities tend to be heterogeneous. There may be majority interests, but there are few signs of a majority interest. Despite Marx, people do not necessarily define themselves solely as "owners" or "share-holders" or as "wage-earners" or "producers". Individuals also take into account their gender, race, age or state of bodily health when designating their prime concerns.

Bosanquet [1965 p 119] argued that individuals do not always know their real interests and this would apply even where individuals were able to categorise themselves competently. In an attempt to resolve this dilemma, Lively [1981, p 114] suggests that, even if people are unable to discern their *interests*, they are usually fairly adept at recognising and advocating their *wishes*. This, coupled with collective popular electoral power, concentrates the minds of their representatives.

However, because individuals are unlikely to share "packages" of characteristics or interests there is a practical difficulty in acquiring suitable representatives, at least in a system where elected individuals go towards making up an all-purpose government.

Even if this were possible, representatives are not delegates, and those who hold positions of political power do not consider themselves as such. Even if they did, it might be impossible to deliver electoral ends. "Events", as Harold Macmillan remarked, have a way of preventing the delivery of commitments, and facts, unavailable outside government, can be equally obstructive.

▪ Instrumentalist ends reconsidered

The foregoing discussion points to two conclusions. The first one is that achieving common ends in a heterogeneous society is almost impossible, and the second that, even if it were not, common ends are unlikely to be achieved through the medium of representation. Inasmuch as these conclusions are valid, two premises follow – first that, to achieve instrumentalist democratic benefits, society needs to become more homogeneous, and second that its inhabitants need to have the will, the ability and the means to participate directly in addition to simply electing representatives. The next part, which considers the possibility of *organic* "demo-benefits", suggests a solution to both of these dilemmas.

2.3.   *Organic democratic outcomes*

Organic democratic outcomes look beyond the achievement of material democratic benefits – freedom, equality, want-satisfaction etc – although they do not discount them. Their attainment requires the creation of a new type of citizen [Mill 1988 p 234; Rousseau [1990]; Pateman 1972 p 46], one to whom citizenship and participation are essential parts of existence. Such individuals are as conscious of their citizenship as of their status as family member, worker, female or male etc. Born from democratic practice, these new "democrats" interact with it so that their being becomes intrinsically democratic. In such circumstances, members of a society have a common interest – in democracy – and the society in which they live achieves a political homogeneity.

▪   What is the democratic personality?

Reference to democratic practitioners and theorists enables the compilation of the characteristics of the democratic personality. Thucydides [1972 p 147] cites Pericles, in his *Funeral Oration* as believing that a primary trait is a willingness and a capacity to inhabit the public sphere as well as the private:

> We do not say that a man who takes no interest in politics is a man who minds his own business; we say that he has no business here at all.

Tocqueville [1980 pp 52-53] believed that holding certain values such as a love of liberty *and* equality was a prerequisite.   The democratic personality will be both self-conscious [Plamenatz 1973 p 28; Barber 1990 p 223] and dynamic [Phillips 1992 p 76]

Fig 1.3 below summarises the beliefs and behaviour of the active democratic citizen:

Fig 1.3.: Characteristics of the democratic citizen

Values/Qualities	Behaviour
•Lover of equality	•Citizen first, private individual second
•Lover of liberty	
•Self determining	•Puts public interests before personal interests, or sees no conflict between them
•Self aware	
•Dynamic	•Guards democratic rights
•Believer in popular sovereignty	

▪ The emergence of the modern democratic personality

No such citizens exist. Participation is usually carried out at arms' length. The general view of the job of representatives is that it is not their business to exhort their constituents towards the common good, but rather to satisfy their demands. Electoral promises make the presumption that the voters are mainly concerned with their own desires. This makes the prognosis for the development of the democratic personality a negative one.

However, some modern theorists have argued that factors that engender apathy and self-interest are not universally and permanently applicable. Various theorists, otherwise holding very different views about the desirability of active participation, agree that apathy results from perceived inefficacy [see eg., Parry *et al* 1992 pp 172-179; Brittan 1989; Pateman 1972 p 46; Lively 1981 p 74; Held 1987 p 161 and p 198; Dahl 1967]. The argument to which this leads is that if popular efficacy were to increase, apathy would disappear[4].

▪ Can participatory democracy produce democrats?

Some commentators think that it is unlikely that democracy produces democrats [Held 1992 p 280; Lively [1980 p 140]. The inference is that government needs to change its character before the *demos* will be both able and willing to cast off its inertia and apathy and participate sufficiently for the development of democratic personalities. It needs to be closer to the people than it is at present, to be amenable to popular control, and to be seen to relate closely to people's needs and interests.

Arblaster [1991 p 24] disagrees. He sees some hope for an increase in the will to participate at national levels since he thinks that the circumstances which gave birth to ancient Greek democratic practice (realisation against entrenched privilege; the need then, as now, for communal spirit) "recur in the modern evolution of democracy". His conclusion is that it is democracy that creates democrats rather than democrats who create democracy.

---

4 Although there is a paradox here, in that the gains attributable to direct popular participation (effectiveness) need to have been made before the populace could actually lose the sense of inefficacy which ensures that they do not participate.

- Problems of organic democratic outcomes

The foregoing presupposes that it is the barriers to the development of the democratic personality which cause problems for democracy. The emergence of the democratic personality, according to this premise, provides a solution both for democracy and for government. The preconditions for direct and effective popular participation are then set. Society has become sufficiently homogeneous in its commitment to democracy and its citizens are sufficiently politically motivated and skilled to devote their energies to a government which will not only serve their interests but also provide one of their main *raisons d'être*. There will be no artificial separation between state and society; each individual will be a unit making up the organism of society and will so regard her/himself.

The desirability of this proposition has been contested. Many theorists and political practitioners from Plato onwards have criticised democracy on the grounds that it is a means of allowing amateurs to rule. Until the nineteenth century most took it for granted that democracy is undesirable. Rousseau is an exception, and is regarded as being a democratic philosopher on the grounds that he required every eligible person to take part in his polity. However, it is Rousseau who points, albeit inadvertently, to the *dangers* posed by democratic participation based on a General Will. All of Rousseau's citizens are participants to a degree [Shklar 1969 p 180]; but their collective homogeneity has caused theorists to fear the consequences of their participation. For example, Sartori [1987 p 360] warns:

> There is definitely a point ... beyond which equality destroys freedom and, with it, liberal democracy. If the state becomes all-powerful, it is by no means certain that it will be a benevolent, equality-dispensing state; on the contrary, it is highly probable that it will not. In that case, our equalities will go with our freedoms.

Schumpeter and the Classical Élite Theorists thought that people cannot be democratic because of their inherent weaknesses. If the people cannot act as democrats, one would need to fear how they *would* act if entrusted with political power. The prospect of majority tyranny for tyranny's sake becomes clearer.

The liberal concern about power concentration is slightly different. To Popper [1991 p 121] the question about government is not so much about how power may be *applied* in the interests of the people, but rather how it may be *restricted* in their interests. In his critiques of Plato, Hegel and Marx and their "enmity" to "the open society", Popper extends this by implication to democracy itself. The *demos*, he suggests, are easily manipulable and he points out that the Fascist leaders "succeeded in realizing one of the boldest dreams of their predecessors; they made the revolt against freedom a *popular* movement" (author's emphasis) [Popper

1974 p 60].

"(All) power to the people" does not provide an equally satisfactory solution unless it can be proved, which Rousseau does not, that collective power will not be used against the individual [Sabine 1963 p 593]. Rousseau's system could enable the *demos* to victimise and demoralise anyone whose priorities were different or whose values were other than those commonly accepted.

2.4. Democratic outcomes reconsidered

This Chapter looked at democratic outcomes acting on the supposition that people expect benefits of one kind or another from any system of government. The discussion however has thrown up various paradoxes of democracy:

- How can a *demos*, whose limited powers are justified because of their limited responsibility and ability, restrain the powers of rulers?

- How can interests be established with sufficient clarity so that they may be accurately represented? Heterogeneity in society makes this even more problematic.

- How can popular apathy, which ensures incompetence as well as relative impotence, be overcome?

- How can the potential dangers offered by the concentration of popular power be counteracted? If the people become state as well as society, there can be no court of appeal against their decisions

This last concern may be premature and unfounded. In practice individual freedom has been threatened far more in non-democratic than in democratic polities. Lacking conspicuous evidence of the fulfilment of minimal or material democratic outcomes, it may be more pertinent to consider how to institute democratic practices than to restrain them.

Democratic proponents argue that popular rule is a good in itself but they can only defend their proposition negatively – that the alternative would be worse. However, there is a better practical argument. If democracy were only regarded as better than other options, individual polities would veer between these options in an attempt to discover which system was the best. The point about democracy, apart from appreciation of its particular benefits, is that it is popular in the common as well as the specific sense of the term. People – and their rulers – *like* democracy.

This gives democratic theorists the confidence to concentrate on *how* the people may make an effective input. The task becomes to discover a form of polity that reduces what now may be termed the *disbenefits* of democracy. To this end the next two sections examine forms of democratic practice.

3.   Democratic inputs (1) – representation

A principle underlying representative systems of government is that decisions made by representatives will be binding on the people. The issue is how far the delegation of decision-making should extend. Elections offer an answer, since they serve the dual purposes of enabling the people to make choices in the first instance and enabling them to change their minds at a later stage if necessary. However, elections have a variable significance and the theory of representation upon which they are based is equally important for democratic outcomes.

3.1.   *Non-elected representation*

It is not only elections which enable representation. Pre-democratic theorists concentrated upon representation of *interest*. Hobbes' sovereign represents the citizens' desire to remain alive and unmolested by their fellows. Locke's government similarly represents the citizens' common will to protect their "lives, liberty and estates".

The democratic critique of this form of *virtual* representation rests on the argument that the identification of common interests is not part of the rôle of government. Hence the democratic theorist normally discounts *unelected* virtual representation as a form of democracy, although, as will be seen later, this is perhaps an unjustified stance.

3.2.   *Defining electoral representation*

Birch [1969 p 13] suggested that the term "representative" does not only mean that the representative is expected to protect and/or advance the interests those represented. He submitted [1969 p 15] that it is the election itself which confers the title of "representative" upon the elected person although he concluded tentatively that elections must involve "some obligation, however slight, to advance the interests and opinions of their electors".

If this were not the case, elections could not be accounted democratic since elections *per se* do not automatically imply representation of nor the possession of the political power of voters. A pope, as Plamenatz [1973] points out, owes his position to election by a College of Cardinals who can subsequently neither direct his actions nor withdraw their mandate. Elections within a representative system, however, assume that the electorate possesses both competences.

3.3.   *Theories of electoral representation*

If the notion that sovereignty cannot be represented is discounted, the degree to which representatives reflect electoral views or interests is relevant. Fig 1.4 [below] demonstrates the electoral representative spectrum, beginning with elected *virtual* representation and ending with *mandatory* representation. The spectrum is divided between representation from sharing characteristics with those represented (essential representation) to representing people by means of taking a kind of action (active representation).

Fig 1.4.: Spectrum of representation

A. ESSENTIAL REPRESENTATION

1. *Virtual representation*
   (territorial.sectional)

Universal election not needed;General interests represented byindividuals expected to share them (eg. capital/land/labour)

2. *Individual representation*
   (liberal)

Election of individuals whose various characteristics/interests are shared by electors (assumed that this enables them to reflect them [Arblaster 1991])

B. ACTIVE REPRESENTATION

1. *Judgmental representation*

Election of individual expected to exercise her/ his judgement as s/he sees fit [Burke 1961p 73

2. *Political representation*

Election of individuals expected to follow party programme, with the majority of the electorate assumed to support that programme

3. *Mandatory representation*

Election of individuals whose characteristics/ interests are irrelevant. Expected that they will follow the mandate of the electoral majority [Ware 1986 p 123]

The representative spectrum permits a variety of responses depending more upon the theory rather than upon the system of representation adopted, although different systems of representation may encourage or foster the adoption of one theory of representation rather than another[5].

This does not necessarily indicate that a representative system is also a democratic system. It was argued above that a polity needs to deliver democratic benefits if it is to be awarded the term "democratic". Not all

---

5 for example, a system providing proportionality amongst its representatives would allow essential than active representation.

representative systems have the same capacity to deliver democratic benefits.

3.4. Types of elections within representative systems

An election that provides significant expression of the popular will should meet the following criteria:

*   Regularity (to avoid conferring indefinite hence corruptible mandates).
*   Frequency (to enable changing electoral preferences to be reflected)
*   Constitutionality (under a constitution not wholly subject to the will of current office holders)
*   Choice (preferably among representatives and political programmes).

Elections that are frequent, regular, constitutional and which offer effective choices to voters furnish better prospects for popular power than rare, irregular elections held at the whim of the current leaders.

The status of the election is also important because it is the only certain opportunity for voters to exercise a form of political power, thenceforth delegated unconditionally to the elected representatives until the next election. Voting is both a significant act – since it is the only act – of the wielding of political power, and an insignificant act – since the political power which it represents is usually very limited.

Much debate about the ideal electoral system has been engendered amongst political theorists. On the one hand single member constituencies link electors to their representatives making the latter more responsive and accountable towards the former. This makes the single member system a better vehicle for *active* representation. The system also enables "strong government" by discouraging the emergence of small parties [Hague *et al* 1992 p 195; Hancock *et al* 1993 p 47; Dearlove & Saunders 1991 pp 178]. This has been linked to electoral democracy by theorists who argue that those (presumably the majority) who back the winners have the opportunity of seeing their chosen party able to govern in their interests.

On the other hand, proportional representation [PR] better enables essential representation. It links electors more closely to their political preferences and interests rather than to individual representatives [Mill (1861) 1972 p 278], since each elector has a better chance of getting at least one representative to express these preferences than under a single member system. Whilst this may be linked to "weak government" with a proliferation of small parties represented at governmental level, it may also require the formation of coalitions and the growth of consensus politics. This helps to ensure that most electors have their interests and preferences advanced to some degree.

The broad choice which kinds of electoral systems offer is between strong governments satisfying most of the interests of some of the electorate or weak governments satisfying some of the interests of most of the electorate.

3.5.   *Electoral representation and democratic benefits*

All *systems* containing an element of elections in theory enable the delivery of the benefit described as "constraining the power of leaders". This is partly because elections act as mechanisms for removing unpopular leaders, and partly because "the fact of the vote casts a long shadow in front of it" [Beetham 1992 p 47]. However this does not mean that electors can fulfil the functions required of them. It seems unreasonable to expect this given that the main reason advanced for not giving more power to voters is that they suffer from ignorance, lack of intelligence, and (understandably, given the first two disadvantages) apathy.

Different theories of representation may deliver different instrumentalist democratic outcomes although these are more elusive. This is partly because of the conflict amongst them but there is also a difficulty in defining majority interests and justifying them when the minority has to pay the price. Electoral systems, as shown below, are blunt instruments.

- the representative spectrum

- *Virtual representation*

The territorial or Tory view of virtual representation, which was influential in the UK before the 1832 Reform Act, was defined by Burke [1964 p 24] as occurring when there is one person or body (originally the monarch) which represents a community of interests. The sectional or Whig version of virtual representation assumes that some communities and interests are not necessarily represented by directly elected individuals, but that the parliamentary body itself is sufficiently diverse to do this. The Whigs defined such interests as primarily economic. They suggested, for example, that it was not necessary for a cotton town to have its own directly elected representative, since members elected for other major industrial towns could be relied upon to further the interests of any industrially based area [Birch 1964 p 53].

Virtual representation is not a form, of itself, to be especially concerned with democratic values. It cannot be unless those values both constitute the main interests of electorates and are known to and shared by their representatives or by their representative body. In practice, virtual representation hitherto has been more concerned with economic rather than social or ethical interests. Nor is majority *want-satisfaction* the primary target since virtual representation does not deal with majorities, but rather with a collection of competing minorities.

- *Individual representation*

The Whig theory of virtual representation gave way, in the later nineteenth century, to a liberal theory of individual representation. It was assumed that people could be identified in terms of their differing opinions. These were not necessarily reflected by their economic circumstances, but could instead be related to other characteristics such as age, gender, race, state of bodily health and so forth. Individual representation therefore depends upon a parliament being comprised of a sufficient range of individuals to represent the range of their electors' interests because they shared and hence empathised with them.

Institution of individual representative presents the problem of devising a system of election that would enable all electors' material interests or characteristics to be represented. However if this difficulty could be surmounted, there would be no reason why instrumentalist democratic outcomes could not be achieved so long as electorates could agree upon them. This would be assisted (not assured) because every parliament would be an accurate microcosm of the people as a whole. It would also be unwieldy, however. In any case, whilst minorities would inevitably be represented in a microcosmic parliament, there would be no guarantee that their interests would (ever) prevail unless the majority who did not share them allowed it. Hence individual representation appears to be a poor vehicle for minority rights.

- *Judgmental representation*

Judgmental representation leaves all decisions to the judgement of the elected individual, and so could deliver any of the named instrumental democratic benefits. However, there can be no guarantees. This is because it is left to the individual representative to determine her/his stance on every issue, and because it is not that individual's rôle to do more than "consult" her/his electorate in general terms [Birch 1961, p 73]. Faith in rather than power over the representative is the basis of this form of representation.

- *Political representation*

Despite the fact that a party representative has at least two additional loyalties – to her/his party as well as her/his electorate – political representation offers a means of delivering some kind of recognisable democratic benefits. A political party may stand for such values as "equality" or "freedom" and it will be concerned to determine the overriding concerns of the majority of the electorate. It will try to address these concerns as far as possible without rendering itself indistinguishable from its opponents.

However, political parties tend to be rather cumbersome vehicles, delivering packages rarely containing all of the items that the individual voter would choose voluntarily. Thus the party finds it difficult to strike a balance among conflicting values without offending enough voters to endanger its chances of gaining political power. A second problem is that individual representatives are dependent as much upon their party as upon their voters for their election and they are more dependent upon their party for their advancement.

- *Mandatory representation*

There are two options for mandatory representation. Representatives could be mandated in advance by stating in their manifesto what they proposed to do if elected, and agreeing to hold themselves answerable to their voters for the accomplishment of these aims. The election of a successful candidate would carry with it the assumption that s/he had been chosen for the purpose of achieving certain objectives. This may be termed the *general political mandate.* In the alternative form, mandates could be continual with representatives carrying out regular referenda amongst their electorate to seek their guidance when important issues were proposed, with the understanding that the representative would be bound by the result. This may be termed the *issue specific mandate.*

At first sight, mandatory representation seems a better way of achieving instrumental democratic outcomes since all that the representative needs to do is to follow her/his electors' instructions. It was this that led the early socialist parties to pursue this as an option. The fact that they soon abandoned this platform, as the corridors of power became accessible [Ware 1986 p 123] indicates that it would not be very popular with elected persons. In any case there would still be issues of resolving conflicting preferences and reflecting minority interests.

Even without these disadvantages, so-called "puppet" representatives, unable to exercise their own judgement against the will of their electorate could be inadequate vehicles for the consistent delivery of any particular benefits.

- Representative systems and organic democratic outcomes

Representative systems can achieve instrumentalist democratic outcomes to some degree, although none of them can guarantee to deliver any of them. Representative theories appear to have no part to play in the delivery of organic democratic outcomes. Where a people is united in its inherent interests, there is no need for a representative to express, protect or enhance them; the people can do that for themselves. If, however, such a homogeneous polity were also a large polity, it might be possible for the people to select some of their number for convenience so that they might act literally on their behalf. In such a situation, mandated representatives could prove to be a partial solution.

3.6.   *Representative systems reconsidered*

Much of the writing on representative democracy emphasises popular *input* – that is the way in which elections are organised and votes cast. However, focusing on democratic *output* – what advantages people gain from democracy – shows that it is insufficient to claim that an institution or those who comprise it should hold power simply on the grounds that its members are directly elected.

This survey of representative theories and the way in which they may be adapted within representative systems demonstrates that electoral representation alone is an inadequate vehicle for the delivery of democratic benefits.

4.   Democratic inputs (2) participation

Heterogeneous polities are the products as well as the sources of liberal representative systems. As indicated above this presents some difficulty for devising an adequately democratic *representative* system. However a proponent of participatory democracy has to devise a system which engenders higher expectations of ends which are just as conflicting.

Hence whilst the potential for democratic benefits under a participatory democracy is greater than under a representative democracy, the danger of outcomes becoming disbenefits is also greater. Participatory democrats have tended to neglect this and their concentration upon the form of participation assumes a beneficent outcome. Nevertheless, since democracy has so far had more positive than negative benefits, it can be argued that deeper democracy would be better democracy.

4.1.   *Problems for participatory democracy*

There are three problems confronting the participatory theorist in devising appropriate forms of democratic input. First we are too many for participatory democracy; second we are too apathetic; and third we are too diverse. Most theorists have directed their emphasis upon one or two of these problems, although a few have tried to devise a system that counters all of the objections.

- Size and participatory democracy

The objection relating to size can be resolved it by modern technology, which offers some potential for ascertaining the majority will. Whether the form decided upon is universal referenda, sample polling or electronic voting on televised debates, a means could be devised to discover the will of the majority of people taking part using modern technology.

- Apathy and participatory democracy

Aristotle claims that "man is a political animal", although he means simply that man naturally belongs in society rather than in isolation. However individuals who present themselves as potential decision-makers as opposed to voters are limited in number and tend to be unrepresentative of heterogeneous polities. It is this which causes democratic theorists to pause on the problem of the perceived lack of interest and hence of knowledge to be found amongst the *demos*. The difficulty is to discover a system that will maximise active and informed participation.

- Diversity and participatory democracy

The discussion on instrumentalist ends demonstrated the problem posed by heterogeneity. If people are to make decisions for themselves and on behalf of their fellows, the responsibility for and hence the difficulty of delivering democratic benefits can make the choice to participate an irrational one. The heterogeneity of modern western societies, to some extent a product of their size, can be a reason for apathy amongst its citizens. Size, apathy and diversity are therefore different facets of the same problem.

In devising an adequate form for popular participation, these difficulties need to be taken into account. Fig 1.5 [below] indicates some of the forms of participatory democracy.

Each "grouping" of participatory form is based upon a different premise. If "all of the people" are to make decisions, the assumption is that either that "all of the people" have an interest in the decision or that only "all of the people" possess the collective wisdom necessary to make good decisions. If a sample of the people is to be selected, then the presumption is that it is possible to select a sample of the people sufficiently *able* (in all senses) to represent the rest. The basic premise is still that ideally "all of the people" *should* decide. However more recent theorists, attempting to address the problems of apathy and diversity, have begun to question the assumptions relating to the collective interests and/or capacities of "all of the people". Taking account of heterogeneity, the principle upon which they base their argument is that those closest to the effects of a decision should be the people to make that decision.

Fig 1.5.: Forms of participatory democracy

Participation by:	Form	Proposed by:
1. *All of the people*	a. Public debate	Greek democracies
	b. Referenda	Various theorists
	c. Media debate with electronic voting	McLean 1989 Arblaster 1991
2. *Samples of the people*	a. "People's Parliaments"	Fishkin 1994
	b. "Citizens' juries"	Stewart 1994
	c. Opinion polling	-
3. *Only the people affected*	a. local democracy	Mill 1861; Miller 1992
	b. Industrial democracy	Pateman 1972
	c. Demarchy	Burnheim 1987
	d. Voluntary organisations	Hirst 1994

4.2.   *Problems and opportunities offered by participatory forms*

▪   All of the people

The quandary facing the advocate of decision-making by all of the people is not now so much the difficulty of enabling such decision making to take place, but rather the problem of enabling satisfactory decisions to be made. Liberal democratic theorists concentrate upon problems such as defending minority rights especially within a heterogeneous polity [Dahl 1967]; taking account of "intensity of preference" [Sartori 1987 p 225], and enabling public accountability [Sartori 1987 p 112]. They depend upon these arguments to refute the case for universal participation.

Participatory theorists believe that these defects are also present within representative systems, and they concern themselves with ensuring quality of more widely disseminated decision-making. Burnheim [1985 p 13] doubts that people would "perform substantially better either morally or intellectually than they do at present" if they were called upon to take on additional democratic duties in this way, but Barber [1990 p 153] thinks that dependence necessarily creates dependability. Voting without the benefit of informed debate debases decision making [Burnheim [1985 pp 2-3]. However, there is a problem in ensuring sufficient full and unbiased information [Sartori 1987 p 119; Barber 1990 p 154], and of ensuring that such information is taken into account when votes are cast [Sartori 1987 p 116]. There is also the problem of deciding who will pose the issue and formulate the question to be decided.

- Samples of the people

It may be objected that using *representative* samples from the population to engage in decision-making on the people's behalf bears more affinity to the "individual representation" theory of representative systems than to direct participatory democracy. There are, however, three main differences. First, individuals who make up the samples are chosen by lot rather than by election. This means that the only authority to which they can aspire is that bestowed by representativeness or knowledge not by status. Second, because of this, decision-making by using samples is a form that lacks permanent leadership, unlike any form of elected *government*. Third, *any* member of the public may be called upon to take part. There is therefore no place for democratic élitism within this form of decision-making.

Some of the potential disadvantages of decision-making by all of the people also apply to random sampling. However its exponents point out that *selected* individuals may be more effectively targeted from the point of view of giving them information [Fishkin 1994]; that they may take more time to debate issues [Stewart 1994], and that they are likely to take their responsibilities seriously [Stewart 1994][6]. This last also applies where individuals take part in random polls rather than being called upon to debate, since the expectation of being called upon to make decisions rather than give opinions could encourage people to become well informed at least upon current issues. Since individuals could be named, they could also be held accountable.

- Only the people affected

Some participatory theorists criticise decision-making by samples of the people on the same grounds as Sartori, asking with what legitimacy individuals who have a limited interest in the outcome of an issue could make decisions which affect other people far more intensely [Burnheim 1985]. These theorists make the assumption that *only* people who "have an interest" in an issue – for example as members of a community, workers in an industry, possessors of certain characteristics – should be in the position of making decisions about it. It is this assumption upon which supporters and members of interest groups base their claims to be heard.

There is little agreement amongst these theorists about how these "interests" should be grouped. Mill [1984 p 378], influenced by Tocqueville [1980 p 59], believed that democratic participation was itself an education that equips the individual intellectually to take part, and so

---

6 Following the principles set by the jury system

advocated involvement in local government.   Miller [1992 p 89],
developing Mill's principle, prescribes local assemblies[7] making decisions
about local issues (and advising their representative about national issues).
Pateman [1972 p 108] argues for direct participation in industry, on the
grounds that people always identify their interests with their working
environment and may have a realistic expectation of being able to influence
events. The question, then, is one of establishing a relevant community.

Burnheim [1987] has developed a scheme that he terms *demarchy*. This
system is characterised by the involvement of individuals with an
established material interest in a sphere of political activity making
decisions relating to that sphere.   Hirst [1994], synthesising some of these
ideas, argues for self-governing voluntary associations publicly funded and
politically accountable which would deal with social provision, whilst
economic regulation would be achieved through public-private partnerships
operating under self-governing industrial districts in which individual firms
are subject to democratic control.

These theorists share the assumption that individual "issues" can be
isolated so that the way in which they are resolved leaves all other "issues"
unaffected.   This ignores the universalisation of modern polities.   The
problem with a community of "us" is that it necessarily involves a
corresponding "them" who will also compete for resources.   The question
that still needs to be resolved is how far can decision-making be devolved
so that satisfying "our" interests does not detract from promoting "theirs".
Many issues cross national boundaries and many other issues have – for
example – financial implications which affect many more people than those
immediately benefiting from or being disadvantaged by the outcome
[Mather 1995]. The institution of "single issue" or "single area" decision-
making arenas resolve some problems for democracy, but fail to provide
answers for others, in particular those which Zolo [1992] relates to trans-
European "complexity".

4.3.   *What is democratic decision-making?*

The foregoing discussion presupposes that "decision-making" is an act
with only one definition.   There is an "issue" or "problem" which only
needs to be addressed in some way so that it may be contained or resolved.
However, the decision-making procedure is more complex than this. Lukes
[1980 p 11; p 16; pp 23-25] isolates three dimensions of power: the power
to decide; the power to exclude areas from the decision-making agenda;
and the power to control the political agenda, thereby preventing the
emergence of latent real interests.   The possibilities named above imply

---

7   These actually take place already in some areas of New England [Ware
1987]

that citizen participants will enter only the first dimension of decision-making – the power to choose from a named variety of options proposed by others [Stewart *et al* 1994].

The possible exception is the third group of possibilities, since people who have a material interest in an area have a greater potential to set their own agenda for it. However, if these local or industrial democrats, "demarchists" or members of associations, stick within their self-prescribed limits, radical changes, such as a fundamental redistribution of income and wealth, are unlikely.

4.4. Participatory democracy and democratic benefits

- Minimalist democratic ends

Participatory democracy, like any other form of democracy, offers the prospect of achieving minimalist democratic ends. No one can dominate when all have equal power. Disseminating decision-making then offers some prospect of limiting the power of leaders. In some cases, some solutions may result in limiting the permanence of leadership altogether.

- Instrumentalist democratic ends

The extent to which instrumentalist democratic ends may be satisfied by more participatory democratic practice depends upon what those ends are. If the end of democracy is the satisfying of majority interests, then a system in which all of the people take all of the decisions (or at least every important decision) might be assumed to fulfil expectations. This, however, would depend upon the people in general being fully conscious of their interests, and knowing the best way to act in order to satisfy them. It is, though, more likely that full citizen participation would enable the satisfaction of majority preferences (wants rather than needs) [Lively 1981 p 114]. Use of samples may improve awareness, as would use of interest groups, although the latter would have difficulty in ensuring that their deliberations satisfied *majority* preferences.

If instrumentalist ends include the acquisition of democratic values, practical democratic experience may either lead to an appreciation of the underlying values such as freedom and equality [Mill 1988; Tocqueville 1980; Pateman 1972], or may enable the people's will towards freedom and equality to emerge [Rousseau 1990 p 277]. This argument was countered by Schumpeter [1976]. He believed that it is unwise to rely upon people even to defend democracy.

If this is so, participatory democratic practice can lead to the achievement of instrumental democratic ends upon two conditions. It will occur only if Rousseau is right in believing that "the people" have a "general will" towards equality, and if participatory theorists are also right when they suggest that democratic participation of one form or another enables that will to emerge.

- Organic democratic ends

Liberal and liberal democratic theorists fear that when all of the people share all of the power, they may not limit its use. They may begin as liberal and end up as totalitarian democrats. They will force everyone to be "free" in a way that can only be recognised by redefining the concept of freedom, and they will enable equality only at the expense of the more traditional concept of liberty.

There are three arguments that meet these charges. First, there is no empirical evidence to support this point of view [Arblaster]; second, popular sovereignty, if it may not be represented, may be divided [Tocqueville; Mill; Pateman; Burnheim; Hirst]; third, the question may be put another way. If *democracy* itself is the first principle, or if such a principle were to be developed, the resulting commonality of purpose could square the circle. Particular democratic benefits would be universally acceptable and thereby achievable. For Barber [1990 p 153], therefore:

> Strong democracy creates the very citizens it depends upon... because it mandates a permanent confrontation between the "me" as citizen and the "Other" as citizen, forcing us to think in common and act in common.

In such a case, totalitarian democracy becomes a solution rather than a problem.

However, only one group of options suggested giving "all the people" the opportunity to participate. Other options suggest that people may be expected to be either "part-time" participants ("samples of the people" options) or "single issue" participants ("only the people affected" options). There seems to be no method that allows more than the occasional use of "all of the people" restricted to deciding only among options put forward infrequently by others. In practice, therefore, there is little prospect of any of the suggested participatory forms leading to the development of the democratic personality, at least in the short run. Hence the dangers of and potential offered by totalitarian democracy both recede.

5.   Conclusion

This survey of democracy gives some indication of which potential benefits and disbenefits are offered by representative and participatory forms. It has taken a fairly wide view of democracy, which should be borne in mind when considering what prospects are offered either by the EU or the recently reconstituted British polity for enhancing its practice.

CHAPTER TWO

PRE-BLAIRITE DEMOCRACY IN BRITAIN

1.   Development of the UK Parliament

Parliament, as a representative of the people (or some of the people), had evolved from the Norman kings' *Curia Regis* and Edward II's "Commonality" to form the Houses of Lords and Commons respectively. After an eventful development[1] by the early eighteenth century Parliament had evolved into a body to which the monarch was answerable, the Commons being chosen by as well as "virtually" representing their fellows [Mount 1993 p 21].

   Burke [1961 p 73] gave his version of the role of the representative in 1774. He argued that a member of Parliament was bound to listen to and consider seriously the opinion of his constituents, but that it would be contrary to the constitution for electors to issue "authoritative *instructions; mandates issued, which the member is bound blindly and implicitly to obey, to vote and to argue for, though contrary to the clearest conviction of his judgement and conscience*" [original emphasis].

   Burke assumes that that parliament was the embodiment of "one *nation, with* one *interest*" [1961 p 73] which could be represented by such aspirants to wisdom and virtue. This supposition did not remain unchallenged. Members of Parliament, according the early nineteenth century Whigs, should represent the *various* interests of the nation. In particular, powerful economic interests appeared to be poorly represented within the sovereign body. This argument was given impetus by its exponents' financial success, which predominated in the nineteenth century.

   The idea of representation of different economic interests expanded with the Reform Acts of 1832, 1867 and 1884. These Acts extended the franchise first to the newly enriched middle-class, then to certain categories of the working class. Elections became a means whereby these interests gained political expression, rather than an opportunity for individuals of

---

1 which included the successful dethronement and beheading of King Charles I.

high birth and supposedly high principles to gain access to the House of Commons for the purpose of exercising their judgement on the nation's behalf.

During this time also, "democracy" as it related to government became less a term of opprobrium, and became first acceptable and then favoured. By the end of the century, arguments about the extension of the franchise had become framed in terms of utility rather than of principle. The problem about extending the vote concerned electors' ability to exercise it responsibly, rather than their right to possess it.

2. The UK's constitution

2.1. *Parliamentary sovereignty*

Britain is said to have no written constitution. In fact, there are constitutional documents that form the doctrines and conventions underlying British political practices and identify Britain as a state that operates under the Rule of Law. These include the Magna Carta (1215) and the Bill of Rights (1688). The significant principle relating to these documents is that they are permanently subject to the will of Parliament. Parliament may, acting on its own initiative alone and by a simple majority vote, change their provisions or even abolish them entirely. The doctrine of parliamentary sovereignty developed fully during the nineteenth century, by the end of which the notion of the supremacy of Parliament had a status exceeding that of statutory law. Interestingly, though, as Dicey [1915 p 456] points out, this too, is a convention rather than an institutional part of the law. It could not be otherwise, where there is no encoded constitution.

Hence Britain is governed by a Parliament which is agreed to be sovereign at least since the reign of Queen Anne. This means that there is no higher court of appeal against a Parliamentary decision, except in the sense that no one parliament may bind its successor [Dicey (1885) 1982 p 88]. Hence, the UK's parliament can exercise sovereignty not because the British constitution is unwritten, but rather because it is impermanent.

In practice, in the UK few constitutional amendments have been enacted or proposed in recent times before 1998-1999. Most have been concerned with the extension of the franchise (1832; 1867; 1883; 1918; 1928; 1968). The main exception was in the area of local government [see below].

2.2. *Parliamentary democracy*

Although parliamentary sovereign practice is acquired from the convention of having an impermanent constitution, the *legitimacy* of the exercise of parliamentary power derives from its representative function. Popular sovereignty is delegated rather than direct. The UK is therefore regarded as having a parliamentary *democracy* as well as parliamentary sovereignty. This is minimal democracy [see Chapter One] since electors cannot initiate, sanction or repeal Parliamentary legislation.

Hobbes is generally not given much credit for the impact of his theories, but the UK Parliament has some similarities with Hobbes' *Leviathan*. Leviathan acts with complete independence and answers to no higher body (save God) for his decisions. He has no constitutional limit to his powers [Hobbes (1651) 1988 pp 230-235 *passim*]. The sovereign is subject only to a law which he is empowered to make and repeal as he sees fit [(1651) 1988 p 313].

There are only two differences between Leviathan and Parliament. First, unlike Hobbes' sovereign, Parliament has within it internal checks and external interpreters [Dicey (1885) 1982 pp 50-60 *passim*]. Second, the most powerful part, the House of Commons, consists of elected representatives who must submit themselves for re-election at least once every five years.

2.3. *The composition of Parliament*

Parliament consists of the House of Lords, the House of Commons and the monarch, together constituting Bagehot's "Queen in Parliament". This was the effect of the 1688 Act of Settlement, which gave Parliament its present constitutional permanence [Urwin 1982 p 25]. It is this parliament, rather than the Commons alone, which is held to be sovereign [Dicey (1885) 1982 p 39].

- The role of the Lords

The House of Lords before 11 November 1999 [see below Chapter Nine] was composed of about 900 peers: the Lords Temporal – the hereditary peers (who formed over 700 of the total [McKie 1994]) and the life peers – and the Lords Spiritual – bishops and archbishops. According to Bagehot [(1867) 1964 pp 121-122], it was part of the "dignified" section of the constitution, by which he meant that its purpose is to enhance the respect which the British subject is supposed to have for her/his rulers.

Since Bagehot's times, when the Lords possessed the formal right to veto legislation, the power of the Lords has been diluted. At present it is limited to revising some legislation, delaying some bills, saving Parliamentary time by giving a first hearing to non-controversial bills, and offering advice [Birch 1967 p 58]. The effect of the 1832 Act prevented the Lords from exercising control over the composition of the Commons. This Act asserted the Commons' supremacy for the first time and made government responsible only to the Commons. The rejection of the People's Budget in 1909, which followed a string of legislative measures turned down by the

Lords from 1884 to 1906, had the effect of reducing the Lords' power further. The 1911 Parliament Act removed their control over finance bills and restricted their authority over other bills to delaying them for a maximum of two years. This period was reduced to one year under the 1949 Parliament Act.

Critics of the House of Lords observed that, despite its limited powers, its existence constituted a democratic shortfall since none of its members were elected by the people [Kennedy 1994 p ix]. The majority held their seats by virtue of birth; the rest by means of – theoretically royal but in practical terms political – patronage. Unlike upper houses in other EU member states, however, the UK's House of Lords does not represent the territorial areas of the country.

Any power that it exercises is therefore non-democratic by definition, except in the sense in which it was regarded during and before the nineteenth century, as *representative* of the aristocracy. Peers, along with the monarch, criminals, people certified as insane, metics (at least until the enactment of the TEU 1992) and minors, did not have any other formal means of representation[2].

- The role of the Monarch

The monarchy is Bagehot's other part of the *dignified* section of the constitution. It exists to produce loyalty, to augment religious support for government (the monarch is head of the Established Church), to act as the head of society, to be the head of *morality*, and to enable changes in the political structure to take place "without heedless people knowing it" [Bagehot (1867) 1964 pp 82-97 *passim*]. Bogdanor [1995 p 62] explains that the monarch's rôle as a unitary representative is depreciated to the extent that s/he exercises "efficient" functions, since when doing so s/he represents only the faction(s) which happen to support her/his actions.

The actual powers of the British monarch are limited. They are also purely formal inasmuch as few of them are exercised in person by the monarch. S/he may:

- open and close Parliament
- create life peers (in consultation with the Prime Minister) and award other honours
- sign military commissions as Supreme Commander of the forces
- dissolve a Parliament (although the request to do this has not been refused for the last hundred years)

---

2   This was changed in 1999. The House of Lords Act [Clause 7(3)] enables the Secretary of State to make transitional provision for ex-hereditary peers to vote if he considered it appropriate.

- invite someone of her/his choice to lead her/his government (although in practice this is usually the leader of the largest party in the House of Commons).
- The monarch must also formally assent to a bill before it can become law (this has never been refused since 1707 and since 1854, it is not the monarch her/himself who signs an act, but the Lords Commissioners, acting as the monarch's representatives. They, of course, act in accordance with the advice of government ministers).

The monarch is head of the executive and this itself creates something of a democratic deficit. It means that ministers are servants of the Crown rather than of Parliament and act on her or his behalf, rather than according to its bidding. The Prerogative of the Crown, which is usually wielded by the ministers of the Crown[3], includes the power to:

- form diplomatic relations with other states
- formulate treaties
- command the armed forces
- declare war and make peace
- appoint judges, bishops and archbishops
- initiate criminal prosecution and pardon offenders [Birch 1967 p 64].

These powers are not merely formal. Puddephatt [1996] estimates that they have been used 1400 times since 1980. Ministers who exercise these powers are answerable to the monarch and s/he may question their actions, although s/he is bound to accept their advice [Anson (1892) cited by Bogdanor 1995 p 66]. In theory this has a "democratic" element since the monarch is said to be giving effect to the will of the electorate who have elected the government whose ministers advise the queen/king [Bogdanor 1995 p 68]. However there exists no democratic *control*, although in practice ministers acknowledge the need to win and retain the support of Parliament.

- The role of the judiciary

Unlike the American Supreme Court that may *overrule* acts by President and Congress, British judges are empowered only to *interpret* the decisions

---

3 Bogdanor [1995 p 66] estimates that "probably over 95 per cent" of prerogative powers are exercised either by or on the advice of ministers. The only exceptions are at the beginning or conclusion of a ministry when by definition ministerial advice is unobtainable. Even here, as Bogdanor goes on to demonstrate [pp 84-112 *passim*], a monarch will seek advice from appropriate (ex) ministers.

of Parliament. There is some debate about how far "interpretation" could be regarded as judicial decision-making in practice [see eg Dearlove and Saunders 1991 pp 216-218; Denning cited by Zander 1989 p 312; Radcliffe cited by Zander 1989 p 316]. However, the principles of applying one of the three Rules[4] limit the options for law making by the judiciary, and leave the ultimate power in the hands of the UK Parliament. The reason for the limited powers of the judiciary is that there is no constitution in Britain to stand above the sovereignty of any existing governing body[5].

3.   Democracy within the British constitution reviewed

The UK's constitution exhibits non-democratic characteristics. It rests upon the sovereignty of a Parliament which is made up of three institutions, only the Commons being elected by the people. The Commons derives its authority from popular elections, but it is accountable only occasionally (at election time) and at all other times it is almost entirely unrestrained[6].

If democracy requires the existence of popular rights, the British constitution provides for none. Parliament may make provision for freedom of expression, for regular elections, for freedom of the individual from arbitrary or unnecessary interference. Parliament may legislate to increase equality in any or all of its manifestations. However, Parliament need do none of those things and it has the ultimate authority within the Constitution to abolish popular rights, and to rewrite the constitutional documents that have hitherto enshrined them.

It is the House of Commons that has the practical power to change the constitution and to do so it would invoke the authority vested in it as the expression of the voice of the people. Hence the final test for the democratic nature of the UK parliamentary system rests upon the extent to

---

4   These are: the Literal Rule (literal interpretation of Parliamentary statute) [Esher, J 1892, cited by Zander 1989 p 90]; the Golden Rule (attempt to interpret what Parliament wished to achieve) [Jervis, C J 1854, cited by Zander 1989 p 91] and the Mischief Rule (attempt to decide what mischief Parliament wished to resolve) [Heydon 1594, cited by Zander 1989 p 92]

5   Unlike the US where the Supreme Court is enabled to rule, as a last resort, against a law enacted by President and Congress, by showing that the Constitution of the United States forbids this or that action.

6   This view contrasts with the notion of the "flexible" constitution which enables popular gains such as those proposed by Public Choice Theorists to be instituted relatively easily [see Harden, I [1992]: *The Contracting State* [Buckingham and Philadelphia, Open University Press]

which the House of Commons exemplifies a democratic body. There are three prerequisites for this:

- Electoral representation must be an adequate vehicle for democracy
- The representative nature of the Commons should enable the achievements of democratic outcomes
- It should be able to check the power of the unelected executive

As Bagehot [(1867) 1964 p 135], not primarily concerned with the claims of democracy *per se* observed: "The most dangerous of all sinister interests is that of the executive Government, because it is the most powerful".

4. The British House of Commons and representative democracy

4.1. *Introduction*

The House of Commons is the only institution at national level that can support the assertion that UK government is a representative democracy. There is a dual foundation for this contention. First, the House of Commons is the only institution to have been selected on the basis of the – nearly – universal franchise. Second it is argued that the House of Commons now dominates to the extent that its power is now usually sufficient to overcome the other two constituent parts in legislative matters. Hence the Commons combines potentially the two components of democracy: *demos* (people) and *kratos* (power).

4.2. *The UK's electoral system and democracy*

Chapter One showed that elections offered the potential for the expression of the popular will. It also presented a series of criteria to enable this, suggesting that constitutionally provided elections, held regularly and frequently, offering a range of choices among candidates were more significant for democracy, than those held rarely and at the will of current leaders offering little choice between candidates. With this in mind, the organisation of UK elections is considered below.

- General

Elections for the House of Commons in Britain are held at least every five years [Parliament Act 1911], although a current Prime Minister may call a General Election earlier than five years after the last, at a time of her/his choosing. Since May 1997, the British House of Commons comprises 659 representatives from each of the constituencies that make up the United

Kingdom of Great Britain and Northern Ireland. Each member has been elected on the basis of obtaining more votes than any other single candidate in her/his constituency. This system is termed a "relative majority system" (i.e., it is not necessary for the winning candidate to have received absolute majority of the possible votes in the election, nor an absolute majority of the votes cast), or "single member, simple plurality" [Crewe 1993 p 116]. It is also popularly referred to as "first past the post".

▪ Plurality of candidates

Anyone who can raise the necessary deposit of £1000 may stand for election at a General Election, or at a by-election held in any one constituency [Rule 9 (1) Representation of the People Act (RPA) 1983 as amended by Section 13 (a) of RPA 1985]. In practice, potential candidates tend to be deterred not so much by the level of the deposit, but by the cost of fighting a significant campaign. The amount for each candidate is limited to 5.2p in a county constituency or 3.9p in a borough constituency per name on the electoral register plus £4,642 [Section 76 (2) (a) of RPA 1983, as amended by RPA 1994 and Section 6 (1) (a), RPA 1989]. However, development of the mass media and its potential to reach the electorate has meant that this is only a small fraction of the amount a political party will need to spend in order to win sufficient seats to form a government. This amount is not limited in law, and no efforts to restrict this have been made to date in the UK.

▪ Degree of political choice

A political party which wishes to become a governing party therefore has need of extensive resources both in terms of finance and personnel. This limits the number of parties that may hope to form a government. In the UK today this is effectively confined to the Conservative, Labour and Liberal Democratic parties, which are the only ones with sufficient resources to be able to fight 330 or more constituencies in general circumstances[7].

The House of Commons, therefore, mostly consists of Members of Parliament [MPs] who are also members of the Labour Party (419 seats in 1997), Conservative Party (165 seats), or Liberal Democratic Party (46 seats). In addition, in the 1997 Parliament there are, to date, six Scottish Nationalist, four Plaid Cymru (Welsh Nationalist), 18 Northern Ireland MPs and one Independent. During most of this century, governing parties

---

7 With the exception of the occasional "maverick" party financed by a wealthy individual such as the Referendum Party of 1997.

have been able to command an absolute majority of seats in the Commons, with exceptions only for relatively short periods in 1924, 1929-31 and 1976-79 (all Labour governments) and for a very short period in 1997 at the end of the Conservative government.

▪ Status of elections

There exists at present no constitutional provision for any form of voter input into the British political system other than via elections at national or local level. Referenda may be held at the behest of Parliament, but they are unusual[8]. Hence elections in Britain are the only *significant* participatory democratic actions undertaken by the majority of the British people.

▪ UK elections and democracy

Elitist commentators tend to admire the UK system as delivering "strong government" [see above, Chapter One], but it scores fairly low in terms of democratic input. Elections are held reasonably frequently[9], but the degree of voter choice is limited, and elections are usually held at the behest of the leader of the governing party, rather than in response to electoral demand. Crewe [1993 p 117] points out that the system "is designed to produce single party government, not fair representation". Whilst "consultations" of various kinds with various groups and individuals relating to policy changes are being held continuously, formal decision-making remains in the hands of Parliament, as advised by the governing executive.

4.3.   *The British House of Commons as a representative body*

Wright [1994 p 36] argues that the UK lacks a convincing theory of representation. This does not mean that there are no theories of

---

8   To date only six have been held in the UK.   In 1975, Wilson's government held a referendum to determine Britain's continuing membership of the then EC. In 1978, referenda restricted to the inhabitants of Scotland and Wales were held to determine the level of support for Scottish and Welsh assemblies respectively [Adonis 1993 p 12] and in September 1997 these were repeated on the question of a Parliament for Scotland and an Assembly for Wales.   A referendum in Northern Ireland was held on the Good Friday Agreement 1998.   Future referenda are likely on electoral changes and upon the UK's entry into the EU's single currency

9   Although they are held more infrequently than within states where the executive and legislature(s) are elected separately such as the US and France

representation operating within the UK system. However, representation is not democracy in itself [see above Chapter One].

Chapter One described five theories of representation: *virtual, individual, judgmental, political* and *mandatory*. It argued that whilst *elections* could be counted amongst forms of popular input, democracy in outcome – Sartori's *demo-benefits* – seemed to be more readily delivered by some forms of representation than by others.

- The House of Commons and virtual representation

This was the traditional form of representation applauded before the 1832 Reform Act. The UK House of Commons is still composed of members who are expected to represent the unity of the state, which makes the Tory or territorial view of representation applicable.

However, the range of economic activities that its members encompass does not reflect proportionately all of those experienced by the electorate, making the sectional or Whig view of representation inappropriate. Fig 2.1. [below] shows the composition of the 1997 Parliament. It includes 48.3 per cent "professionals" (legal, medical, engineering, accountancy, teachers etc.); 20.4 per cent "business" (i.e. at executive/director level) but only 3.3 per cent "other white collar", 6.1 per cent manual workers and 1.2 per cent farmers/landowners. There is also a large number (20.7 per cent) of MPs whose previous occupation can only be placed in the category of "political". Such MPs have been employed either by the political party, a trade union or by local government.

- The House of Commons and individual representation

Speaking in the House of Commons during the second reading of the House of Lords Bill [*Official Record* 1 February 1999: Column 615], the Leader of the House, Margaret Beckett, commented of the Lords:

> Almost all those people are men; almost all are white; most have little, if any, experience of school, health care or housing in common with most of their fellow countrymen and countrywomen.

This description might also be applied to the Commons. One of the frequently repeated criticisms of the House of Commons is that it is not, *except* in some sort of political sense, representative of the electorate. Mulgan [1994], for example, points out: "Parliament remains a deeply unrepresentative institution – overwhelmingly male and middle-aged and still far short of any fair representation of Britain's ethnic minorities". A survey of the members of the 1992 and 1997 Parliaments bears this out. In 1992, 9.5 per cent were women; in 1997 this had risen to 18.5 per cent. In

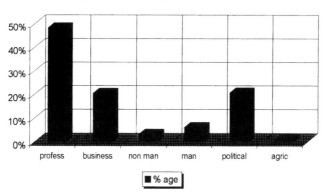

Fig 2.1: MPs 1997: by previous occupation

profess:	Professional background
man:	Manual worker background
business:	Business background
political:	Background in professional politics
non man:	non-manual
agric:	Farming or agricultural background

[Source: *Times Guide to the House of Commons* 1997 - adapted]

1992, 8.6 per cent were aged over 40 1.4 per cent were over 70 and 1.8% over 70 when first elected. In 1997, 14 per cent were under forty and 1.4 per cent were over 70 [see Fig 2.2. below].

This disproportionality in itself suggests that the Commons is deficient as a *virtually* representative body. However, the shortfall poses a deeper problem for voters whose *interests* might otherwise be represented *individually* by members of the House of Commons. Economic interests are poorly apportioned amongst House of Commons members, but so are many of the other interests, such as those related to age, gender, race etc., which voters possess

- The House of Commons and judgmental representation

Burke's notion of an MP being elected to exercise his (*sic*) judgement in the best interests of his constituency is a theory still deeply rooted in the practice of the British House of Commons in the 1990s. In most cases, an MP cannot be guided by a majority view held by her/his electorate since no

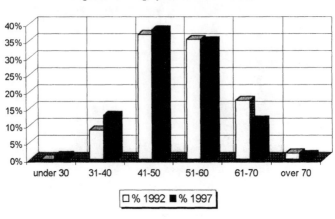

Fig 2.2: MPs' age profiles 1992 and 1997

[Sources: *Times Guide to the House of Commons 1992; Dodds Parliamentary Companion 1993; Times Guide to the House of Commons 1999* – adapted]

such majority view actually exists, at least where issues that may be deemed to be party political are concerned. In such a case, it follows that an MP has no alternative but to exercise her/his own political judgement.

The way in which the UK system is organised tends to maximise this difficulty. The results of the 1997 General Election show that 345 constituencies are held by MPs who received more than 50 per cent of the votes cast, but this is an unusually high number [see below].

- The House of Commons and political representation

It can be argued that every Parliamentary constituency should be extremely marginal, so that each elector would be conscious that her/his vote would be likely to influence the eventual choice of representative or of government. Most constituencies are not very marginal. For example, the Conservative majority of 21 seats in 1992 resulted from only 2478 votes (an average of 118 per seat) – the sum of the majorities in the eleven most marginal constituencies [Ezard 1993]. The Labour "landslide" of 1997 represented majorities totalling 949,532 votes in the 146 seats that the Labour party gained in the General Election (an average of 6503 votes per seat). Although 185 changed hands in 1997, only 40 constituencies changed at the 1992 election, and the average number is about 69 taken over the last six elections.

On the other hand, it may be argued that seats should be as "safe" as possible, so that the member representing that seat could be fairly sure of representing the views of most of her/his electorate. The fact that a number of seats were won by more than 50% of the votes cast in 1997 is, however, coincidental. This was not the aim of the 1993/4 Parliamentary Boundary Commission that was more concerned with geographical representation [Boundary Commission for England news release, 6 May 1993].

A proportion of the electorate – 18.5 per cent in 1997 – is underrepresented politically because they failed to vote. This underestimates the total number of potential votes. There are also a number of people in Britain who have not registered as electors. Just over one million voters, or just under 2 per cent of the total disappeared from the electoral register between 1987 and 1991, giving a registration rate of 95.6 per cent [Office of Population Censuses and Surveys, cited in the *Guardian* 19 April 1991].

If the political structure of the House of Commons is not greatly affected by individual voters' preferences, this is not to say that political *representation* is necessarily absent. Political representation of the electorate within the House of Commons has several different facets. First, the Commons may be said to be politically representative since it roughly represents the way in which individuals cast their votes for party candidates in the preceding General Election. Second, it may be contended that the preferences of the largest number of voters are reflected by the fact that the party which wins the most seats is, in most cases, able to enact its legislative programme.

Third, it may be argued that internal party democracy operates at least in the selection of candidates so that the winning candidate represents those who are most keenly politicised. It may also be said that this internal democracy may continue to operate in the way in which a sitting MP (or at least one who wishes to be reselected) is guided. Finally, the claim can be made that a firm party stance may clarify matters for voters when choosing their representative.

The question of political representation is therefore a more complex and more contemporarily relevant one than the question of virtual or judgmental representation.

- *Voting and seats*

In the six elections held between 1974 (February) and 1992, the Conservative Party won an average of 40.7 per cent of the votes cast [Crewe 1993 p 96]. From 1979, it was able to form a majority government on each occasion. This meant that at least until the majority was eroded by the results of several by-elections by the end of 1994/beginning of 1995, it was able to be fairly certain of winning the vote in the Commons. The way in which seats are allocated in this system does not reflect the way in which votes were cast. If seats had been granted by the "national constituency" form of proportional representation, the 1992 Conservative majority of 21 would have been cut to an overall *minority* of 96 seats [calculated from figures compiled by Adonis 1993 p 38]. The system was, however, rather disadvantageous for the Conservatives in 1997 when their 30.7 per cent of the votes cast resulted in only 25 per cent of the seats, whilst Labour's 43.2 per cent gave them 63.4 per cent of the seats.

▪ *Voting and legislative programmes*

In a "winner take all" system such as the British system, a political party that has won over half of the seats is able to form a government and the leader of that party becomes the Prime Minister with the authority to form an executive. Except in extreme circumstances[10] all of the ministers will be members of the governing party. Hence the winning party is enabled to carry its legislative programme through the Commons virtually unimpeded, apart from the efforts of the representatives of the other parties.

It could be argued that a "majority" of the electorate may, by this means, have its political views incorporated into the legislative process. However, it is not the *majority*, in practice, but rather that which usually constitutes the largest *minority* (13,516,632 out of a total 31,286,597 voters in 1997) whose views are incorporated in this manner. The wishes of the rest of the voters may be effectively ignored. In any case no party sees itself as being entirely bound by a manifesto which few of its own supporters have read or would support in its entirety if they had.

▪ *Voters and political parties*

Marquand [1994] argues that political parties have reduced the power of Parliament. His case depends on his contention that relationships between MPs and constituents have been adversely affected.

Once elected to the Commons, MPs have several loyalties with which to contend: to the parliamentary party, to the local party, and to their electorate. These may conflict. Where an MP has been elected by the majority of her/his electorate, the conflict may be reduced, and may be confined to local and individual issues (where the governmental or party line delivers disbenefits to a particular area or to individual voters). However, since in many cases an MP has been supported by less than half of the electorate, any political loyalty that s/he expresses toward the party must inevitably conflict with the political views held by the majority of her/his electorate sooner or later.

Occasionally, independently minded members take note of other considerations. For example, McKie's [1994] analysis of MPs voting on

---

10 For example following the financial crisis of 1931 or during the two world wars

the Criminal Justice Bill shows that some MPs consulted either their local parties or lobbyists or were influenced by consideration of the views of the electorate or of their own religious affiliation before deciding which way to cast their vote. A survey conducted by Hull University's Centre for Legislative Studies, reported by the *Guardian* [11 December 1998] showed that to that date 78 Labour MPs had defied the whip on occasion. Four fifths of them, however, had remained loyal.

- The British House of Commons and mandatory representation

No member of the House of Commons regards her/himself as being a delegate from her/his constituency, although many of them feel under an obligation to act as constituents' advocates at national level and all have a caseload of constituents' cases. The extent to which an MP gives priority to such work is a matter for her/him to decide, however, and the voter has no means of ensuring that her/his representative takes action when it is required. An MP may consult with interested parties when deciding on what course of action to adopt on some aspects of legislation, but the representative is usually careful to emphasise that the results of this consultation will not be binding.

- The British House of Commons as a representative body reviewed

Chapter One pointed out "that all *systems* containing an element of elections must in theory enable the delivery of the benefit described as 'constraining the power of leaders'". It was also suggested that it was illogical to expect those who were regarded as being incapable of making other forms of political choice to be effective curbs on those abler than they.

The Commons' function as a representative body is hard to define. It has been shown that the Commons is an imperfect vehicle for the Whig version of virtual representation or for individual representation. It is all but prevented from becoming an efficient politically representative body given the way in which the electoral system is organised and the way in which parties operate within the system. It is not, and has never aspired to become, a body consisting of mandated delegates, and, again, the relative majority basis for deciding the victor in parliamentary elections precludes her/his electorate from forming a common view in many cases.

What is left to the House of Commons, therefore, is its function as a body that is elected to exercise its judgement inasmuch as it is free to do so on behalf of its electorate. The conclusion in Chapter One was that judgmental representation could produce all forms of instrumental democratic benefits, but that none of these outcomes could be guaranteed.

The House of Commons, conforms best to the pre-democratic Tory or territorial version of "virtual representation", and the Burkeian "judgmental representation". Otherwise it represents its electorate only in the way described by Birch [1964 p 17]: "... it is the manner of choice of members of the legislative assembly, rather than their characteristics or their behaviour, which is generally taken to be the criterion of a representative form of government". This is inadequate as a democratic form.

- The Commons and the Executive

Central government, comprising ministers of the Crown, acts as the executive of Parliament.

Above it was noted that the power of the monarch and of the second chamber of Parliament have declined in relation to the power of the Commons over the last hundred and fifty years. Hence it is the House of Commons alone which may need to answer accusations of increasing the democratic deficit. Whether or not it is in a position to defend itself is another matter, however, if arguments about the relative decline of the Commons itself contrasted with the power of central government are validated.

Empirical evidence for this is not entirely conclusive. Representatives' consent is necessary (albeit insufficient) for a bill to become law and there are examples of government defeats (Kettle [1994] notes eight occasions since 1979) or threats of defeat in the Commons[11]. The House of Commons backbench committees can also call government to account[12].

On the whole, however, it has been generally acknowledged that central government is in a strong position *vis-à-vis* the House of Commons. The two main reasons for this are its constitutional status – members of government are ministers of the *Crown* – and its institutional position (House of Commons backbench committees may express opinions, but they have no executive function).

However, there are other reasons. For example, opportunities for non-governmental members to institute debates or to feed into Parliamentary procedures are limited. In addition, members of government are in a better position to acquire information, and are made privy to some information that is unobtainable by anyone else[13].

---

11 For example, Michael Heseltine was forced to back down from his proposed privatisation of the Post Office; the 1994 Autumn Budget was clearly going to be defeated on the question of VAT on fuel bills.

12 For example, the Public Accounts Committee condemned the spending of tax payers' money on the Pergau Dam in Malaysia.

13 This was illustrated when Lord Trefgarne, who was Margaret

Despite this, few attempts have been made to increase extra-governmental strength within the Commons. Marquand [1994] believes that "for 90 per cent of the time, 90 per cent of the speeches in the House of Commons have no effect on anything, except perhaps the egos of those who deliver them". He believes that the House of Commons has changed from being an "efficient" to a "dignified" part of the constitution[14].

That proportion of central government's *de facto* political strength that is not derived from its constitutional position is acquired through its party political power. A government with a large majority in the House of Commons is likely to be able to ensure that the Commons supports the main part of its legislative programme, and in fact, the Commons provides it with a delegated legislative function. There is no guarantee that the UK system of electoral representation will deliver majority governments, but the system of electing representatives on territorial boundaries is more likely to deliver absolute majorities than systems of proportional representation [Chapter One].

The only remaining requirement for executive dominance is the application of executive power over political representatives, and there is evidence to suggest that this occurs. Government has grown in size during this century, and this means that there is plenty of opportunity for loyal backbenchers to be rewarded for their fealty. In addition, backbenchers may be constrained by the overall programme which they accepted when selected as Parliamentary candidates, and may feel honour bound to support "their" government even when they do not agree with it. In such a case, even the "judgmental" function of British representatives is flawed, so that the judgement of elected representatives is itself delegated (albeit conditionally) to its internal élite.

Thatcher's trade and defence minister, informed the Scott enquiry that he did not believe that there was a duty to tell Parliament about the government's decision to relax guidelines governing defence sales to Iran.

14 Bagehot too thought that the Commons had its "dignified" function, as Crossman points out in his Introduction to *The English Constitution* [1964 p 37], but Crossman [1964 pp 43-46 *passim*] like Marquand, was of the view that the emergence of the modern party system had significantly reduced the Commons' "efficiency"

5. The UK parliament and democracy

The above shows that the House of Commons is an inadequate vehicle for democratic input. MPs do not empower their constituents. There are three main reasons for this: the doctrine of parliamentary sovereignty, the theory of representation that is practised (which is the only one possible given the way in which the electoral system is organised), and the authority of party. The people function only as a mechanism for installing a ruling government. Their faith in their representatives (government support) and in the system that supplies them (regime support) provides the necessary ingredient of consent to enable the system to function.

Although the House of Commons falls short of enabling effective democratic input, its potential for supplying democratic outcomes still needed to be ascertained. It appeared that only the loose "judgmental" representation theory could operate. This theory falls short of *guaranteeing* democratic outcomes, but with a democratically-minded and powerful House of Commons, there is a possibility that demo-benefits may accrue.

Hence the next step is to look at the way in which Parliament has treated democratic issues, answering the question: "how far has Parliament shown itself to be receptive to the notion of devolving power to the people?" Local government is an appropriate case study, not because the term *local government* is of itself synonymous with popular participation, but because local government:

- is also elected
- is closer to the people [Mill (1861) 1988 p 380]
- offers the opportunity to more people to become involved in the political process [ibid p 378]
- most importantly, local government offers Parliament the potential to delegate some of its power and thus preserves the liberty of the individual against centralised power.

It may be argued that the extent to which Parliament is willing to delegate to local government, therefore, provides a suitable test of its inclination, or lack of inclination, to devolve its power.

6. Central and local government in the UK

Chapter One showed that there are various ways in which people, as opposed to those who represent them, could become decision-makers. Some of these options may be viable in the UK in future, but at present local government[15] is the only available form of decentralised government in the UK whose participants are independent from central government, since their legitimacy depends upon election rather than appointment or patronage. Local government, therefore, offers prospects for popular participation in political decision-making in the manner originally prescribed by Mill [(1861) 1972 p 378].

There is a debate about the significance to UK democracy of the existence of sub-national power sources [see below]. However, to date this debate has not been at the core of government's thinking on local government [see below]. Evidence suggests that the impetus behind reform of local government from 1979-1997 was a desire to centralise rather than to decentralise power.

6.1. The constitutional position of UK local government

One of the advantages of having an impermanent constitution is that, although it is difficult to apply it to define the scope and activities of the sovereign body, it is unambiguous about all other aspects of political activities. Where Parliament is sovereign, no other body is. This is because a person or institution with permanent rights, enforceable under the constitution, would be sovereign in respect to her/him/itself. The only powers which local government, for example, exercises are those which are granted by Parliament. This, as Widdicombe [1986 p 45] points out, includes the right to exist[16]. Preston [1997[17]] notes that "Local government in the UK has a precarious constitutional status".

Under British common law, given statutory force in Section III of the Local Government Act 1972, local government is counted as a body corporate. As such it may only do what it is authorised to do by Act of Parliament. Any other activities are deemed *ultra vires* – that is beyond the powers of the corporate body [ibid]. Hence, local government's activities are restricted to those that Parliament has authorised.

---

15 There was no elected regional government in the UK until 1999.

16 Although MacKenzie [(1961) 1975 p 51], arguing for the significance of constitutional practice rather than theory, believes that in such a case: "in some sense or other, local self-government is now part of the English Constitution, the English notion of what proper government should be".

17 The article cited is unpublished. It is cited by permission of the author, who has, however, asked that it be specified that the paper is an interim one.

6.2.   *Parliament and local government before 1979*

It was noted above that Parliament has not concerned itself overmuch with constitutional changes during the last two centuries. This does not apply to local government. In this respect, the UK's Parliament has been fairly active.

Local government in a guise that would be recognised today was instituted by an act of the Whig Parliament in 1835 that established elected municipal corporations. It was reformed and extended by acts in 1875 (sanitary districts), 1888 (creation of elected county councils), 1894 (creation of elected district councils), 1961 (creation of the Greater London Council) and 1972 (creation of metropolitan counties with metropolitan boroughs and non-metropolitan counties with non-metropolitan borough and district councils). The cumulative effect of this legislation was to remove from local government the last vestiges of the autonomy previously granted by royal charters [Elliot 1983 p 45]. Henceforward, local government had no *de jure* independence.

Although Parliament has never left local government entirely to itself [Stoker 1988], local government has enjoyed a certain amount of *de facto* autonomy, so that before 1979 the doctrine of *ultra vires* was not always too constricting. During the nineteenth century, for example, some local authorities took it upon themselves to decide what actions needed to be undertaken within their boundaries and requested the authority from Parliament to proceed. Usually this was granted, and enabling legislation, which extended a similar competence to all local councils, often followed – for example, the Sanitary Act of 1866. During the earlier years of the twentieth century, some councils found it possible to provide more extensive services than others did, and there were few cases which involved a direct clash with Parliament[18].

Nevertheless, the range of services which was placed within the remit of local government did vary during the first half of the twentieth century. This meant, for example, that councils were and then were not responsible for social security; were and then were not responsible for health care. By 1979, however, it was generally accepted that councils were primarily responsible for education, social services, planning, housing, environmental health and recreation and that they had a role to play in monitoring police, fire and transport services [Butcher *et al* 1990 p 11].

This general understanding about the role of local government was not restricted to service provision. The Redcliffe-Maud Report [1969 p 10]

---

18 The actions of the Poplar councillors of the 1930s who wanted to give out more generous dole payments than the Parliament found acceptable were a fairly rare exception [Butcher *et al* 1990 pp 18-19].

also agreed that local government had a part to play in extending the democratic activities of a local population wherein local people were able to decide for themselves which services should be provided. The Bains Report [1972 p 6] awarded local government a general role for overseeing the well-being of the whole community. The Layfield Report on Local Government Finance [1976 p 284] said that: "the role of local government is to enable decisions to be taken democratically to cater for local needs and preferences".

This consensus prevailed until 1979, although it would be an exaggeration to suggest that the activities of local government were of limited concern to the centre until that time.

6.3.   *Parliament and local government 1979-1997*

Since 1979, however, the fact that local government spending has an effect on the national economy has become increasingly significant. Jones and Stewart [1983 p 51] note that Brittan, Chief Secretary to the Treasury in 1982, believed that "local government expenditure, even though financed from the rates, is no different from departmental expenditure and should be determined by ministers in central government". As demands on central government for social and economic management became greater, the centre's concerns about local government expanded [Pearce 1980 pp 5-9] and consequently pressure towards centralisation increased.

Conservative governments during the 1980s and early 1990s found local government to be out of harmony with the prevailing ideology [Stoker 1988 p 218]. It was also seen to be out of line with what was perceived as economic necessity [Budge *et al* 1988 p 127]. It was believed that public expenditure needed to be reduced [Hutton 1995 p 69], and the attempts of local councils to resist this met with Parliamentary legislation aimed at diminishing their capacity to obstruct [Blunkett & Jackson 1987 p 198; Young 1994 p 88].

In total, over 200 acts affecting local government were passed between 1979 and 1995 (not including separate Acts for Scotland and Wales). About forty of these, enacted between 1979 and 1987, constrained local authority expenditure [King 1993 p 200][19]. Hence local government finance acts passed during the 1980s and 1990s had the effect of limiting local government financial autonomy relating both to raising and to spending money[20].

---

19 although some of this legislation reflected the failure of earlier acts to achieve governmental aims [Budge *et al* 1988 p 129 & p 132]

20 Local Government Planning and Land Act 1980; Local Government Finance Act 1982; Local Authorities (Expenditure Powers) Act 1983;

At the same time local councils were obliged to put their services out to competitive tender, so that council "blue collar" work could only be carried out by an in-house workforce if it bid the lowest price, other than in exceptional circumstances[21]. The Secretary of State at the Department of the Environment was frequently enabled, by statute, to use his discretion about how and when he could intervene in a council's conduct of its business[22], despite Michael Heseltine's contention [1991] that competitive tendering *empowered* local councils.

Widdicombe [1986 p 52], whilst accepting that there would always be a need for locally delivered services, suggested that there were other means than local government through which they might be provided. Following his report, many local government services were "hived off" to Quasi-Autonomous Non-Governmental Organisations [Quangos] and joint boards. King [1993 pp 205-206] characterises these as "informal local government" – bodies which are not *directly* accountable, and only rarely *indirectly* accountable. They include urban development corporations and training and enterprise councils as well as public/private partnerships and central government initiatives such as City Challenge.

Central government's willingness to exercise its powers over local government to the extent acknowledged in the Widdicombe report was demonstrated in 1986 when a tier of local government (the Greater London Council and the metropolitan counties) was abolished in its entirety [Local Government Act 1985].

Other initiatives have been taken which have had the general effect of reducing local authorities' direct management role even where they retain overall responsibility for public services. These include:

- privatisation
- devolving spending power to individual schools[23]
- enabling schools to "opt out of local authority control[24]

Local Government (Miscellaneous Financial Provisions) Act 1983; Rates Act 1984; Rate Support Grants Act 1986; Local Government Finance Act 1987; Local Government Finance Act 1988; Rates Support Grant Act 1988; Local Government Act 1992].

21 Local Government Planning and Land Act 1980; Local Government Act 1988

22 Local Government Planning and Land Act 1980; Rates Act 1984; Local Government Finance Act 1987

23 Education Act 1986

- devising a *national* curriculum for education
- creating separate boards for different service areas
- switching resources from councils to Housing Associations
- enabling Housing Action Trusts to take over housing ownership and management[25]
- requiring councils to sell houses to tenants[26].

In 1968-69, local authorities were responsible for redistributing 15 per cent of the Gross National Product [Redcliffe-Maud 1969 p 12]. By 1994, local government spending had been reduced to £60 billion in England and Wales from over £62 billion in 1991/2. At the same time, the estimate for non-departmental bodies[27] for 1993-1994 was £60 billion. The result was that some financial control over services as well as direct service delivery itself was removed from local government.

One of the arguments used by recent governments is that removing power from local government demonstrates the desire of Parliament to decentralise decision-making from local councils and thus to empower individuals, particularly as consumers [King 1993 p 204] to make their own decisions [Young 1994 p 94].

The phrase "the enabling council" was adopted by government [Governmental White Paper: *Housing* 1987]. This changed the role of the local council to a regulatory one, but also suggested that the centre was concerned to *extend* the role for the localities by encouraging them to work more imaginatively in partnership with their communities and local businesses. In addition to this, local authorities were required to take on additional direct responsibilities – for example in implementing "care in the community" packages. Local authorities have complained that the financial resources to take on these extras have not been forthcoming [Willis 1995 p 134].

Bogdanor [1994] challenges the notion that recent changes have provided a net gain for democracy, arguing that a market democracy in public services does not exist. He says that "We are, after all, something more than consumers" and he believes that "appointed managers and officials

---

24 Education Reform Act 1988

25 Housing Act 1988

26 Housing Act 1980; Housing and Building Control Act 1984; Housing Act 1985

27 These include Housing Action Trusts, Health Boards and Trusts, Urban Development Corporations, Grant Maintained Schools, Training and Enterprise Councils

who will be protected from the public both by distance and by time ... would weaken the power of the people – as consumers, as decision-makers and as voters". Stevens [1995 p 43] argues that decentralisation to individuals may lead to a transfer of their dependence upon centralised bodies, such as the Department for Education and Employment.

Bulpitt [cited by Stoker 1990 p 142] questions the assumption that local interests and local authority interests are the same, but for Stoker [*ibid*] this raises the interesting question of:

> ... whose democracy? If central government seeks to protect and promote certain local interests it favours, is it any more than "humbug" to accuse it of attacking local democracy?

That there may be two views about what constitutes local democracy was demonstrated by the challenge to local authorities supplied by the Audit Commission, which was required by central government to direct local authorities to provide "Citizens' Charter" indicators. The Audit Commission indicated that it expected the process to improve local democracy by providing local people with information about the services they should expect. However, the format of the indicators was centrally decreed, and conflicted with initiatives developed by individual councils such as York, Hertfordshire and Sheffield. All of these councils claimed that they considered their electors to be citizens as well as consumers.

Support for the concept of the "enabling authority", initially welcomed by some academics and local authority organisations[28] was later qualified. "Enabling" can mean getting other organisations to carry out work after the Ridley model of 1988 ("The Local Right: Enabling, not providing") rather than "enabling communities to resolve their problems and meet their needs in the most effective way" [Stewart and Stoker [1995 p 204]. In addition the Ridley model removes from councils their role as representatives of the local community. Stoker [1990 p 138] also thought that the potential for enabling was dependent upon funding, and that where resources were available – for example in community care – it would have more significance than where they were not – for example in housing.

6.4. *Centralisation, decentralisation and democracy*

Actions of British Conservative governments over the last two decades were directed towards centralisation, rather than democratic decentralisation of power. Local authority freedom to raise and spend money and to decide the level and method of service delivery has been

---

28 Such as that expressed in the Association of District Councils' [ADC] circular 1991/160): "Views on the Structure of Local Government in England"

curtailed. Some local councils have been abolished. In addition, the governments of 1983-May 1997 refused to sign the European Charter of Local Self Government that was published in Strasbourg in 1985. In the House of Lords, Baroness Blatch [Hansard, 1986], then Parliamentary Under-Secretary of State for the Environment, explained why:

> My lords, to give just one example, the government objects to the powers of general competence contained in the Charter. That provision means that local authorities would be empowered to do absolutely anything they wished outside the provisions proscribed by Parliament.

The government indicated, thereby, that the power to tell local government what *not* to do was insufficient; it wanted to retain the power to tell local government what it *might* do as well.

If the general arguments in favour of democratic enhancement by means of local decision-making proposed by Mill are accepted, it gives the centre a *prima facie* case to answer for an apparent reduction in democratic practice. However, there is also an argument that suggests that local councils may be just as unresponsive to public opinion as the centre. Besides, local councils too are elected on the relative majority system, so citizens whose participation is limited to the act of voting may be equally ineffective in influencing the political stance a council can take.

These arguments may be countered by noting that whatever else may be said about local government, it is *closer* to the people [Jones and Stewart 1983 p 5]. Fewer people are needed to elect a councillor, but fewer people are needed to elect her/his opponent. A councillor who lives locally and who depends for her/his council seat on the continuing support of hundreds rather than thousands of voters, may be expected to feel more directly the effects of Beetham's "long shadow" of the fact of voting [see above, Chapter One]. Parry *et al* [1992 pp 368-369] also noted that, whilst the voting level for local councils is relatively low, if "participation" is extended to include visiting council officers and consulting elected members, then far more people "participate" in local government than in national affairs.

The *prima facie* case that the centre needs to answer may also be countered by arguing that central government had *decentralisation* in mind when carrying out its policies in relation to local government. But, as noted above, this contention is not easy to sustain, given that there are varying interpretations of the meaning of local democracy and that devolution to unaccountable bodies is not evidence of democratic impulse. Also, as argued in Chapter One, democracy has its dynamic aspect and it is therefore a difficult concept to enforce from the top down.

In the UK case, the extent to which Parliament has concerned itself with other sources or potential sources of elected political authority illustrates not only the supremacy of Parliament, but also its determination that such supremacy should not be successfully challenged. Hence this Chapter concludes that the nature of UK's constitution and the way in which its institutions operate have created a democratic deficit. The actions of central government towards local government between 1979 and 1997 had the effect of increasing it[29].

---

29   but see below [Chapter Nine] for a discussion on the attitude of the 1997 "new" Labour government towards local government

CHAPTER THREE

THE UK, THE EUROPEAN UNION
AND THE LEGITIMACY DEFICIT

1.   The prima facie case for reducing the UK's democratic deficit

The last chapter showed that the UK system of government displays a
democratic deficit, and that, at least until the election of the Labour
government in 1997, there was little prospect of remedying this by means
of British political practice. This chapter examines the *prima facie* case
for the prospects of a reduction in the UK's democratic by means of
membership of the EU.

This could come about in two ways. First, the EU could enable or
enforce constitutional changes within the member states. Enforcement, as
is shown in Chapter Six [below], is not likely at present, although there
are prospects for encouraging or instituting change [Chapter Seven].
Second, the way in which the EU's governance develops can empower its
citizens by giving them control over a number of policy matters that are of
significance to them.

The EU now has many competences, and looks set to add to them. Its
"first pillar", under which the EU's main institutions are involved in the
decision making process, covers policy making in the areas of:

- agriculture
- audiovisual regulation
- common commercial policy
- competition, consumer policy
- cultural affairs
- economic and monetary issues
- economic and social cohesion
- education, vocational training and youth
- development policy
- employment and social issues
- energy
- enterprise policy
- environment
- equal opportunities

- external relations
- fisheries
- humanitarian aid
- information and communication
- the information society and telecommunications
- industrial regulation
- the internal market
- public health
- research and technology
- trans-European networks
- transport.

The Treaty of Amsterdam [ToA] adds matters relating to internal and external frontiers, visa policy, asylum and immigration and judicial co-operation to the "first pillar" (albeit with a five year transitional period). In addition the ToA gives the EU an expanded role in foreign and security policy ("second pillar"[1]) and in provisions on police and judicial co-operation in criminal matters ("third pillar") – issues which have been held traditionally to be the essence of national sovereignty.

Of course, the degree to which the EU's involvement with policies varies. In some areas, for example, Common Commercial Policy, Common Agricultural Policy and Common Fisheries Policy, most decisions are taken at EU level; in others, for example, competition or the environment, the EU is a significant player. In yet others, for example, education, health, housing and pensions, EU involvement is limited. Nevertheless the above is a formidable list of competences and means that the question of popular control over EU-level decision making is a significant one. An EU which was composed of fully accountable decision makers, or one which was able to devolve its powers "as closely as possible to the citizen" [Article A, TEU], would be one which had successfully enhanced democracy within all member states. The UK, in particular, could acquire a democratic gain from such developments.

2.   European Union influence over the UK

The EU, of which the UK is a full, participating and permanent member, is the greatest external political influence upon British governance.

There are several reasons for this. First, legislation passed at EU level becomes part of UK law. EU law mainly consists of regulations (directly applicable), directives (wherein the method of application is left to

---

1 Decision making under both the second and the third pillars is mainly in the hands of the Council and its bureaucracy

member states) and decisions (usually specifically directed, but directly applicable) all of which take precedence over UK law.   Also, EU policy competence, as shown above, is quite extensive.

Second, politicians from national and sub-national governments are taking part in EU policy processes at all levels – notably in the Council, the Commission, the EP, and the CoR.   Member state bureaucrats too are active in the administrative levels of these institutions.   Representative of most major interests and interest groups participate either as advisers[2] or as lobbyists.   The involvement of decision-makers and opinion-formers at EU level makes an impact within home member states because the act of participation in Europe-wide governmental processes gives rise to new ways of thinking and amongst all political actors.   It does this by means of exposing UK citizens to a range of cultural influences and constitutional traditions unlikely to have been experienced without "ever closer political union" with other member states.   These include, for example, other European states' attitude towards local government.

Third, the EU dimension has a significance in the evolutionary relationship between state and nation which offers a new dimension in the field of political science [Newton & Valles 1991; Haseler 1994 p 66] which, in the First World, has previously focused upon liberal representative government.

3.   The European Union and legitimacy

However, it is difficult at first sight to see how prospects for democratic enhancement are likely to arise from the EU, given popular attitudes towards it.

Weber [1967] defines three sources for the legitimate exercising of power: tradition, charisma and legality (see Chapter One).   The EU has not had time to achieve the first and its political actors are too remote, too numerous and too impermanent to be able to acquire the second.   This leaves legality (which is in any case now more common in modern liberal democracies) to form the basis for legitimate EU government.   The EU has a very substantial written constitution in the form of the treaties which give it shape and scope and which have received the formal consent of all member state governments.   This, however, is perceived to be insufficient.

Beetham and Lord [1998 p 3] argue that the use of political authority is legitimate only if it meets three criteria.   It should be it legally acquired and exercised; the rules that underpin this legality should be popularly and

2   For example, as members of the Economic and Social Committee [ECOSOC] or of the Commission's Expert and Advisory Committees

universally acceptable and it should be essentially temporary – that is to say, subject to continuous consent. They call this "rule legitimacy". Part of the problem for the EU is that legitimacy in all of these facets is limited. Initially political authority was legally acquired, but the extent to which that authority stretched was much more constricted than it is today. Additional competences have, of course, been appropriated legally, but, for people accustomed to rule-making shaped by and subjected to the popular mandate, treaties and neofunctional spillovers alike furnish a legality that may appear spurious. Renewed consent is limited to referenda in some member states or agreement by other member states' parliaments to the treaties. The implications of these treaties are often neither presented nor understood clearly at the time of their ratification.

Bogdanor [1996 p 105] argues that the EU is in danger of providing "That deepest and most intractable of all political cleavages, a cleavage between the people and the political class". Weiler [1992 pp 22-31] thinks that public acceptance of the EU has been delayed by the scope and range of legislation which emanates from within it and by the popular perception that the EU operates under different rules from those operating within more generally understood left/right party lines [*ibid* pp 31-35].

The most usual criticism of EU legitimacy is based upon its "democratic deficit". This term has been coined to describe a popular unease with decision-making processes within the EU in particular. It has been interpreted in a number of different ways. It may focus upon the unelected and hence unaccountable nature of the EU's primary decision-makers. It can also mean a general shortfall in practical arrangements for ensuring responsible democratic government. Of the five stages of policy making (proposing, advising, deciding, implementing and enforcing), the directly elected element – the EP – has a role only within the initiation and legislative stages [Goodman 1997]. In a wider sense, it can be defined as a failure to provide opportunities for self-government.

Weiler [1992 pp 18-27] agrees that governmental legitimacy is equivocal in the EU, but he feels that the legitimacy shortfall results only partially from a *democratic* deficit. He accords equal weight to problems issuing from the integration of polities which enjoyed popular legitimacy in isolation, but which may become less acceptable and therefore less socially legitimate in aggregate. The EU is also too heterogeneous to be accepted readily by the peoples of Europe. Weiler concludes that, whilst the EU has a formal (legal) legitimacy, it may lack a social (empirical) legitimacy. Beetham and Lord [1998 pp 23-30 *passim*] agree that there are several facets of governmental legitimacy. They suggest that these include performance (in relation to scope of competence and effectiveness of delivery) and identity (the lack of a sense of homogeneity among the EU's citizens) as well as democracy.

Beetham and Lord [1998 pp 30-32] note that the interactions between the EU and its member states confers a varying sense of EU legitimacy within the different states. They point out that people from member states whose governmental system has a low level of popular support are more likely to warm to the EU. They also argue that opportunities provided by the EU enhances the capacities of smaller states and (significantly) of regions within states. Thus the people of those states or those who identify strongly with those regions are more likely to have a favourable impression of EU membership.

This does not appear to apply to the UK. The notion is that the EU, usually epitomised as "Brussels", endangers national sovereignty, or the right of a nation to self-determination. A *Eurobarometer* survey conducted in spring 1999 found that of the EU15, an average of 56 per cent felt positive attachment to Europe, with 40 per cent making a negative response. It noted that UK citizens were the least likely to feel positive attachment to Europe (37 per cent) and the most likely to feel "not very" or "not at all" attached (57 per cent).

Although this may be a reflection of geographic rather than nationalist sentiments (the next least enthusiastic country was Greece, which shares no land borders with the rest of the EU), these figures indicate that the EU's legitimacy is conditional. Figures apart, in general the EU's citizens present an indifferent response to initiatives intended to extend its authority. They also deny it the distinction of taking part in its embryonic democratic processes [see Chapter Five].

The validity of such criticisms is sufficient to indicate that prospects for democratic enhancement via membership of the EU are in the long rather than short term.

Quite apart from this, a sketch of the EU's own "democratic deficit" (which is related both to the way in which power is distributed, and to the way in which it is exercised) provides further justification for pessimism [see below, 5].

If the EU is subjected to Beetham's analysis, therefore, so far it has acquired neither system nor governmental legitimacy. However, the most commonly proposed solution is to attempt to resolve the deficiency in governmental legitimacy in the expectation that this will lead to the provision of system legitimacy.

4.   The European Union and the British public

The EU is generally unpopular with the UK public in particular. The outcome of ten *Eurobarometer* surveys from 1982-1999 is shown below [Fig 3.1.].

Fig 3.1: The UK and the EU - citizens' attitudes 1982-1999

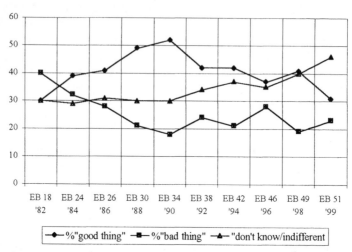

[Sources: *Eurobarometer* no 49, September 1998 and *Eurobarometer* no 50, June 1999 – adapted]

Although only in 1982 did the "negatives" towards the EU from amongst the UK respondents outweigh the "positives", it is noticeable from the surveys that it was only in 1990 that the "positives" were a higher percentage than the combined "negatives" and "don't know/indifferents". It is also noticeable that in spring 1999, immediately before the last set of European Elections, there were more "don't knows" than there were positives.

The study indicates that most of the UK public is either opposed to involvement with the EU or doubtful about it.   These anti-EU and sceptical views connect with the democratic deficit, when those who express them cite also the unelected nature of those who operate within the EU and comment adversely upon their methods of operation.   A similar percentage of UK respondents (32 per cent) expressed themselves as satisfied with EU democracy as were generally satisfied with the EU (31 per cent) in the *Eurobarometer* survey of 1999.

However, there also appears to be a widespread perception of over-bureaucratisation[3] and of a lack of transparency in the EU.   This implies that non-participants in the political process believe that "Brussels" reduces their control over their lives and suggests that non-politicians

---

3 This despite the fact that the Brussels bureaucracy corresponds roughly to that of a large metropolitan borough council in the UK

include a degree of the self-determination which was listed above [Chapter One] amongst the benefits of living within a "democratic" society.

5. European Union institutions and repairing the democratic deficit

The question of the distribution of power is considered below [Chapter Four], but it is noted here that power within the EU tends to be concentrated among the *unelected* bodies. This is the case both in constitutional theory and institutional practice at present, (although the *elected* element – the EP – is continuing to accumulate additional powers). In addition, these unelected bodies are neither effectively controlled nor adequately scrutinised by any means that may be regarded as democratic.

There are five main institutions directly concerned with EU government:

- *The European Council* which is composed of the heads of member states/governments and their foreign ministers[4], the Commission President and one other Commissioner

- *The Council of Ministers* whose membership varies, but which comprises member state ministers who hold national portfolios in the various EU policy arenas

- *The College of the European Commission*, whose members are selected by member states' governments

- *The European Court of Justice* [ECJ] whose members are also appointed theoretically "by common accord of the Governments of the Member states", although in practice each member state appoints one member

- The *European Parliament*, which is composed of individuals elected by the people of the member states.

It is the division of powers among these bodies that has been the primary source of accusations of a "democratic deficit". An examination of the unelected institutions [below] indicates that the bodies themselves are

---

4 Except in France, where the accompanying Minister may be the Prime Minister

unlikely to become the vehicles for enhanced democracy.

5.1.   *The European Council*

The European Council is the EU's agenda-setter, dealing with issues of a constitutional nature, although, since it is composed of heads of member states' or of their governments, its remit is both as wide-ranging and as specific as its participants wish [Nugent 1994 p 166].

Its members have been elected, but not specifically as members of the supranational body. A directly-elected President may have been chosen as much for her/his skills as a trans-European participant as for her/his other abilities in the fields of foreign and domestic policies. Nevertheless, the composite figure of national President has many dimensions besides that of EU negotiator, and the EU is not inevitably at the forefront of people's minds when they are casting votes for their President. The British Prime Minister has not been directly elected as the head of government.

5.2.   *The Council of Ministers*

As the EU's main legislative body, the Council of Ministers could be a key actor in promoting devolution within the member states. However, the way in which the Council is constituted – with its consequent unaccountability, the nature of its proceedings – which has led to criticisms about its openness – and its constitutional limitations, all indicate that it is no more likely than the European Council to repair the democratic deficit.

Members of the Council of Ministers are usually appointed by the heads of member states' governments. Individual members will probably be elected representatives, but they are even less likely than heads of state/government to have been elected for the purpose of representing their constituents' interests in, for example, agriculture, trade, or environment at EU level.

The Council of Ministers, like the European Council, has not been elected as a body on a European manifesto [Martin 1993] and, since their members have not been elected as such, neither body can be held collectively accountable [Wistrich 1994 p 112]. This problem has increased since the institution of the Single European Act [SEA] 1986, the TEU 1992 and the ToA 1997, all of which increased the EU's competences and extended qualified majority voting [QMV] in the Council of Ministers. It is theoretically possible for all the members of a national parliament to dissent unanimously from an EU policy. However, they cannot control the outcome if there are sufficient ministers from other member states who hold a different view, although in some circumstances (but not under the second and third pillar areas), elected representatives in the EP can intervene [see below Chapter Four]. Paradoxically, however, it has also been argued that the impact of Qualified Majority Voting has made it harder for the Council to exercise control over the decision-making process, and thus has paved the way for the Commission to substitute its own policy making methods [Marks *et al* 1996b p 364].

The Council of Ministers has also been criticised on the grounds of the secrecy of its proceedings. The record of Council's votes is published following the October 1993 revision of its rules of procedure, but the way in which decisions are reached is not. Gestures towards more openness have been made, but these have not always been substantiated. Although the ToA adds a declaration – that '...decisions are taken as openly as possible...' to the TEU's Article A [Common Provisions] –, the right of access to documentation only applies to the first pillar and empowers the Council (albeit in consultation with the EP) to determine limits to those rights.

Since the Council of Ministers is not a directly elected body it holds its democratic culture at second hand. There is no reason to suppose that such a body would be primarily concerned with devolution of power. Such evidence that exists supports the contrary [see below, Chapter Five]. No members of the Council of Ministers deal specifically with regional policy. The Council does not often discuss regional matters although regional policy ministers now meet informally at intergovernmental summits, and some Belgian and German regional ministers are members of the Council of Ministers on relevant occasions [see Chapter Six].

The Council of Ministers would, in any case, have difficulty promoting devolution of its own accord. Its members may hold positive views on the subject, but as part of an intergovernmental body, they are discouraged from interfering with the internal arrangements of a member state [under Article 3b, TEU] without that state's consent. After the Italian government proposed to change its electoral law to allow single member majority voting instead of proportional representation, MEPs asked the Council to take steps to "guarantee political pluralism and the rights of minorities to be represented" (in support of the EP resolution under the rapporteurship of De Gucht). The reply from the Council was simply that as this related to the internal political organisation of a member state, "the Council is not competent to reply to the Honourable Members' Question" [*Official Journal* No C283 p 48, 20 October 1993].

5.3.   *The European Commission*

The European Commission's primary task is to initiate and execute legislation, although it also has a range of political functions related to giving effect to Treaty provisions.   Members of the College of Commissioners are awarded their portfolios after their appointment by the President of the Commission, her/himself appointed by the agreement of the heads of member states' governments, although now they are also examined by the EP whose consent is needed [see below, Chapter Four].

The College of Commissioners has a five year tenure of office and its members usually retain the same portfolio throughout.   (The Commission's bureaucracy is permanent although the addition of officials from newly-joined member states prevents full entrenchment of existing staff.)   Critics have argued that the role designated for the Commission inevitably supplies a democratic deficit and that this was the intention of the EU's Founding Father, Jean Monnet [Featherstone 1994 p 162].

The Commission's role in devolution and diffusion of powers is, however, an ambiguous one.   Although unelected, the Commission may contain Commissioners who are individually committed to the principle of devolution.   This was certainly the case with the former Commissioner responsible for the regional portfolio, Bruce Millan.   Monika Wulf-Mathies, Regional Commissioner from 1994-1999, had a reputation for extensive consultation and co-operative dealing among sub-national actors.   In any case, whatever her/his personal views, the Commissioner in charge of regional policies needs to encourage greater participation by sub- and non-governmental levels of decision-making to gain the necessary information and expertise to serve its purposes, for example, effective distribution of the Structural Funds [see Chapter Seven].

There may be more ideologically-based reasons.   The Commission can utilise its relationships with sub-national actors to bring about a more closely integrated EU [see below, Chapter Six].   It is particularly advantageously placed to do this successfully, given that it has the advantages of continuity and consistency.   The Commission's legislative proposals are considered in detail by the Council of Ministers and by the EP, but it is the Commission that initiates policy proposals, giving it the opportunity to set the EU's agenda.   In addition, the College of Commissioners is likely to be composed of extremely experienced and senior politicians [Page and Wouters 1994], which enables it to accomplish its leadership function.   Insofar as the Commission is an agent for EU integration, it is also an agent for devolving and diffusing the EU's policy-making processes.   The Commission may have a part to play in the *de facto* devolution of power.

Nevertheless, the Commission operates within strict limits. The conclusions of the Edinburgh meeting (11-12 December 1992) of the European Council stress the importance of the Commission's role with relation to Article 3b [TEU] only – that is in implementing subsidiarity in relation to the member state level [Part III (a): Procedures and Practices]. Hence, irrespective of personal views of Commissioners, the Commission is bound to work according to the agenda laid down in the Treaties as clarified by the Council of Ministers.

5.4.   *The European Court of Justice*

Members of the European Court of Justice [ECJ] are appointed on the basis of their general legal background – typically they have legal qualifications, but have limited experience in judicial practice – and have normally been involved with their member state's government in some capacity.

The ECJ's role is to apply and to interpret the provisions of EU law, when cases are referred to it by Commission, Council, member states, or, in restricted circumstances, by private individuals or companies. After the ratification of the TEU, some commentators speculated what the ECJ might do if it were asked to judge conflicting interpretations of subsidiarity [Newman [1996 p 125]. This has not yet happened, and looks increasingly unlikely since the CoR was unsuccessful in its bid to acquire recourse to the ECJ concerning breaches to the subsidiarity principle affecting regional and local authorities under the ToA.

The ECJ has a *de facto* as well as a *de jure* role, however. Marks *et al* [1996b pp 369-371] point to research which indicates that the ECJ has created the basis for an integrated EU polity and suggest that, like the other EU institutions, it is interdependent with other actors upon whom it relies to set its agenda and support its pronouncements. This has led to a an acceptance of ECJ decisions which, they claim, has the effect of "shifting expectations about decision-making authority from a purely national-based system to one that is more multi-level."

6.   The European Parliament and the democratic deficit

Despite their own shortcomings as a vehicle for delivering decentralisation and providing popular accountability the EU's institutions hold the view that there are prospects for reducing the democratic deficit at European level and believe that it is the EP which holds the main key.

The recognition of the EP's case found expression in the preamble to the SEA [1986]. This reads in part that the European Council was:

> Convinced that the European idea, the results achieved in the fields of economic integration and political co-operation, and the need for new developments correspond to the wishes of the democratic peoples of Europe, *for whom the EP, elected by universal suffrage, is an indispensable means of expression.*
> (author's emphasis)

The "Birmingham Declaration" expressed similar sentiments. In its statement, *A Community close to its Citizens*, the European Council stressed "the European Parliament's important role in the democratic life of the Community" [paragraph four], although the emphasis in the clause was placed more heavily upon national parliaments. The Irish Tanaiste and Minister for Foreign Affairs, Dick Spring, declared in his 1997 statement on the Inter Governmental Conference [IGC] summarising a draft outline for a Treaty revision, that: "A strong European Parliament is an essential part of a democratic Union".

The European Commission's view was stated in its *Declaration on the two IGCs* published on 27 November 1991. It thought that "Injecting greater democracy into Community life should be achieved *primarily* by giving the European Parliament greater powers" (author's emphasis), and it looked to the Parliament "to become fully a co-legislator". The Commission's report for the Reflection Group [1995], which looked at options for the 1996-1997 IGC, confirmed its belief that the need for EP approval for the Commission and increase in the EP's legislative powers had contributed significantly to the strengthening of the EU's democratic legitimacy.

David Martin, one of the Vice Presidents of the EP, asks: "can we really accept that over 100 million voters should be asked to vote every five years for a democratic figleaf on an undemocratic system?" [Martin 1988]. This question, echoing Spinelli [1966 p 171] implies that the Parliament would render the system democratic if only it had sufficient power. Martin's [1989] view is that directly participatory democracy remains "an idea to be aimed at rather than a principle which we can put into practice...". He thinks, therefore that: "It is the job of the politician and political scientist to make sure that our representative democracy represents the people who elect it and not other interests".

Martin seems to speak for the Parliament. In its resolution on the IGC submitted to the European Council of 1989, the EP declared in its preamble that "... the democratic structure of the Community will remain incomplete until Parliament possesses joint decision-making rights on an equal footing with the Council in all important policy decisions...". In its proposals for the 1996 IGC, the EP claimed "equal status" and rights of co-decision with the Council of Ministers, on the grounds of its elected status.

The idea that the EP has the potential to reduce the democratic deficit is also shared by some of the member states. In their joint declaration on strengthening the powers of the EP during the IGC, of 10 April 1991, Germany and Italy noted: "*it is no longer admissible that the Institution,* which is the direct expression of the will of the people, *be kept on the edge of the legislative process* of the Community and that the "last word" in this process be left to the Council alone." [emphasis in original]. They added that the EP and Council together represented "popular sovereignty" and "governmental legitimacy".

Federalist academics also look to the EP to improve EU democracy. Boyce [1993] comments that the EP enjoys democratic legitimacy, but that this is of limited efficacy because of the limits of EP power. In a Fabian pamphlet published in 1991, Lodge argued that: "The democratic deficit can only be rectified by increasing the power of the European Parliament to perform a legislative function and to exercise democratic scrutiny and control over the legislative process". In her 1994 article [p 356], Lodge believed that "Until [the EP] is given genuine co-decision rights with the Council across the board, the deficit will remain". However, she thinks that there are other components to the democratic deficit. In 1996 [p 189] she points out: "... democratic legitimacy implies also that government is lawful and that its authority is accepted; something that could not be deduced merely from Euro-elections".

An elected EP may be insufficient. For the EP to feature in enhancing democratic practice within its member states, it is necessary for it to be an institution that is powerful and also one which may prove to "represent the people who elect it and not other interests". If it were not both, it could hardly fulfil the requirements for providing a vehicle for "people power".

However, the empowered EP is required not only to democratise but also to legitimise and popularise the EU in the eyes of its people. To rely upon the evolution of EP powers to resolve the crisis of legitimacy may be to place too much emphasis on one institution. There is another point that should be taken into account as well – that liberal democratic governments throughout the EU are also suffering crises in confidence.

The role of the EP in this context is examined in the following Chapters. It is argued therein that the EP itself has evolved in accordance with previous notions of a liberal democracy. These notions may not now serve citizens who have come to demand and require more self-government and who have now the resources to secure their ends in the long term.

7. Other prospects for democracy within the European Union

It has been argued above that the EU has more than a democratic deficit with which to deal. However, there may still be a democratic answer to these concerns, which have to do with the devolution ("subsidiarity") or to the diffusion ("multi-level" or "multi-sector governance") of power.

Two schools of thought have developed about the way in which the EU is developing.   On the one hand is the presumption of state centric governance or intergovernmentalism, wherein member states dictate the pace of integration, and the function of supranational agencies is to serve the member states.   State-centricity, which interprets the concept of subsidiarity as simply entrenching "states rights" [see Chapter Six], offers little hope for devolution of powers as a means of resolving the democratic deficit.

In the event, state-centricity, whilst it may be the preferred *prescription* for some members states' actors (notably some member states' governments), may not be an accurate *description* of the process which is taking place.   Nation states, faced with globalisation factors as well as the "spill over" effects of EU policy making, may not be able to continue to divide their competences solely between themselves and the EU.   This leads some observers[5] to suggest that the alternative "multi-level governance" model gives a more appropriate portrayal of the EU polity. In this model, both legitimacy and policy competence is derived from across supra-national, national and sub-national levels of government [Marks *et al* 1996b p 342; Banchoff and Smith 1999 p 2].   At present the supra-national and national levels exercise *de jure* powers, but a growing number of commentators [Marks 1996a; 1996b; Hooghe 1996] argue that lower levels practise *de facto* competences and influences.   Scott *et al* [1994 pp 58-59] suggest that moving the EC towards regionalism, by giving sub-national government these kinds of opportunities for participation in the EU decision-making process is an alternative method of resolving the democratic deficit.   This may also solve the problems for democracy related to "diversity and participatory democracy" as described above [Chapter One].

These problems could also be resolved by a third option that the evolving EU may provide.   Held [1993] has suggested that the problem of legitimacy may be related to the international order wherein economic decisions by one nation state impact upon another whose inhabitants have no power over the decisions taken by the first.   His alternative prescription is for "agencies and organisations which form an element of, and yet cut across, the territorial boundaries of the nation-state".   His suggestion is therefore, not so much for "multi-*level* governance" but rather "multi-*sector* governance".   Hirst's [1994] "associative democracy" fits into the same group of theories.

There are, then, a number of options to consider when determining what

5 For example Marks *et al* 1996a and 1996b; Hooghe 1996

are the prospects for the EU to enhance democracy and democratic practice in one of its more centralised member states. These will be considered in the following three chapters.

CHAPTER FOUR

POWER AND THE EUROPEAN PARLIAMENT

1.   Relations of power

The possession and exercise of power of an institution in a liberal democracy is legitimate only inasmuch as the institution expresses the voice of, or carries out the will of, or is accountable to the people. The conventional position is that the EU's democratic deficit would be reduced if only the EP had more power [see above Chapter Three]. This Chapter, however, shows that whilst the EP has been steadily gaining powers, this has not yet been sufficient to reduce the democratic deficit.

To reach this conclusion, this chapter looks first at the general question of power and legitimacy and second the formal powers of the Parliament. Third, it examines examples of the way in which power has been exercised. Finally prospects for enhancement are surveyed.

2.   Power, legitimacy and the European Parliament

The existence of the EP is defined constitutionally. However, because the constitution that created and supports the EU itself has only conditional legitimacy itself [see Chapter Three] it may not be taken for granted that it has endowed the EP with popular legitimacy. If popular consent to a political *system* is limited, then to look to one of its *institutions* – in this case the EP – to resolve this situation, before that institution has achieved consent in its own right, places too much pressure on it. It also perhaps strains the liberal democratic system of electing representatives.

3.   Status of the European Parliament

There are two fundamental problems in defining the status of the EP. The first relates to its *de jure* status. The Treaties which incorporate the EU do not give EP constitutional sovereignty (unlike the UK Parliament). If a parliament is not sovereign, then its function is less easy to define. The status of the EP – then entitled "European Assembly" – as envisaged in the Treaty of Paris 1951 and Treaties of Rome 1957, was that originally signified in the term – a talking shop or consultative body. This hardly describes the position of the present EP.

The second relates to the EP's *de facto* status. If this depends upon power, the EP's is uncertain. Jacobs *et al* [1992 p 6] point out that the problem is compounded because all EU member states have distinctive parliaments themselves giving rise to different expectations about the role of a parliament. They claim [*ibid*] that the EP "is a unique institution with an involvement in all of the roles associated with parliaments". However the task of assessing whether this "involvement" makes the EP a *real* parliament as well as a unique one is problematic and subjective. Those committed to parliamentary democracy may argue that only a parliament supreme in the exercise of its legislative function is truly a parliament. The democrat may suggest that the only *real* parliament is one which rules in the name of the sovereign people who have elected its members and have the power to reject those members for whatever reason they choose.

Neither of these definitions applies to the EP. However, a parliament that is not sovereign should at least operate as a constraint on the executive, as required by a liberal polity. It may not declare the law, but it should be able to have some form of legislative input, it should be able to scrutinise the executive and legislature and it should have some input into budgetary matters. Spinelli [1966 p 153] thinks that a parliament should also be able to legislate, to impose taxes and to participate decisively in the choice of the head of government.

The EP's powers, although both readily quantifiable and easily catalogued in one sense (since they are conveniently laid down in the various Treaties [see below, 4.] are harder to define in another because they are still expanding. At the same time, the EP's overall significance is also changing in relation to the balance of powers held by other EU institutions[1].

From the point of view of enhancing popular democracy, however, it must be the potential for the EP to expand its powers and grow into a parliament which is "real" in either of the democratic senses which is of greatest significance.

4.   Formal powers

4.1.   *The Treaties of Paris and Rome*

The functions laid down for the Assembly in the Treaty of Paris 1951 for the Common Assembly were strictly advisory. Those of the Treaties of

---

1 see, for example, Dankert [1997 p 212] who argues that the emphasis on intergovernmentalism in the second and third "pillars" of the EU and the enhancement of the European Council's role both present particular challenges to the EP.

Rome (EEC and Euratom) 1957 were also mainly consultative. Article 137 [EEC] stated that:

> The Assembly, which shall consist of representatives of the peoples of the States brought together in the Community, shall exercise the *advisory* and *supervisory* powers which are conferred on it by this Treaty.

[author's emphasis].

Hence the Treaties provided not for a "Parliament", but rather for an "Assembly" or talking shop consisting of 198 members from national parliaments [Article 138 EEC], whose members spoke as representatives not of the people, but of their bodies of origin.

This reflected the wish of its French instigators to avoid any suggestion of supranationalism [Greenwood 1992 p 31]. Jacobs *et al* [1992 p 7] comment: "Having created a Parliamentary assembly... the Member states were extremely cautious about giving it any powers".

Apart from fairly extensive consultative provisions, there were three other measures relating to the Assembly by the EEC Treaty that proved to have a lasting significance. First, under Article 122, the Assembly was given the power to "invite" the Commission to draw up reports on any particular problems concerning social conditions. This effectively empowered the founding members of the Assembly to request legislative proposals.

Second, the infrastructure of the relationship between the Commission and Assembly was laid down. The Commission was given the right to attend all meetings of the Assembly [Article 140] and the Assembly was required to discuss the Commission's report on an annual basis [Article 143]. The Commission was required to publish this report not later than one month before the opening session of the Assembly [Article 156]. Also, under Article 144, the Assembly was empowered to censure the whole Commission, which, if this received a two-thirds majority, was required to resign. More than forty years later, this was to become of more than theoretical significance.

Third, the European Assembly was given a means of control over the Budget under Article 203, which empowered the Assembly to adopt the budget (with a three-fifths majority). This was another power that was to be exercised effectively almost a half century later. It could also increase the total amount under its right of amendment, although there is a limit set upon the amount by which it may propose an increase.

The EEC Treaty provided for direct elections to the Assembly, although this was not executed until more than twenty years later. The provision indicates that the originators of the European Economic Community foresaw and intended an enhanced democratic role for the EP. When implemented, the elected status did have an impact upon the EP's efforts to develop its powers. Steppat [1988 p 8] notes that the EP's activities increased substantially after the first set of direct elections in its policy making, system developing and interactive functions.

4.2. From Rome to the Single European Act

In 1962, the European Assembly adopted for itself the title "European Parliament", presumably believing that this title would enhance its authority. However the self-styled "Parliament" was still not directly elected, and its title was not incorporated into EC legislation until 1970.

Most of the statutory increases in the EP's powers between 1957 and 1986 were within the field of budgetary control. In 1970, a *Treaty amending certain budgetary provisions* gave the Parliament the right to propose modification to compulsory expenditure (mainly upon agriculture); and to propose "amendments" to non-compulsory expenditure (all but agriculture). A second *Treaty amending certain financial provisions* (1975) empowered the Parliament "acting by a majority of its members and two thirds of the vote cast [to] reject, if there are important reasons, the draft budget and ask for a new draft to be submitted to it." [Article 203 (8)]. This was an important step in that it enabled the Parliament to reject the whole budget if it objected to the final draft. In 1980, the ECJ ruled in a controversial interpretation of this Treaty that the EP could effect this by instructing its president to refuse to sign the final draft [George 1985 p 3]. Again, at the end of the 1990s, this became a significant issue.

The Parliament's control over the budget was refined by the *Joint declaration of 30 June 1982 by the EP, the Council and the Commission on various methods to improve the Budgetary Procedure*. This permitted the EP to require the Council and Commission to legislate to institute new budget heads for matters within the EC's jurisdiction not already covered in the existing budget. Expenditure limits were to be placed within the Parliament's dominion – the budgetary process – rather than in the legislative process.

4.3. The Single European Act [1987]

The SEA amended the provisions of the Treaty of Paris (1951) and the two Treaties of Rome (1957). The main significance to the EP was to bring into operation *co-operation* and *assent procedures* that supplemented the *consultation* requirement of the original Treaties. The co-operation procedure gave the EP limited control over some areas of the

EC's policy competences[2] where decisions were taken under QMV [Nugent 1994 p 50]. In such cases, Article 149 required the Council to explain to the EP the reasons for Council's common position and to give the EP the opportunity to amend or reject the common position. In this instance, the decision was to be referred back to Commission that must take into account the EP's objections/amendments and then to refer the amended proposition back to the Council. At the same time the EP was given a final say in matters relating to the EC's enlargement. The EP's assent became necessary for the accession of new members to the Community [Article 237] and for Association Agreements between the Community and third countries [Article 238]. This power too was later to be exercised effectively.

The SEA provided other additional powers to the Parliament. Even where the Council acted unanimously "to ensure co-ordination of general economic policies of Member States", the EP was to be entitled to express an Opinion [Article 145]. Also the EP was included as a consultee in proposed legislation intended to aid the functioning of the internal market [Articles 99; 100A] and to bring about economic and social cohesion [Articles 130a-130s]. It must also be consulted when considering matters relating to the ECJ [Article 140a; 168a; 188].

The overall effect of the SEA was to make some progress towards co-decision making powers for the EP; and to give it some right of action relating to the constitutional and institutional structure of the EC.

Parliamentary activity increased following the SEA, although this may have been due to greater involvement rather than augmented powers. Duff [1994] calculates that in 1987, Parliament adopted 522 resolutions; asking 2942 written questions and 1109 oral questions. These were increased to 733, 4111 and 1604 respectively in 1993.

4.4.   *Treaty on European Union (Maastricht Treaty) 1992*

Thus, as the process of formalising and accelerating the pace of European integration began, the EP was already accepted as a legitimate institution whose claims could not be ignored during the discussion process. However, since the discussions were intergovernmental, the Parliament had limited opportunity to take part and did not have the constitutional power to ratify the Treaty.

In 1984, the EP had supported by a sizeable majority a draft Treaty that would establish the EU. However in the final version of the TEU the Parliament was only included in the amendments to the original Treaty of

---

2 The most significant were measures undertaken for the completion of the Single Market

Paris and Treaties of Rome[3]. These were listed in Articles G-I29 – the "revised EC articles". Article D required the Council to report to the Parliament after each of its meetings and annually upon progress achieved by the Union. Article E required the Parliament along with the Council and Commission, to act in accordance with the provisions of the Treaties [Nugent 1994 p 67].

It was also given rights regarded by Westlake [1995 p 65] as "weakly consultative" and by Dankert [1997 p 218] as "minimal" on the two other "pillars" of the Treaty: in Article J.7 – Common Foreign and Security Policy – and in Article K.6 – Justice and Home Affairs. Martin [1993] comments: "As far as the EP was concerned, Maastricht was not a dream come true".

The EP's power to influence legislation was, however, strengthened by the adoption of the co-decision procedure of Article 189b. Article 189b enables a conciliation procedure when the Council and Parliament fail to agree. In this a Conciliation Committee (comprising equal numbers of members of Council or their representatives and members of the EP) tries to agree joint texts. Should this prove to be unrealisable, the EP has the final say if it chooses to reject by an absolute majority the Council's text. Article 189 also includes the EP as a third institution to act jointly with Council and Commission to make regulations, issue directives, take decisions, make recommendations or deliver opinions.

The TEU also introduced a number of new areas wherein the Parliament must be consulted, which covered areas of citizenship, competition, taxation and making financial regulations. In other areas, for example adopting broad guidelines for economic policies of member states, the EP's statutory right to be kept informed is enshrined in the TEU.

Under the TEU, the Council, the European Central Bank [ECB] and the Commission are required to report to Parliament on a regular basis. The EP has the right to confirm the appointment of the President and to approve the appointment of the Commission.

The TEU enhanced opportunities for the Parliament to initiate legislation, laying down the provision for the EP to "request the Commission to submit any appropriate proposal on matters on which it considers that a Community act is required for the purpose of implementing this Treaty" [Article 138b]. Martin [1993] comments that this amounts to giving the EP "half a right to initiate legislation".

Parliament's control over the budget was increased. Article 204 enables the EP, on three fifths of the vote cast, to adopt a different decision on additional expenditure from that of the Council if the expenditure does not

---

3   That is the "pillar" which is based on the existing European Communities

fall within the provisions of the Treaty or acts adopted in accordance with it.   The EP is responsible for giving discharge to the Commission regarding the implementation of the budget [Article 206 (1)] and the Commission must act upon its observations [Article 206 (3)].   The Parliament may ask the Commission to give evidence about the execution of expenditure or operation of financial control systems that the Commission must provide [Article 206 (2)].   The EP's supervision of the budget has been given greater impetus via the appointment of the Court of Auditors [Article 188a].   Its role is to provide the EP and Council with assurances as to the reliability of accounts and legality and regularity of the underlying transactions.   It is also intended to assist the EP and Council over the implementation of the budget.   In the months before the 1999 European Elections, the EP's right to auditors' reports were to lead to a crisis in the EU's affairs [see below].

EU citizenship was given a boost when individuals were given the right to petition Parliament [Article 8d] in accordance with Article 138d, which means on any matter which comes within the Community's field of activity and affecting an individual directly.   Complaints may be referred to an Ombudsman, whose duties are laid down by the EP after seeking the Commission's Opinion and the approval of the Council [Article 138e]. The TEU has also given the EP an investigative or supervisory role by enabling it to set up temporary Committees of Inquiry to "investigate alleged contraventions or maladministrations in the implementation of Community law" [Article 138c].

4.5.   The Treaty of Amsterdam [ToA]

The ToA in response partly to the demands expressed by Commission and the EP itself, supplied enhancements to the powers of the EP.   The EP's Assent is now required under a new Article Fa that enables the EU to suspend any member state: "in the event of a serious and persistent breach of fundamental rights by a Member State".   The co-operation procedure has been reduced to a very few issues relating to Economic and Monetary Union [EMU] only and a simplified co-decision procedure (dropping the third reading) has been substituted for all other issues previously included under it[4].   These changes, of course, represent major extensions to the EP's powers – not only because of the number of areas now subject to co-

---

4   These include employment [Article 5], social policy [Article 119], public health [Article 129], principles for transparency [Article 191a], countering fraud [Article 209a], statistics [Article 213a] and the establishment of an independent advisory authority on data protection [Article 213b]

decision, but also because the omission of the third reading means that where conciliation does not work, the proposed instrument will be dropped [Petite 1998]. However, the EP was not given the power of assent over amendments of the Treaties (Article N) for which it had lobbied.

5. Has the European Parliament sufficient formal power?

Irrespective of the evolution of powers, the EP still lacks the competences to make it the sovereign voice of the people, although it exercises the key functions outlined above [3.]. It has some form of legislative input, it has some input into budgetary matters and it does scrutinise, to some extent, the EU's executive. Westlake [1994 pp 174-181] lists the means whereby the EP can exercise this function:

- posing questions to Council or Commission (written and oral and during 'Question time')
- following up on the Commission's undertakings
- utilising the 'comitology' proceedings to secure access to Commission working groups' papers
- establishing temporary Committees of Enquiry [power granted by the TEU]

Nugent [1994 p 174] although he accepts that the EP's constitutional powers are fewer than those normally the prerogative of national legislatures, concludes that developments over the years have given the EP "not inconsiderable" influence within the Community. On the other hand, Dankert [1997 p 214] thinks that the EP is "relatively weak compared to most national parliaments".

Although, as with other non-sovereign bodies, the extent of the EP's influence outweighs its formal powers [see below], it still lacks the status of the *sovereign* voice of the people that it was elected to represent. This is because none of the enhancements to its competences endow it with the independent and final decision-making powers. Therefore, neither Parliamentary nor popular sovereignty forms the political infrastructure of the EU.

6. The European Parliament's use of power

The reality of power, though, depends equally upon the use to which it is put. This part of the chapter looks at significant instances of the way in which the EP has used its powers since the TEU in an attempt to discover whether its powers have been utilised effectively.

6.1.   *Parliamentary Assent before the accession of new countries*
         [Article 237]

This example was chosen because it shows that the EP does not make only
nominal use of its assent powers; it may also use them successfully as
bargaining counters towards greater influence in unrelated issues.   The
experience of the ratification of the new member states justifies Dankert's
[1997 p 212] claim that the extension of the assent procedure to this area
was "progress".

Under Article 237 EC, the agreement of at least 260 MEPs is needed to
enable new countries to accede.   The first four countries to apply for
membership since the SEA was ratified were Austria, Finland, Norway
and Sweden.   In 1994, the negotiations for EU membership for these
countries were concluded[5].

The EP was initially favourably disposed.   The EP minutes of 17
November 1993 include a resolution on negotiations on the enlargement of
the EU to include the four states [a.133-1553 and 1554/93].   Heads of
government from the three countries (excluding Norway) duly proceeded
to Brussels to lobby the Parliament.

However, it began to be clear that not all MEPs were enthusiastic about
the project.   Boyce [1995 p 152] comments that some members were more
concerned to "deepen" before "widening".   This gave rise to fears that,
despite the initial majority within the EP for "widening", insufficient
MEPs could be mustered for the vote.   These fears were expressed in the
EP's April plenary.   Its minutes contain a resolution on enlargement
which complains that the Council had failed to respond to the EP's request
for the full text of the treaties on enlargement and that there had been no
discussion on the institutional reforms needed [B3-0148, 0150, 0151,
0152/94].

The Greek Presidency responded by promising the EP a greater role in
shaping political union if it agreed to admit the new applicants to the
Union.   In addition to a few minor concessions relating to enlargement
[Corbett 1999 p 102], the EP was assured that it would be formally
included in the consultations in the lead-up to the 1996 review of the
TEU, as it had not been during discussions regarding the original Treaty.
Honours presumably being satisfied following this pledge, at its May
plenary the EP voted convincingly for the accession of the four countries
with between 376 (Norway) and 381 (Sweden) votes in favour.   The EP's
President: "... noted that the Parliament's vote in favour of accession was

---

5   Although the result of a referendum held in Norway later led to the
Norwegian government to withdraw its application.

an historic moment and welcomed the new member states to the European family" [EP minutes, 4 May 1994 C205/143].

The Greek foreign minister, Theodoros Pangalos, confirmed that the EP would be invited to join member states in preparing the discussion documents for the 1996 conference. The Corfu European Council, 24-25 June 1995, formally granted this concession [Duff 1994] and the EP was allowed to participate in the work of the IGC's Reflection Group [Dinan 1997 p 188]. Whilst the EP was not granted full participation rights in the IGC itself, two of its representatives were allowed to attend some of the working group meetings, and it was agreed that the representatives, with the President of the EP, would be consulted at the start of the monthly IGC meetings of foreign ministers [Corbett 1999 p 103].

6.2.   *Budgetary scrutiny*

One of the EP's key powers [see above 4.3. and 4.4.] lies in its control over the budget. This example, therefore, was chosen to demonstrate the way in which the EP exercises this authority.

The EP's substantial powers over the budget were utilised to good effect by the 1994-1999 Parliament. For example, in December 1994, MEPs forced the Italian government to allow a budget increase by threatening to make savings in regional, thermonuclear fusion and fisheries polices and in-travel allowances which enabled national officials to attend Brussels meetings. It even kept the travelling allowances for national officials in reserve, releasing it only when the EP had received and analysed full reports on the activities of the "Comitology Committees" attended by officials[6]. The EP published the full text of the 1995 budget in December 1995 [OJ L369. 31.12.95, pp 1-1913].

This Parliament kept sight of its ability to use its power over the budget to deliver other ends that it deems desirable. In his report for the 1996 budgetary procedure, for example, James Elles [UK EPP] stated that the Budgets Committee:

> insists that there must be more transparency in the decision-making nature of the Council of Ministers; to this effect, urges that conciliation meetings between the EP and the Council in July and November be held in public.

[Report on the guidelines for the 1996 budgetary procedure, Section III –

---

6   Terry Wynn MEP, letter to author, 28 February 1995.   NB the 'comitology' procedure has been the basis of heavy criticism relating to the bureaucratic nature of EU decision-making (see Corbett [1994 pp 220-221]).

Commission, Committee on Budgets 24 March 1995].

During the same procedure, the EP successfully used its powers over the budget to press EU committees, staffed by national civil servants and experts, to open up their proceedings to MEPs [*European Voice*, 10-16 October 1996]. By threatening to withhold funds, the EP had previously managed to obtain access to agendas for committee meetings and results of any votes taken. In October 1996, the EP indicated that it might freeze the running costs of such committees, unless Council and Commission agreed that MEPs could attend them automatically, except where delegates decided unanimously with explicit reasons, that they should be debarred.

Budget controversy continued into the late 1990s. The Commission approved the preliminary draft budget for 1999 on 29 April 1998 (*Bull.EU*, No.4, 1998, p73-77) and the Council adopted a first reading draft on 17 July 1998 (*Bull.EU*, No.7-8, 1998, p112-118). The European Parliament voted on the first reading on 22 October 1998 and the Council approved a draft 1999 budget at a second reading on 24 November 1998 (*Press Release* (Council), PRES/98/406 (24.11.98). The EP however held out for the inclusion of a strategic reserve, which resulted in a further Budget Council and trialogue held on 8 December 1998 to resolve these disagreements. The compromise eventually reached did not include the reserve, but the Council agreed to accept elements of flexibility within the context of negotiations for a new inter-institutional agreement [*Press Release* (Council), PRES/98/436 (8.12.98)]. The EP then agreed to adopt the 1999 budget on 17 December 1998 [Thomson and Mather 1999].

6.3.   *The European Parliament and the Commission*

On the same date that the EP ratified the 1999 budget, it received a Court of Auditors' report on the 1996 budget, which had been discharged by the Auditors' by a fine margin. During the previous months, various allegations of fraud, particularly in the areas of tourism, aid and education had been made. The EP refused to ratify the budget report, rejecting it by 270 votes to 225, attracting a vehement response from the Commission President, Jacques Santer. For reasons that appeared obscure at the time, the leader of the Party of European Socialists [PES], Pauline Green, declared her intention to table a motion of censure, and at the same time announced that she would not be supporting it. This motion was debated on 11 January 1999 [EP Briefing: 11-01-99] and on the 14 January 1999 it was defeated by 293 votes to 232, with 27 abstentions. In response to demands from the PES during the debate, Santer promised to deliver a timetable for modernising Commission administration by 3 March 1999, with new rules to be in place by 28 April 1999 and a revision of financial regulations in June 1999.

The EP, however, was still dissatisfied and decided to appoint a committee of experts, to be known as the *Comité des Sages* (mostly former auditors) to report on the varying accusations directed at the Commission [EP Daily Notebook: 14-01-99]. The Commissioner who attracted most adverse criticism was the French Edith Cresson, Commissioner for science, research and development, human resources, education, training and youth. On 23 February 1999, the EP called for her resignation, but Cresson refused to depart.

As Santer had undertaken, on 3 March 1999 the Commission agreed on two codes of conduct governing the behaviour of EU Commissioners and their relations with the Commission's department, but on 14 March 1999, advance copies of the formal inquiry report were circulated. At this, the EP issued an ultimatum that Cresson be dismissed, threatening to dismiss the whole Commission if this demand was not met. The EP was preparing to force a motion of censure during the week starting 15 March 1999, which it expected to win easily. The official issue on 15 March of the *Comité des Sages* Report showed it to be heavily critical of the Commission. It was particularly censorious of Cresson, Marin (External relations with Southern Mediterranean countries, the Middle East, Latin America and Asia) and João Pinheiro (External relations with African, Caribbean and Pacific countries and South Africa). The issue of the report prompted the entire Commission to resign. Santer [DN: IP/99/172 Bruxelles, le 16 mars 1999] issued a statement:

> In the light of the report by the independent experts, the members of the Commission have decided unanimously this evening to tender their collective resignation. The Commission thus takes on its responsibilities, in conformity with the undertaking which it has taken to give following the report of the Committee of independent experts. Tomorrow, I shall inform the Conference of the Presidents of the European Parliament, and I will make a declaration in the name of the Commission at the end of that conference.

The following day, Santer muddied the waters by arguing that no Commissioner had been found to be involved in fraud, corruption or personal gain, and that the conclusions of the report were not justified by the evidence contained therein. He pointed to the significance of past and future reforms within the Commission and he suggested that the Commission's resignation was a gesture of collective responsibility rather than of an acceptance of guilt. He announced the Commission's intention of continuing to exercise its functions until replaced. This, however, was unacceptable both to the EP and the member states' governments. Romano Prodi, ex-President of Italy was chosen to be the new President of the Commission, although the remaining Commissioners stayed in office until new nominees were proposed, just before the 1999 European

Elections, and were accepted by the EP after a series of hearings after the elections.

The implications of these events for the Commission are likely to be far reaching, but the impact upon the authority of the EP may be less significant. When Pauline Green proposed her motion of censure, but announced her intention not to support it, this apparent inconsistency seems to have been due to her realisation that the UK government would be unhappy about an EU crisis at this point. Significant issues relating to the new currency, enlargement and the UK's rebate on the budget remained unresolved. On the other hand, during the debate on censure Ms Green implied that her actions were undertaken merely "so that those who felt the Commission to be culpable over the 1996 budget should face up to their responsibility and the logical consequences of their vote". Since there is no procedure for putting forward a motion of confidence, Ms Green decided to propose a vote of censure so that the EP could indicate its support for the Commission negatively by *not* censuring it. She insisted that the majority of the Party of European Socialists [PES] thought that the Commission had made significant progress in responding to Parliament's concerns. She added that those who had voted against the discharge of the 1996 budget did so with the "smell of election in their nostrils or a particular domestic agenda to which they were playing" [EP: Daily Notebook: 11-01-99].

At no time, nevertheless, was any criticism of the EP's actions made apparent by member states' governments, and this might suggest that the EP was acting with the tacit approval of the Council. This was despite the *Comité des Sages* report's contents, which, as Santer claimed, had provided no evidence of fraud within the Commission and had exonerated the majority of the Commission from actual malpractice [Committee of Independent Experts 1999]. A Commission diminished in stature might serve the wishes, if not the purposes, of the Council as much as those of the Parliament. However, the EP has succeeded in wielding its powers to the utmost and no future Commission, however strong and effective, will ever be able to lose sight of this. Whether a future Commission will be more dependent upon the good will and approval of Council or Parliament (or both) remains to be determined.

7.   Use of power reconsidered

"The process of stepwise development", according to Corbett [1999 p 105], "... has taken the European Parliament a long way from its origin as a largely consultative assembly". The above examples indicate that the EP has been the primary architect of this incrementalist approach. The 1989 EP made immediate use of the additional and extended powers granted to it under the TEU. The Parliament that was elected in 1994 also exercised these powers to the limit. It is also significant that on one occasion, the Parliament was able to engender circumstances wherein by exercising one power [6.1] it has gained at least the promise of extra concessions as the price for its co-operation.

The examples examined indicate that the degree to which the Parliament has been successful is dependent upon two factors. The one relates to the calibre of MEPs and their ability to act as a united body. However, the second relates to the nature of the "adversary". In the presence of the two other powerful institutions, the Commission and the Council, the question concerning the EP's power is relative. In the examples cited above, it appears that the EP showed complete success when dealing with the Commission [6.3.] but that when negotiating with the Council [6.1 and 6.2], the EP had to work harder for its gains.

One answer may be for Parliament to engage with one of the institutions in its struggles against the other, but this may now become more problematic. The EP's supranationalism gives it an affinity with the Commission, but it is not certain that full co-operation between the two will still be possible now that the EP has demonstrated its readiness to use its power over the Commission. On the other hand, the weight of parliamentary assistance might seem to the Commission to be worth retaining. The Council's powers in comparison with both EP and Commission are still considerable.

The linking of the Parliament to the Commission under Article 158 (2) by enabling their terms of office to be virtually co-terminous began the process of giving the EP an accountable executive. However, this has not yet been attained in full. Martin [1993] comments that the six month gap between the Euro-elections and the start of the Commission's term of office may be too long for Community citizens to link the two together. The unusual situation in 1999, whereby the Commission was appointed in effect for a five and a half year term, may resolve this problem in the short term.

Existing relations with the Council do not seem to offer much prospect of enabling the Parliament to become stronger. The absence of strong ties need not be a disadvantage, however. Attina [1990] commented that a lack of "loyalty" towards the executive branch of EU government on the part of the Parliament is not a form of weakness: "because the absence of this requisite renders it free from the binding condition of having a majority subordinate to the political executive branch...[it] is rather a liberating element for EP members."

The unencumbered Parliament's demands for additional powers may become irresistible on the grounds that it embodies the will of the people upon whom nation-state leaders depend for their own status. Lodge [1986 p 52] believes that "The EP's position in Union decision-making is justified in terms of its claim to democratic legitimacy, having been directly elected", but governments throughout the First World are experiencing a crisis of confidence which "having been directly elected" appears to be insufficient to resolve. The EP, less hidebound by tradition than older national parliaments and born at a time when this crisis of confidence was just beginning to become apparent, may have the potential to gain legitimacy, alongside additional powers. To do this it will need to demonstrate the extent of its democratic and popular credentials beyond those appertaining simply to "having been directly elected".

Hence the significance of Parliamentary powers – the *kratos* part of democracy – is inseparable from the significance of its popularity – the *demos* form. The EP needs powers in order to be a demo*cratic* assembly; but it may gain powers in proportion to its ability to prove that it is a *demo*cratic institution. The Parliament has shown that it can utilise existing capacities with a degree of success, and that it can use them to bring about future increases in powers. An extensive increase, however, is beyond its ability to deliver by these means. For its long-term future, the Parliament needs to rely also upon its function as the voice of the people.

In relatively few instances so far has the Parliament used its existing powers directly and effectively on behalf of the people. However, the notion that people are served only when legislation that benefits some of them is enacted is a simplistic concept of the benefits of representative democracy [see Chapter One above]. The portrayal of MEPs as being representative or non-representative on this basis is similarly naive. The next Chapter examines other means by which the EP may fulfil its role as a representative institution. It also considers the significance of elections in relation to the EP before reconsidering theories of representation and the way in which the EP embodies them.

CHAPTER FIVE

DEMOCRACY AND THE EUROPEAN PARLIAMENT

1. *Kratos* and *Demos*

The previous chapter concluded that the EP's existing powers are still insufficient to enable it to function as a demo*cratic* institution. However, the EP is steadily reducing its "power deficit" as the EU evolves.

There are two grounds upon which demands for increased powers can be justified. First, the EP could assert that it is a legitimately *constituted* body with such a role included or implied in the constitutional documents that give it substance. Second the EP could base its claim on the fact that it possesses Weber's legal legitimacy as the only *elected* body within the European Union.

The examination of the Treaties of Paris and Rome [see Chapter Four] shows that the EP was never intended by the member states to play a more active role upon the European stage than it does already. In fact, additional EP powers granted so far have two main sources that have little to do with the EP's constitutional standing. First, there are the activities on the part of MEPs who occasionally utilise existing competences as a means of acquiring additional ones [see Chapter Four]. Second, there is the perception of a democratic deficit, which, it is assumed, would be corrected if the EP were further empowered [see Chapter Three]. Bolstering this assumption, MEPs claim that they act in the name of the voters and call for an extension of their powers for the same reason.

To some extent their assertion has been accepted. The EP's powers have grown despite the reluctance and occasional antagonism of the representatives of member state governments. Today the EP may look forward confidently to retaining its powers, and probably increasing them under the next IGC. Yet the only change which has taken place in the EP's own constitutional arrangements since 1979 is that it is now directly elected. This indicates that even those who would prefer it otherwise reluctantly admit the claims of the elected representative[1].

---

1 Steppat [1988 p 10], notes that the Commission paid more formal attention to the EP's opinions during its first electoral period than before

This chapter examines the basis from which MEPs demand increased powers and assesses the justification for this by exploring the question of electoral representation in relation to the EP. First, European elections are examined so as to estimate the degree and quality of democratic input. A case study of the 1999 elections is presented. Second, previously outlined theories of representation [see above Chapter One] are applied to the EP so that prospects for democratic outcomes may be established.

2.   European elections and popular power

It is important to establish whether the degree of democratic input delivers a representative *system* or a representative *democracy*. These were differentiated in Chapter One by defining a representative system as one in which elections produced representatives who remained free to exercise their judgement and a representative democracy as one wherein elections were regarded as vehicles for expressing the popular will. It was argued that democratic benefits were more likely to accrue from the latter than from the former.

Chapter One also proposed criteria for elections that could offer significant expressions of the popular will. These were: regularity (to avoid indefinite mandates); frequency (to enable changing electoral preferences to be expressed); constitutionality (to avoid preferential rule changes) and choice (to offer meaningful options). It was argued that elections held rarely, those held at the will of leaders and/or which provide the voters with little opportunity to affect the outcome were inadequate vehicles for representative democracy.

Elections to the EP fulfil the first condition. Elections are held regularly – in June every five years. The second criterion is not therefore entirely fulfilled, but there have been few popular demands for an increased frequency. The third requirement – about the organisation of elections – is laid down within the Treaty and may not, therefore, be disregarded.

It is the fourth criterion that is not fulfilled adequately. First, elections do not have the same effect upon policies as national elections, *because* there is no government as such which is formed after an election [Nugent 1994; Gallagher *et al* 1992 p 276]. As Bogdanor [1996 p 107] comments, European elections

> ... do not determine the political colour of the Community, how it is to be governed, for they do not affect the composition of the Commission, nor, of course, of the

1979 and that the Council was also readier to interact more closely with the EP [*ibid* p 20].

Council of Ministers. Therefore, they do little to help determine the policies followed by the Union; nor do they yield personalized and recognizable leadership for the Union.

Also, so far the results of the election have never given a majority of seats to one party, so that there can be no expectation of any particular set of policies which are likely to be pursued. Second, given the numbers of parties operating at EU level, it is unlikely that votes for any one MEP or even group of MEPs will affect significantly the policies pursued by the EP itself over the ensuing five years. Third, taking into account the indeterminate nature of party groupings at EU level, elections do not provide voters with any assurance that those whom they elect will pursue the policies upon which they stood for election.

3. Electoral systems and the European Parliament

Chapter One looked at electoral systems, considering the advantages and disadvantages of simple majority and PR systems. It concluded that the theory of representation underlying an elected body was of greater significance than the manner of electing a representative.

The experience of voting in European elections in the fifteen member states has added little coherence to the system debate, and by extension, little coherence to the manner in which decisions are or ought to be reached within the EP. Each member state applies its own system of electing representatives to the EP. Article 138 of the Treaty of Rome stated that:

> The Assembly shall draw up proposals for elections by direct universal suffrage in accordance with a uniform procedure in all member states. The Council shall, acting unanimously, lay down the appropriate provisions which it shall recommend to Member States for adoption in accordance with their respective constitutional requirements.

"The Act Concerning the Election of the Representatives of the Assembly by Direct Universal Suffrage" needed to implement Article 138 was not signed until 1976 and it was not until 1979 that members of the Assembly were directly elected[2]. The problem then was that the first part of the cited paragraph of Article 138 clashed with the second. "Uniform procedures" are bound to conflict with member states' "respective constitutional requirements" – unless they are prepared and able to change them. In

---

2 Britain being the only country to fail to meet the Community target for direct elections.

practice, there are a variety of PR systems used by the member states. When the UK joined the EEC in 1973, its "constitutional requirement" for electing representatives was not PR in any form; it was a single member simple plurality system. The UK parliament, apparently fearing the impact of PR on its own composition, effected a cabinet revolt at the prospect of change [Greenwood 1992 p 106]. It was not until the 1999 elections that the UK altered the "constitutional requirements" to enable it to "act unanimously" with the rest of the Council to draw up proposals for a "uniform procedure" for elections to the Parliament.

4.   Democratic input: European Parliament elections

4.1.   *EP awareness and electoral turnouts*

Reif and Niedermayer [1987 pp 160-161], basing their conclusions on data obtained from *Eurobarometer* no 19, March-April 1983, concluded tentatively that public awareness about the EP and its functions was very low. They noted that over half of non-party members contacted were unaware that its members were elected. Steppat [1988 pp 26-27], in his study on the first elected parliament, reached similar conclusions relating to public awareness. The case study herein presented shows that increased awareness has not led to increased participation since that date.

Public consciousness has tended to fluctuate depending upon media attention.   Media focus on the EP is highest around the European Elections and normally is at its lowest point when the previous elections are most distant and before the campaigning begins for the next [*Eurobarometer* 49, September 1998] as indicated in fig 5.1. below:

Fig 5.1: Popular awareness of EP 1979-98

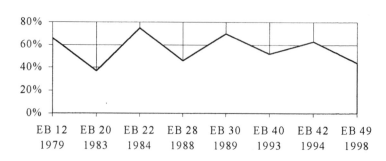

[Source: Eurobarometer 49, September 1998 – adapted]

However, there is no direct correlation between the percentage of popular awareness and the percentage of popular participation as demonstrated by fig 5.2 below:

**Fig 5.2: EP awareness and electoral turnout
1979-1994**

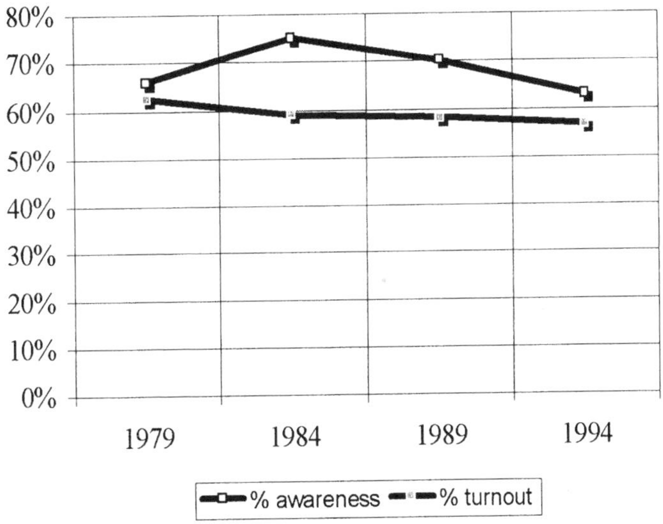

[Source: Eurobarometer 49, September 1998 – adapted]

4.2.   *Voter effectiveness*

"Voter effectiveness" refers to the utility of the electorate. Given the number of different systems under which MEPs are elected at present, there is bound to be an imbalance of voter effectiveness throughout the member states. The basis of the lists (regional or national) gives voters more or less opportunity to familiarise themselves with candidates, so that they may make informed choices. The method of counting votes gives more or less weight to individual votes; the degree of "openness" of the lists provides voters with more or less influence upon which individuals are elected.

Fig 5.3 [below] summarises the main characteristics of the 15 member states' EP election systems:

Fig 5.3.: European Elections 1999: Electoral systems

Member state	Regional/ national basis	Open/closed list	Proportional representation/ single transferable vote
UK (excl NI)	regional (11)	closed	PR (de Hondt method)
N Ireland	national	open	single transferable vote
Austria	national	closed*	PR - 4% threshold per list
Belgium	regional (4)	open electoral) colleges (3))	PR
Denmark	national	closed*	PR (de Hondt method)
Finland	national	open	PR (de Hondt method)
France	national	closed	PR - 5% threshold per list
Germany	regional (16)**	closed	PR - 5% threshold per list
Greece	national	closed	PR - 3% threshold per list
Ireland	regional (4)	open	single transferable vote
Italy	regional (5)	open ***	PR - no threshold
Luxembourg	national	open	PR (de Hondt method)
Netherlands	national	open	PR (de Hondt method)
Portugal	national	closed	PR (de Hondt method)
Spain	national	closed	PR (de Hondt method)
Sweden	national	closed	PR - 4% threshold per list

*	individual preferences may be expressed
**	parties may submit a federal list as an alternative
***	a limited form of preference voting is permitted

Sources: Jacobs *et al* 1992; pp 15-17; Lodge [ed] 1996, *EP News* [November 1997]; Christian Andersson, Europaparlamentet info@europarl.se 26 Nov 1998 - adapted].

4.3.   *Voter efficacy*

One of the problems with large electorates is enabling voters to participate meaningfully in the electoral process. The ratio of voters to MEPs varies considerably (see Fig 5.4. below), which means that the efficacy of individual voters also varies in proportion.

Fig 5.4 shows that the proportion of voters to MEPs in the Netherlands comes closest to the EU average in 1999. Luxembourg voters had 12 times more efficacy relating to the election of an MEP than German voters.

Fig 5.4.: Ratio of voters to MEPs (1999 figures)

Member state	Number of MEPs	Total number of voters	Ratio of voters to MEPs
UK	87	45,678,000	525,034:1
Austria	21	6,416,100	305,529:1
Belgium	25	8,041,700	321,668:1
Denmark	16	4,177,900	261,119:1
Finland	16	4,006,500	250,406:1
France	87	45,420,400	522,074:1
Germany	99	66,390,900	670,615:1
Greece	25	8,490,600	339,624:1
Ireland	15	2,701,500	180,100:1
Italy	87	47,425,100	545,116:1
Luxembourg	6	333,900	55,650:1
Netherlands	31	12,293,400	396,561:1
Portugal	25	7,888,700	315,548:1
Spain	64	31,807,300	496,989:1
Sweden	22	6,906,300	313,923:1
total/average	**626**	**297978300**	**476,004:1**

4.4.   *Voting levels*

In general voting levels in European elections are low and are declining. Most criticisms of the British "winner take all" electoral system used to focus on the fact that frequently successful candidates receive less than 50 per cent of their electorate's votes. With the EP, the total *turnout* is lower than this in some member states. In 1999, the average turnout too was less than 50 per cent.

Fig 5.5. below gives the voting figures for member states since 1979. It shows a steady decline over the last twenty years in most member states.

Every member state, except Denmark, whose turnout has fluctuated, has seen a lower turnout in 1999 than it had at the first EP election for that state. The average turnout has declined consistently.

Fig 5.5: Voting in the EP elections 1979-1999

Member state	Percentage turnouts				
	1979	1984	1989	1994	1999
UK	31.6	32.6	36.2	36.4	24.0
Austria	-	-	-	67.7*	49.0
Belgium	91.6	92.2	90.7	90.7	91.0
Denmark	47.1	52.3	46.1	52.9	50.4
Finland	-	-	-	60.3*	30.1
France	60.7	56.7	48.7	52.7	47.0
Germany	65.7	56.8	62.4	60.0	45.2
Greece	78.6	77.2	79.9	71.2	70.2
Ireland	63.6	47.6	68.3	44.0	50.5
Italy	85.5	83.9	81.5	74.8	70.8
Luxembourg	88.9	87.0	87.4	88.5	85.8
Netherlands	57.8	50.5	47.2	35.7	29.9
Portugal	-	72.2**	51.1	35.5	40.4
Spain	-	68.9**	54.8	59.1	64.4
Sweden	-	-	-	41.6*	38.3
Average	63.0	61.0	58.5	56.8	49.4

*	EP Elections in Sweden first took place in 1995; in Austria and Finland in 1996
**	Elections in Portugal and Spain first took place in 1987.

4.5.   *The European Elections 1999*

A study of the 1999 campaign and the election results gives little encouragement to advocates of increased power to the Parliament on the strength of its popular appeal. Despite the focus upon the EP in the months before the EP elections, when the Parliament brought about the resignation of the Commission, a lower proportion of people voted in 1999 than in any other Euro-elections. Voting throughout the member states fell to 49.4 per cent from 56.8 per cent in 1994. It demonstrated (as in 1994) a considerable difference between voters' stated intentions according to a *Eurobarometer* survey and their voting behaviour [see fig 5.6. below]. Only in Belgium and Luxembourg did more electors vote than the survey implied (voting in these countries is compulsory as it is in Greece and Italy); only Ireland, Portugal and Spain experienced an increase in turnout from 1994 [see fig 5.5 above]. In the case of Spain, this was because the municipal and, in some regions, regional elections took place on the same day [Gibbons 2000[3]].

Fig 5.6: EP elections 1999:
voters' intentions v turnout

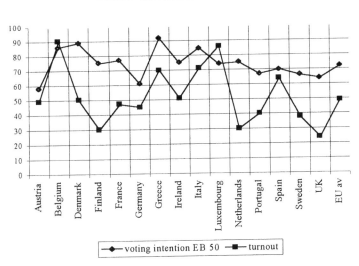

Sources: *Eurobarometer* 50 [May 1999] Election results published by EP [http://www2.europarl.eu.int/election/results/a_tab.htm]

A second worrying factor for the EP was the lack of relationship between support for the EU and the turnout for the EP elections. Fig 5.7 shows that the member state that indicated greatest support for the EU – Ireland – was by no means the one that provided the highest turnout. The Netherlands, demonstrating a very low electoral turnout, appears to have a relatively high degree of support for the EU.

Nor is there a clear relationship, even, between people's notions of the significance of the Parliament and their readiness to turn out to vote for its members. Fig 5.8 [below] shows that electors in member states regarding the EP as important (Finland, Portugal) still show a reluctance to participate in the elections:

---

3 "Spain", in forthcoming book: *the 1999 European Elections* edited by J Lodge, Basingstoke, Macmillan, 2000

Fig 5.7: 1999 EP elections: support v turnout

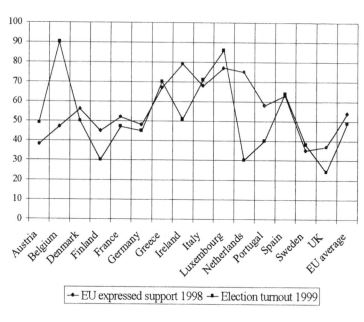

Sources: *Eurobarometer* 50 [May 1999] Election results published by EP
[http://www2.europarl.eu.int/election/results/a_tab.htm]

The elections in the 15 member states demonstrate no discernible trends in voting behaviour. Some states showed a leaning towards smaller, regionally based or factional parties. Others demonstrated an anti-government stance, which gave the result that the 1999 Parliament has a greater centre-right leaning than before, whilst the member states' governments tend towards the centre left.

5.   Towards a representative system or a representative democracy?

Only 49.4 per cent of the EU's electorate cast a vote at the 1999 European Elections. The question that remains, however, is how far these voters would be able to affect the behaviour of that representative thereafter. There is reason to doubt that voter effectiveness extends much further than casting a vote for a successful candidate. After the elections, the elected MEP may act in a different way from that which her or his manifesto implied.

MEPs' group membership is not finally decided upon by their electors.

Fig 5.8: EP Elections 1999:
Perceived importance of EP v electoral turnout

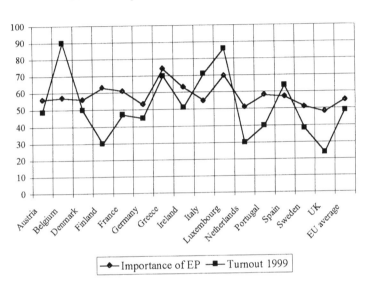

For example, the UK's Conservative MEPs did not decide until after the election that they would ally themselves to the European People's Party/European Democrats [EPP/ED], and even then they indicated that alliance did not mean that they would accept the EPP/ED's manifesto or programme. Nor did it mean acceptance of the group whip[4]. The question of the political significance of individual votes cast for candidates for the EP must be raised when elected candidates decide upon their own orientation without further reference to their electorate or do not declare it with any precision during their campaign.

---

4 Letter to Edward McMillan-Scott, MEP, leader of the British Conservatives in the EP, from Hans-Gert Poettering, Chairman of the EPP, 16 September 1999. Herr Poettering also acknowledges that the UK Conservatives are free to act in accordance with the British Conservative manifesto where it conflicts with EPP policy.

6.   Democracy in input – alternative means of expression

If voters do not affect their MEP's performance directly by means of using their vote, the significance of the representative's function may lie in the interaction between the electorate and the elected member. Steppat [1988 p 26] requires quality as well as quantity of interaction between the two parties. It does not seem, however, that this has been achieved. When Parry *et al* [1992 p 44] researched political participation in Britain, they included "contacting" as one of the categories of participation. However, although they contrasted levels of contacts with UK MPs (9.7 per cent), civil servants (7.3 per cent), councillors (20.7 per cent), local government officers (17.4 per cent) and the media (3.8 per cent), they did not consider potential contacts with MEPs. This, Parry explained[5], was because they did not think that sufficient people would have been in contact with their MEP to make it worth asking the question. Reif and Niedermayer [1987 p 171] reported that in 1983, 57 per cent of MEPs claimed to have met with their "constituency and their voters" "often" or "very often", but respondents were not asked to specify precise numbers of electors. The evidence of an ICM Research poll carried out in May 1994 (that is just before the European Election in June) for the *Daily Express* suggested that contacts were limited. Steppat [1988 p 26] believed that "contacts between voters and Members of the EP have not reached the intensity desired by both sides" and cites as his evidence studies carried out with MEPs and opinion polls showing that voters have little knowledge about the EP and EC.

7.   The democratic significance of EP elections

Despite their regularity and relative frequency, elections for the EP lack the mechanisms for enabling electoral decisiveness, and so far they have not been organised specifically to enhance democratic input within the EU. Non-voters, who now form an absolute majority within the EU, seem to concur with this judgement. Gallagher *et al* [1992 p 276] suggest that "Many voters undoubtedly conclude that in fact nothing much is at stake, and so they don't bother to vote."

If non-voting accurately reflects the relative impotence of the EP, then augmenting its powers may provide a solution. However, there are other difficulties. First, the elections do not settle many questions relating to the basis of power between elector and elected. The party system is too weak for an incoming EP, even with a majority grouping, to determine a set of

5   In conversation with author

policies which could be isolated as characteristic of any single party [Bogdanor 1996 p 112].

Second, if electoral participation is to include contact, again MEPs score low. Parry *et al* [1992] could argue that, given the circumstances, voting is at a surprisingly high level in EP elections since it may hardly be a rational choice to take the trouble to vote.

This evidence leads to the conclusion that EP elections endow the Parliament with the characteristics of a representative *system* rather than those of a representative *democracy*. This leads to a further proposition – that if power should follow democratic legitimacy, European Elections and their outcomes are insufficient to confer this legitimacy upon representatives produced thereby.

8.   Towards democracy in outcome

It has already been argued [see above Chapter One] that to claim that an institution should be powerful on the grounds that its members are directly elected is insufficient. If the manner and effect of its elections are inadequate, this makes the democratic legitimacy of the EP still more questionable. The EP's prospect of exemplifying a representative democracy rests therefore on whether the EP can be shown to be representative on additional grounds than those of having been elected.

Ladrech [1993 p 55] claims that "The fact... still remains that the EP is elected by citizens of the member states, making it the most representative body concerned with Community wide legislation". If the purpose of representation is to enable the voice of the people to be expressed there is a need for a more detailed analysis of the relationship between electors and their representatives. Liberal democracy has always relied upon elections, but democracy *per se* need not, so long as a representative or representative body can be depended upon to present and forward the interests of the people whom s/he or it represents [see above Chapter One]. Theories of representation demonstrate the various means of ensuring that the representative carries out this task. The erstwhile Conservative minister, David Davis, reflecting the position of Euro-sceptics, presented this question in a comment: "It is not clear in what sense the European Parliament *does* represent the people of Europe" [*European* 3-9 February 1995].

There are two possible responses to this implied criticism. First it may be submitted that the EP is a body sufficiently heterogeneous in its complexion to be able to reflect the assorted and sometimes conflicting interests of the peoples of Europe [see Mill (1861) 1972 p 279]. Second the individual MEP may represent in an acceptable democratic sense the people who have elected her or him. In other words, either the EP as a body or its individual members should produce democratic outcomes by means of their form of representation.

Chapter One looked at different kinds of democratic outcomes (termed *minimalist, instrumentalist* and *organic*) and examined various theories of representation (classified as *virtual, individual, judgmental, political* and *mandatory*) with the intention of discerning which of these demo-benefits were likely to be derived from them. It concluded that all of them in theory offered some potential for achieving the minimalist end of "constraining the power of the leaders". It argued that individual representation offered the greatest hope of obtaining *instrumentalist* democratic outcomes such as enhancing democratic values and achieving popular ends. The conclusion was that none offered many prospects of achieving *organic* outcomes, however. The reason for this was that these demanded a popular unity of purpose allied to self government which, by definition, is not available where a people is heterogeneous, where government is via representation and where democracy is indirect and relatively non-participatory.

Any possibility that the EP may enhance democracy within member states must therefore be restricted to deciding whether it may achieve *minimalist* or *instrumentalist* democratic ends.

This Chapter considered whether the EP can, in effect, achieve minimalist democratic ends irrespective of the nature of its representativeness by means of its ability to scrutinise the executive. Since the Parliament itself does not "lead" the political process within the EU, it could utilise its limited powers to constrain those who do so in the name of the people who are, in this case, too remote from the leaders to do this for themselves. The overall conclusion from the examination of empirical evidence was that the Parliament is insufficiently powerful to do this at present, although its ability and readiness to bring about the resignation of the Santer Commission is suggestive of increasing capacity. In addition, new powers provided by the ToA are beginning to redress the balance.

An examination of various theories that underpin representation at the Euro-level indicates what prospects there are that demo-benefits may accrue from the EP as a representative body. With this in mind, the representative nature of the Parliament is examined, drawing also upon MEPs' views of their role, and relevant comparisons are made with the similar study carried out on the British House of Commons in Chapter Two.

8.1. *Virtual representation*

If the EU is taken to be a supranational body, it is the European Commission that "virtually" represents the EU in the territorial (Tory) sense. Each Commissioner may be assumed to have the overall interests of the EU at heart. If the EU is regarded as a grouping of nations, it is the Council of Ministers which "virtually" represents the member states at EU level since each is expected to further the general interests of her/his country of origin. The concept of a Europe of the Regions opens the possibility that the CoR may become a virtually representative body, with each representative embodying the general interest of the region that s/he represents, although by which s/he is not directly elected. This does not leave a role for the EP as a virtually representative body in the Tory sense.

The EP could, however, represent the sectional or Whig version of virtual representation by providing a body sufficiently diverse as to include members, elected for one area, representing the sectional (usually economic) interests of another.

If the EP is examined in this light, however, the range of economic interests held by members is limited. Given that many of the policies related to EU legislation are based upon trading and agricultural interests, proportionately few MEPs reflect them. Few members of the 1999 EP have a business background (6.5 per cent of all MEPs; 19.5 per cent of British MEPs) and only a tiny proportion have a farming background (14 of all MEPs and two UK MEPs list "farming" as their primary economic activity). In fact, the EP is predominantly composed of members with professional and political backgrounds. 62.5 per cent of all MEPs and 50.6 per cent of British MEPs have professional backgrounds (there are 80 "lawyers" and 104 "lecturers" and "teachers" in the 1999 Parliament) whilst 18.9 per cent of all MEPs and 20.7 per cent of British MEPs have a professional background in politics. Manual worker interests are similarly poorly reflected – 1.3 per cent of all MEPs and no UK MEPs have been skilled or unskilled manual workers. Despite this, it seems that UK MEPs are better able to reflect a diversity of economic interests than the membership of the EP in general [see below Fig 5.9.]. Overall, the figures suggest that PR is an inadequate vehicle in the European context to deliver reflective representation of economic interests.

There are, however, elements of the sectional form of virtual representation extant within the EP, if primarily of one section of interests (professional). This is not recognised by MEPs as such, probably because their attention is fixed upon the *elected* nature of their representativeness, but the notion itself may have an effect upon the way in which they exercise their judgement on behalf of their constituents [see below].

Fig 5.9: MEPs' backgrounds, 1999

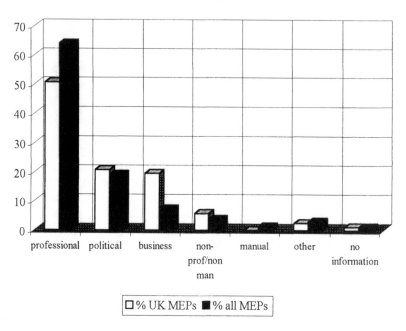

[Source: figures based upon biographies of the 626 Elected members, Directorate-General for Information and Public Relations, September 1999]

8.2. *Individual representation*

There are 626 members of the EP, now representing around 300,000,000 electors. Each Euro-MP, therefore, represents an average of 476,000 people (although German MEPs, for example, represent disproportionately more and Luxembourg MEPs disproportionately fewer people). These electors have a variety of economic, social and individual interests, and it would be implausible to suggest that the few MEPs who represent them all, or that they could do so in a strictly proportional sense.

A study of the membership of the Parliament indicates, though, that individual representation is limited even more than this would imply. In the EP as a whole in 1999, 70 per cent of all and 76 of UK MEPs were male. Most MEPs are middle-aged. On election in 1999, 21 per cent of all MEPs were aged between 40 and 49 (UK: 33 per cent) and 40 per cent between 50 and 59 (UK: 36 per cent). Only two per cent were aged over 70 (UK figure: two per cent) and two per cent were under 30 (UK figures are the same). 9 per cent of all and 16 per cent of UK MEPs were aged between 30 and 39 with 14 per cent of all and 9 per cent of UK MEPs aged between 60 and 69 [see fig 5.10 below].

Fig 5.10: MEPs 1999 - age profiles

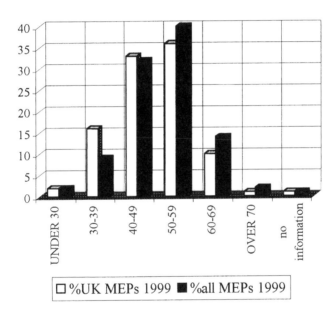

[Source: figures based upon biographies of the 626 Elected members, Directorate-General for Information and Public Relations, September 1999]

By far the majority of MEPs are white. As for disability, one or two MEPs use a wheelchair, but there is no register of MEPs' disabilities, and the majority appear to be able-bodied. The modal average MEP therefore is white, male, middle-aged, and able-bodied. The average European elector is just as likely to be female and either young or old. People who are non-white or who have a handicapping disability are, of course, much more poorly represented.

The ability of MEPs to sympathise with the particular interests of the female or non-white or working class elector or elector with some form of disability is unquantifiable. It is unlikely, however, that they are in a position to empathise effectively. Individual representation therefore does not characterise the EP's form of representation.

8.3.   *Judgmental representation*

MEPs, like British members of the House of Commons, do not consult their electorates about the way in which they should vote in specific matters. There is little tradition of doing this in liberal democracies and there are so many electors to be represented by EP members. Also MEPs operate at a considerable distance in a social and political as well as geographical sense from their constituents and voters rarely have a direct interest in the issues which pertain to MEPs unless they are members of interest groups particularly concerned with EU-wide issues such as pollution.

However, another feature of the EP is that it is attractive to politicians of national and hence prominent status. 31.5 per cent of all MEPs and 16 per cent of UK MEPs had served their countries in their national Parliaments. Also many MEPs hold or have held a seat in local or regional government. This applies to 34.2 per cent of UK and 34.5 per cent of all MEPs. There is a tendency for UK MEPs to have been local councillors, whilst, especially in France, some still serve on local or regional elected bodies. Others have been engaged upon conspicuous political activities of a voluntary nature [see below fig 5.11].

Yet MEPs are not particularly well-known to their electors, at least as MEPs. The ICM poll for the *Daily Express* conducted in May 1994 in the UK included the question: "can you name your own MEP?". Of the 85 per cent who could not, the response seemed to be evenly distributed between both sexes; amongst all classes; across all party affiliations; and throughout England [ICM research 1994]. This, of course, was before the advent of PR with party lists. No conclusions can be drawn definitively from this about the present relationship between MEPs and their electors, although the system of PR tends to create more rather than less distance between representatives and electorates.

Electoral ignorance may be the effect of a lack of attention from the local and regional press. On the other hand, a lack of attention from the press may be a reflection of public indifference. There have been claims that those MEPs who have tried issuing local press-releases usually succeed in getting material published, but this does not appear to have had much effect on public awareness of their identity.

If MEPs are unknown to their electors, this may explain the low contact levels between the two parties.

Fig 5.11: MEPs 1999 - political experience

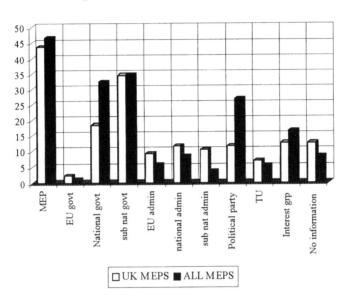

[Source: figures based upon biographies of the 626 Elected members, Directorate-General for Information and Public Relations, September 1999]

If the public is rarely consulted by its MEPs, by default this leaves the representatives free to exercise their judgement. MEPs, perhaps because of their academic/political backgrounds, are skilled in so doing. Specialism is particularly characteristic of the EP [Bowler & Farrell 1995 p 221]. Every MEP has the opportunity to be a *rapporteur* and this means, as Green [1994] commented, that every MEP becomes at least a political, if not technical, expert in something.

This means that job-satisfaction can be high in Strasbourg. There is no evidence, however, that the interests of MEPs are chosen because they are the interests of their electorate.

A high degree of specialisation may lead to heightened respect and hence increased authority for the EP and it may also have its effect upon the quality of EU government. However, it is only likely to have such effects inasmuch as individual MEPs are free to exercise their judgement upon the issues put to them. Therefore there is little incentive for MEPs to devolve decision-making down to their much less informed and also less-involved electorates, and the notion of devolved decision-making receives only qualified support from MEPs.

The conclusion is that the EP depends even more upon the theory of judgmental representation than does the British House of Commons.

8.4.   *Political representation*

The question of political representation has several dimensions. First, the composition of parliaments may represent the political views of their electors. Second, elections to parliament may reflect changes in the political views of the electorate. Third, those *selected* to be candidates for election may represent the political preferences of those who hold them most strongly – that is members of political parties. Finally, the extent to which representatives are influenced by their party rather than by the political preferences of their electorate will affect the degree of political electoral representation.

▪   The EP and electoral views

Most MEPs represent the broad political views of their electors. They stand as political party candidates and are elected on some system of PR. Nevertheless, in those member states where the system does not allow for a preferential vote[6] the eventual choice of representative – and hence her/his political stance – depends heavily upon party preference. When interviewed in 1994, the UK PES MEP, Terry Wynn, said: "Nobody voted for me because my name's Wynn; it said 'Labour Party Candidate' after my name. That's why people voted for me". In 1999, Wynn was the third candidate listed on a slate of candidates for the North West region headed "Labour Party Candidates" and no elector was able to choose to vote for him in any other capacity.

The Parliament as a whole could amend the imbalances within individual states. Whilst no Green MEP was elected in Spain, for example, 38 Green MEPs were elected to the 1999 Parliament from amongst the other member states. This means that voters throughout the member states may be "virtually" if not directly politically represented in the Parliament, although there is obviously no guarantee that they will be nor that their particular political stances will be reflected by those whom they played no part in electing.

The problem with representation as a reflection of electoral political preferences in the EP is common to all parliaments elected via a PR system. There is less chance that the representative selected upon the basis of an individual voter's *political* preference will be in a position to influence the direction the parliament takes because there is a reduced

6 Germany, Greece, Spain, France and Portugal

likelihood of an overall majority for any one political party. This disadvantage is exacerbated in the EP because there are so many parties. There is also an argument that European political groups have not evolved completely, and that MEPs' loyalties belong first to the political group of their country of origin and second to the somewhat broader grouping within the EP formed when that political group joined it.

- The EP and strong political preferences

The EP contains examples of two kinds of party-member input into MEP candidature. The first category applies to those states which have list systems with preferential votes[7] or which offer a single transferable vote to electors[8]. This system offers less power to the party than systems without preferential votes, although the party formulates the whole list which is put forward and is in a position to promote the campaign of its favoured candidates[9]. In the second category, electors cast their vote from a "closed list", selecting only the party preference, so that the individuals finally elected are those chosen by the party rather than by the electorate

The lack of uniformity within the EU relating to selection of candidates makes it hard to estimate how far strong political preferences are reflected in the composition of the EP, but it may be noted that party preferences figure quite highly whichever system is adopted.

- Party influence

The EP is regarded as being less bound by party influences than is the UK's House of Commons, and this has been viewed as a potential advantage in relation to electoral representation. There are several reasons for the apparent decline in party power at EU level. First European "parties" are amalgamations of several parties. Reif and Niedermayer [1987 p 168] report a survey of MEPs carried out in 1983 wherein the majority of respondents thought that national party leaderships had limited influence over decisions made in the EP.

There is evidence that UK MEPs regard their ties to their (national)

---

7   Belgium – albeit with a "closed list" –, Denmark, Ireland, Italy, Luxembourg, the Netherlands, Austria, Finland and Sweden

8   Northern Ireland

9   For example, in Italy, Berlusconi was placed on the list in all five regional constituencies

party of origin relatively lightly. There are examples also of groups of both Conservative and Labour MEPs rebelling openly against the expressed views of their parties' national leaders on fairly fundamental issues. The Conservatives opposed their party's European policies [*European* 16/22 September 1994] and Labour MEPs refused the party leader's request that MEPs sign a pledge of their behaviour [*Guardian* 10 July 1997].

However, national party ties are still strong. For example, when interviewed in 1999, Simpson said:

> ... my view is that at the end of the day I go down to people who sent me here and that's the British Labour Party, so if there is conflict and I have to fall one side of the fence or the other, I'll fall on the side of the British Labour Party.

As noted above, the UK Conservatives have already made it a condition of their allied membership of the EPP/ED that they will not be considered bound in any way by its manifesto or programme. This reinforces the view that European political parties are not yet fully formed.

The whipping system within the EU level groups is sometimes seen as being less formidable than that imposed in the Commons. There are few formal sanctions, although of course the whip may be withdrawn, and the independence of MEPs is enshrined in the Parliament's Rules of Procedure. Not all MEPs thought that the group whip was ineffective, however. When interviewed in 1994, for example, Glyn Ford thought that there was an effective whipping system when it mattered.

The whipping system may be more flexible because less depends upon the outcome of voting. If this is so, as the Parliament's powers increase, so will discipline amongst its members.

The whipping system used in the EP also recognises that some issues relate more to national than to party boundaries. Simpson drew attention to the national group "conscience clause", although he commented that "funnily enough it's not invoked as many times as perhaps people would expect."

Slacker discipline may also exist because absenteeism prevents effective whipping or because in general the non-UK experience with more consensual government encourages more flexibility for individual members who may be persuaded rather than forced to vote with their party.

Advancement within the EP does not result directly from obedience to Group whips, which means that the whips have limited inducements and sanctions to encourage rigid discipline. The EP, probably because it lacks an executive, tends to be less hierarchical in nature than the UK House of

Commons[10]. UK MEPs interviewed claimed that advancement was not particularly desirable so long as they could involve themselves in matters which interested them, and opportunities to do this were plentiful where MEPs demonstrated sufficient commitment.

The reduced influence of political parties may give MEPs greater freedom of individual action although in their survey on the internal organisation of the EP, Bowler and Farrell [1995 p 243] conclude that, although MEPs may specialise, "they do so under party-group scrutiny and control". In any case, national political parties, controllers of future lists in most cases, do not permit MEPs to take full advantage of the freedom that weaker EU parties may allow.

8.5. *Mandatory representation*

The two forms of mandatory representation – general political and issue specific – [see Chapter One] may be examined in relation to the EP:

- General political mandates (pre mandating of representatives)

European Election manifestos are even less likely to be regarded as an expression of what successful candidates will do when elected than are parliamentary manifestos. This is because the EP has no executive and because – given the evanescent and diffuse nature of EP party structures already noted – it is not possible in practical terms to make "promises" with any guarantee of being able to deliver. Common EP group manifestos are therefore rarely used in election campaigns [Steppat 1988 p 33], although in 1999, left and centre-left parties throughout the member states adopted the PES manifesto. No one party operating within one member state could be large enough to put into effect its chosen policies even if all were elected. MEPs interviewed indicated a lively appreciation of the difficulty of achieving the delicate balance between national and political interests needed to implement any of the undertakings given in their manifestos. Hence statements of intent are sufficiently non-specific to ensure that no MEP once elected could be bound in any but the most general sense by the manifesto.

---

10 There is a hierarchy of sorts, with the Bureau (President and Vice-Presidents with the Quaestors in an advisory capacity) and the Conference of Presidents (President and Chairmen of political groups) but this is mainly concerned with setting the agenda for the Parliament rather than disciplining or rewarding its members.

- Issue specific mandates (continual mandating)

One of the more attractive aspects of being an MEP, according to MEPs interviewed, is that any individual who is prepared to put in the time can attain the kind of authority achievable from such diligence. All MEPs consulted had been rapporteurs; all were able to give details of their special expertise; and all could confirm the high esteem in which their well-informed and industrious colleagues were held within EU circles. Yet there is little evidence that those whom these well-briefed, hard-working and highly-motivated MEPs represented were even aware of their MEPs' specialisations or that these specialisations figured highly among the reasons for voting for them.

This indicates that electors would be unlikely to be able to share their MEP's concerns even if they were balloted as to how their representative ought to act with relation to her or his particular brief. Electors may feel that they have insufficient knowledge or interest to be able to offer responsible guidance on such issues.

There is a practical difficulty in contacting so many electors for issue specific mandating, which may be added to the potential democratic impediments. However, it would be possible to contact a representative sample by means of random polling. The co-decision-making process outlined in Article 189b (TEU) where it is implemented in full is long enough to offer the opportunity for enhanced democratic participation during its procedures[11]. So far there has been no suggestion that this could form part of the interaction between MEPs and their voters.

The evidence presented above indicates that there is no feasible potential for general political mandatory representation. In regard to issue specific mandatory representation there is no evidence that the political will to achieve it exists.

9.   The European Parliament and democracy in outcome

The EP has no defined role in relation to the territorial view of virtual representation. The sectional view of virtual representation is not demonstrated clearly, given the unequal distribution of economic interests exhibited by the Parliament. Individual representation is flawed since the characteristics of MEPs are not sufficiently varied to enable different (not always minority) interests to surface.

MEPs frequently use their judgement about policies. They are well-equipped to do so, and the size of their electorates as well as their geographical and political remoteness makes it hard to encompass

---

11   It has been shortened under the ToA

frequent voter-consultation.

The EP can be reasonably responsive to shades of political opinion within the EU, although the fact that members are elected on state boundaries makes it hard for the party-preferences and preference changes of an EU-wide electorate to be represented accurately. The fact that MEPs have looser ties both with their European party grouping and their national party may enhance their links with their electors, although UK Labour MEPs at least have an instinctive leaning towards their party of origin.

Mandatory representation has no place within the EP, for practical and theoretical reasons.

The most applicable theory of representation for the EP – judgmental representation – is one which overall is an unreliable vehicle for the delivery of positive democratic outcomes [Chapter One]. This is not surprising, since this was the theory that applied before the advent of universal suffrage – the initial requirement for a democratic polity. The EP may therefore be a representative body but it is not a model of representative democracy.

10. MEPs and *demos*

This chapter has argued that the relationship between MEPs and their electors is not primarily characterised by democratic representation of the one by the other. As with most representative systems, the representative function is essentially pre-democratic, resting largely upon members who are free to and who are expected to exercise their judgement to the best of their abilities on behalf of those whom they represent.

Part of the reason for this is that MEPs all share a liberal democratic political background wherein representativeness has long been considered to be adequate simply because the representative has been elected by those whom s/he represents. This is now starting to be regarded as insufficient to satisfy changing electoral needs within the member states, but in the EU the problem is exacerbated because of the large numbers involved. Ladrech [1993 p 66] comments that the EP's solution to the democratic deficit is rooted in traditional notions of the nation state, which is becoming inapplicable to the trends and dynamics which push EC integration. Lodge [1996 p 214] believes that "the issue of defining and rectifying the EU's democratic deficit by reference to the socio-political norms of a bygone age may no longer be entirely appropriate". In addition, its form of electoral representation is destined to founder upon the problems relating to "size and democracy" [Dahl and Tufte 1974 p 140], despite the earnest intentions of existing representatives.

MEPs, including British MEPs, are therefore unable to represent their electors in any meaningful *democratic* sense, although they fulfil adequately the Burkeian function of utilising their judgement on behalf of those who have elected them.

However, the EP may perform an alternative function in enhancing democracy. It has been readier to accept regional and local government as an integral part of the EU's political structure than has the Council of Ministers. This may be because the majority of its members regard themselves as representing areas rather than countries (and some of them have been, or are still, local or regional councillors). The EP has also less to lose at present by a devolution of power and some MEPs, uncommitted to national politics, see devolution as an alternative means of depriving Council and Commission of their level of control over EU governmental processes and therefore indirectly enhancing the EP's own.

It is therefore concluded that the justification for existing and increasing MEPs' powers may depend more upon the EP's readiness and ability to devolve them. The next chapter begins to examine prospects for devolution.

CHAPTER SIX

THE EUROPEAN UNION: VEHICLE FOR PARTICIPATORY DEMOCRACY

So far it has been established that the prospects for enhanced democratic practice offered directly by the EU's main institutions are limited. The EP, the only elected body within the EU, is not an impressive model of representative democracy and as such offers few positive expectations for the future. Although representative democracy within the EU is uninspiring, this chapter demonstrates that there are prospects for the alternative form of participatory democracy provided by the EU. There are two options: a *de jure* and/or a *de facto* means towards devolving powers.

1. Subsidiarity

Subsidiarity, legally enshrined in the EU's treaty, was originally seen by participants in EU governance as the principle that could satisfy both of these requirements. The idea, at its simplest, is that decisions should be taken at the lowest practical level. Spicker [1994] notes that the concept arose in Catholic teaching in the nineteenth century, but found its place in the Catholic doctrine by means of Pius XI's statement in *Quadragesimo Anno* 1931. John Paul II clarified this in an encyclical letter in 1990, where a specific link between subsidiarity and economic activity was also made.

The intention was to protect the rights of the individual against the state, and to protect the lower body from the higher according to the same principle of justice. Spicker observes that this concept originally involved ambiguity. It was the Church's authority and scope, as much as the individual's freedom, which Pius XI was determined to protect, and the Catholic Church, like the member states of the EU, had a circumscribed notion of decentralisation.

However, Spicker goes on to argue that this is only one reason why the application of the principle has quickly reached an *impasse* within the EU. There are, he points out, five other primogenitors of the subsidiary concept. These are:

- The Calvinistic concept of *sphere sovereignty* which is concerned to protect the independence of different groups within Dutch society and economy.

- *Self-determination.* This is a form of liberalism concerned to protect the different levels of governance (neighbourhoods, communities, regions and nations), rather than the individualistic liberalism of the UK. This was significant in French thought [Constant, 1815, cited by Spicker 1994].

- *Residualism,* which epitomises British and German liberalism, sees a role for the state only when social requirements go beyond the capacity of the individual to satisfy.

- *States' rights,* as enshrined in the Constitution of the United States of America, argue for the power of the states so as to restrain the authority of the centre by leaving everything not specifically placed within the remit of the central bodies to the states.

- *Pluralism,* according to Walzer [1983], suggests that different spheres of social action should be judged by different criteria. The regulation needed by the family or the law or commerce are different. This suggests that intervention by the centre is acceptable in some areas, but not in others.

Spicker emphasises that there are conflicts among these ideas. The question is one of determining whose freedom of action should be protected. The notion of subsidiarity carries with it only a *prima facie* requirement to protect all bodies against each other, since any body has the potential to encroach upon another's existing sphere of influence. In the EU this is particularly useful in the circumstances of evolving forms of political interaction. In practice, as demonstrated below, only the *states' rights* concept has managed to survive the strains of these developments, probably because it offers the prospect of least change in an uncertain environment.

The subsidiarity principle was first expressed formally in the 1986 SEA article on environmental protection, but the idea was referred to in the Tindemans Report on European Union 1975 and again in the EP's Draft Treaty on European Union adopted in 1984. The TEU [1992] brought the concept fully into the public domain. At first sight, Article A of the TEU offers grounds for optimism for advocates of participatory democracy.

> This Treaty marks a new stage in the process of creating an ever closer union among the people of Europe, in which decisions are taken as closely as possible to the citizen.

However, Article B of the Treaty states that the objectives of the Union will be achieved by respecting the principle of subsidiarity as outlined in its

Article 3b.   Article 3b gives more comfort to *residualists*.   It declares:

> In areas which do not fall within its exclusive competence, the Community shall take action, in accordance with the principle of subsidiarity, only if and in so far as the objectives of the proposed action cannot be sufficiently achieved by the member states...

Article F (1) of the TEU specifically requires the EU to respect the national identities of its member states.

Peterson comments that the two definitions differ from each other because they were designed to appeal to two groups of national governments with different bases in political thinking.   There were those like Germany's which were interested in protecting the interests of their federal states, and those such as the UK's which were concerned with ensuring the primacy of nation-state decision making [1994 pp 120-121]. Van Kersbergen and Verbeek [1994 p 216] suggest that this minimalist approach was "the touch of genius" enabling political participants to gloss over their fundamental disagreements.   Scott *et al* [1994 pp 49-50] thinks that whilst Article A provides a *substantive principle*, Article 3b supplies the *procedural criterion* determining the occasion and manner of EC intervention.   Scharpf [1994 p 223] concludes that Article 3b "provides few grounds for optimism" in part because he doubts that it could ever be proved that any objective could not be sufficiently achieved by the member states.

In theory, subsidiarity itself could prove an exception to this.   Since it is the EU which defines subsidiarity, the EU should be the body to decide whether or not its implementation has been "sufficiently achieved" by its member states.   If the member states cannot succeed in devolving decision-making "as closely as possible to the citizen", then, according to Article 3b, the Community is empowered to take action to ensure that they do.   This *residualist* notion was laid to rest at the Edinburgh meeting of the European Council (11-12 December 1992) which first defined the *states' rights* approach.   It stressed that the implementation of subsidiarity related to the division of competences between the EC and member states only [Part III (a): Procedures and Practices].   Following this definition, Article 3b has been invoked to prevent the enforcement of any interpretation of subsidiarity other than that of *states' rights*.

In 1993, the Spanish MEP Arbeloa Muru [PES] asked the Council: "Who is Article 3b intended to cover – it appears to exclude all levels of political activity below national level?   How should this be viewed in light of reference to the broader context of the preamble?" [94/C/102/06 E-2930/93 Arbeloa Muru to Council].

The answer was provided in March 1994.   It reiterated the *states' rights* concept of subsidiarity and offered a definitive discouragement of hopes that subsidiarity might offer prospects for *self-determination* within the

EU. The Council stated that:

- Subsidiarity means that the Community will take action only when objectives cannot be achieved by member states.

- The principle of subsidiarity is not governing attributes of powers between the Community and member states, nor, obviously, between the Community and regional/local authorities

- Subsidiarity is a general principle of Community law, but is as yet untested in the courts

and, even more conclusively:

- The Edinburgh European Council felt that "the principle of subsidiarity cannot be regarded as having a direct effect" (President's conclusions, Annex 1 to pt A under 1(4) fifth indenture) [Source: *Official Journal*]

Arbeloa Muru also tried to discover whether any form of *sphere sovereignty* for different groups and for sub-regional levels was to be attainable through the EU instead. In November 1993, he asked whether the concept of subsidiarity as defined in the German government's memo of September 1992 should "extend to the protection of social rights and powers and the rights of regions and groups of regions in dealing with the affairs of local communities?" [10.11.93 94 C 147/02 E-3100/93 – Arbeloa Muru to Council]. The Council's reply, supplied the following March, adhered to the notion of *states' rights* even more unequivocally:

> The principle of subsidiarity (Article 3b, TEU) deals with the exercise of certain powers by the EC, but does not deal with the relationships in each member state between the powers of the state on the one hand and those of the two sides of industry on the other. That relationship is governed by the laws of the individual member states, some of which recognise principles equivalent to the principle of subsidiarity and to the principle of proportionality.

This response implies that if some member states, exercise their rights *not* to "recognise principles equivalent to the principle of subsidiarity", they will not be forced to by invoking a more radical interpretation of Article 3b[1]. Jacques Delors, retiring President of the Commission, confirmed this

---

1 Arbeloa Muru put the same question to the Commission [10.11.93 94 C 147/02 E-3100/93]. Its response in March 1994 followed the Council's *states' rights* line: "It is not for the Commission to interfere in the distribution of powers between the central, regional or local authorities in the member states"

in his address to the inaugural meeting of the CoR: "The Union has no say in what the nature of relations between central and regional authorities is to be" [*European Access* 1994 No. 3, June].

Protocol C from Part Two of the ToA: "Provisions on the Simplification of the Treaties" contains a reference to subsidiarity. It reaffirms the European Council's commitment to the Edinburgh Council's application of the principle, but defines subsidiarity as a "dynamic concept" to be applied in the light of the Treaty's objectives. It emphasises, however, that this may mean that EU action could be restricted or discontinued if necessary. There is no indication that the principle could be applied to activities below the level of the EU.

Both the TEU and the ToA, therefore, have fallen short of enabling issues relating to the implementation of its constitutional agenda to be adequately addressed.

In sum, the EU approves of the concept of subsidiarity, but interprets it only in accordance with the *states' rights* definition. It is not prepared to risk substantial disagreements with those of its member states' governments who believe either that the EU should not take any unnecessary action which may encroach upon national sovereignty or that their own internal sovereignty may be endangered by a devolution of power. The member state that, at least until recently, epitomised this position is the UK. Scott *et al* [1994 p 48] comment that the intensity of the Major government's "ideological aversion to 'subsidiarity at home' [was] unique". This was supported by the response the former UK Prime Minister made to Sir Charles Grey, the leader of the CoR's UK delegation [cited by Sillett 1995 p 6]:

> I do not believe that the community via the Treaty, should try to dictate the relationship between the various levels of government within a member state.

Chapter Two demonstrated this by examining the attitude of the pre 1997-UK government towards devolution of power.

The EU's interpretation of subsidiarity suggests that there are no prospects of the UK's membership of the EU leading to a *de jure* devolution of power via the application of the subsidiarity principle. If the UK government does not want to decentralise power, the EU will not force it to do so. There is to be no federalist solution. This interpretation has been adopted by Major's successor, Tony Blair. In a speech entitled: "The new challenge for Europe", delivered in Aachen, Germany, 14 May 1999, Blair showed that his version of the subsidiarity concept was similar to the Edinburgh summit's, and that "decentralisation" referred only to returning control to the nation state:

> Europe should do the big things better; and it should get out of as many of the small things as possible.

> Our citizens will support the EU. But the one thing they will unite on, in opposition, is where the EU appears to interfere in the minutiae of everyday life for purposes that appear obscure. Europe could legislate less in some areas and achieve more.
>
> As I say, integrate where necessary, decentralise where possible

Nevertheless, the debate about subsidiarity has had the effect of concentrating thought within the EU about the *potential* for decentralisation within its member states [Peterson 1994 p 129, 131; Scott *et al* 1994 p 57]. Sinn [1994 p 86] points out that "the main function of the subsidiarity principle is that it places the burden of proof on those who want more centralization". If actors from the UK, operating at EU or sub-national level, question the centralisation principle as practised by a British government, the subsidiarity concept may be invoked.

There are intellectual allies and support at EU level. Representatives from those states that have already devolved powers substantially, like Germany, Belgium and Spain, express their views within the Council of Ministers, the EP and the CoR. Sub-national governments within these states have already made use of the language of subsidiarity to enhance their arguments about the role they should play *vis-à-vis* the development of EU policies and to demand greater regional autonomy. Nationals from those countries that were earlier signatories to the European Charter for Local Self Government bear its general principles in mind. If these general trends are set within the framework of the concept of subsidiarity, which is formally embodied in the Treaty, they can provide a balancing feature alongside the mechanistic interpretation of the concept that was provided by the 1992 Edinburgh Summit.

If the subsidiarity concept is still ill-defined, there are two *de facto* potential avenues for the decentralising of political activities within the EU. These rely upon a neo-functionalist theory, which relies upon political "spill over", not necessarily intended by the chief actors, from economic or other factors.

First, the CoR may become a mechanism whereby local and regional authorities can affect the decision-making process within the EU [Scott *et al* 1994 p 60][2]. Second, non- or sub-national levels of government themselves may, through their contacts with supranational institutions within the EU, become more autonomous and more effective participants in EU and UK governance. "Multi-sector" or "multi-level" governance may become the practical means of decision-making within the EU. This will be considered in Chapters Seven and Eight.

---

2 Gallacher [1995 p 22] points out that the establishment of the CoR itself extends the principle of subsidiarity below the level of the member states in practice since it prevents the EU from legislating or developing policies in areas affecting sub-national government without consulting it via the CoR.

This chapter concentrates upon the impact of the CoR. It looks at early views of the prospects of the CoR; it considers its functions and structure and finally, the challenges the CoR faces.

2.   The Committee of the regions

2.1.   *Prospects*

The importance of the CoR to this study lies in the prospects it offers for improving the position of local and regional government within the member states, especially within the UK.

Initially there were grounds for optimism. Taylor [1995 p 76] referred to the creation of the CoR as "a significant step towards the recognition that sub-national government deserves to be involved as a formal component of the EU decision-making process". Jones [1995 pp 295-296] hoped that decentralising forces (such as those referred to above) would be encouraged to develop by means of the CoR, perhaps towards the creation of more empowered regional institutions. He also noted [*ibid*] that the "regional element" as determined by member states' governments, had been significantly diluted.

Wistrich [1994 p 68] focused upon the importance of the creation of a statutory body representing sub-national government that could participate in the formulation of EU policies that affect the regions. Keating [1995 p 15] was cautiously optimistic, believing that the establishment of the CoR gave legitimacy to the regional input in EC decision making (although he did not think that the CoR was likely to develop into a regionally based second Chamber of the EP in the short term).

However, Scott *et al* [*op cit*] disagreed with Jones that a powerful CoR would encourage member states' governments to develop distinct regional authorities. They pointed out that this would take place in the face of attempts by the UK [then Conservative] government to veto the conferment of greater powers to Europe's regions, should this issue be considered formally at an IGC. They also thought [*ibid*] that sub-national government in the UK was poorly equipped to play a part in the CoR. Jeffery [1996 p 262], examining the policies of and effect on sub-national government of the powerful German Länder, was also cautious, but concluded that the CoR, including representatives of the Länder, would make the force of regionalism a significant one at EU level:

The CoR is now in its second term. It has not rewritten the political agenda of decision-making at EU level, although it has had its modest successes. This chapter analyses the CoR's impact upon the EU's democratic processes in its second term.

2.2.   *History of the Committee of the Regions*

A Consultative Council of Regional and Local Authorities attached to Directorate General [DG] XVI (Regions) was set up by the Commission on 4 June 1988 as a forerunner to the CoR [*OJ*, C51/25, Questions to Council and Commission 2359/92 and 2358/92, 23 September 1992]. Its members were allocated evenly between local and regional authorities and were chosen by the Assembly of European Regions [AER] and the Conference of European Municipalities and Regions [CEMR]. It had few functions and little influence [Preston 1997[3]] and was abolished in 1993.

The CoR itself originated in the IGC that was set up to consider the form of the TEU [1992]. It was set up partly because of pressure from sub-national government itself, particularly the German Länder and the Belgian regions, upon their home governments [Marks *et al* 1996 p 360]. Local and regional authorities were affected by EU policies and legislation and, as a result of the increasing significance of regional funding (which now stands at about 30 per cent of the EU's budget), sub-national government's interest in the EU was also growing. As interest grew, so did pressure from two pan-European sub-national organisations – AER and CEMR.

At the time of institution the future CoR was welcomed by two of the major EU institutions (the EP and Commission) and was supported by some member states' governments, such as those of Belgium and Germany. Germany in particular saw the establishment of the CoR as an acceptable compromise, made available by the EU, which would assist it in dealing with its Länder [Preston 1997].

The CoR was established under Article 198a [EC] of the TEU which outlined its purpose as a representative of regional and local government within the EU, and gave it an advisory status. It also established the number of members of the CoR.

Article 198b defined organisational details:

- the CoR would elect its own officers who should hold office for two years
- it should adopt its own rules of procedure which needed to be ratified by the Council acting unanimously
- meetings could be convened by the Chairman at the request of Council or Commission or on its own initiative.

Article 198c specified terms of reference. The CoR was to be a consultative committee, consulted where the Council of Ministers or Commission considered it appropriate, with an option for Council or

3 Unpublished interim paper, cited by permission of the author

Commission to set a time limit on its deliberations. It had to be consulted where the [EC] Treaty so provided. These areas related to:

- education and youth [Article 126]
- culture [Article 128]
- public health [Article 129]
- trans-European networks in the areas of transport, telecommunications and energy infrastructure [Articles 129c & 129d]
- economic and social cohesion [Article 130b]
- Structural Funds and the Cohesion Fund [Article 130d]
- decisions on the European Regional Development Fund [Article 130e]

In addition, the CoR should be informed when ECOSOC was consulted and, if it considered that regional interests were involved, it could issue an Opinion on that matter. Whilst the above limited the areas for CoR involvement, the CoR was also given a remit which was potentially limitless – it could issue an opinion either where it considered that specific regional interests were involved, or where it "considered such action appropriate". Opinions were to be forwarded to the Council and the Commission.

- *Effects of the provisions of Articles 198a, 198b & 198c*

The articles that set up the CoR are very short, but the terms in which they are couched have constructed some difficulties for the CoR. Two areas have been of especial concern:

Article 198a neglected to specify the form or style of representation. Inevitably the criteria for the selection of representatives to the CoR differ from member state to member state [see below]. The different bases for membership also presented the CoR with organisational difficulties that inhibit it from becoming a homogeneous body.

The article was vague about the CoR's function. It has the role of commenting on draft EU legislation in areas in which sub-national government has interests either in implementing or enforcing EU law [O'Neill 1995 p 2; Gallacher 1995 p 2]. However, since it is not limited to this in the Treaty, there is confusion about the restrictions on the role.

In other words, Articles 198b and 198c conferred on the CoR opportunities which were simultaneously too extensive and too limited. Opportunities were too expansive since Article 198b allows the CoR to issue "own initiative" Opinions which tempt it to blur its focus. Opportunities were too restricted because originally there were no formal means within the TEU to enable the CoR to report directly to or to liaise with the EP, thus impeding the formation of an effective partnership between the two. The ToA remedied this, but not before poor relations had already developed between the two institutions.

2.3.   *Allocation of members*

Among the fifteen member states, Germany, France, Italy and the UK were allocated 24 members apiece; Spain: 21; Belgium, Greece, the Netherlands, Portugal, Austria and Sweden: 12; Denmark, Finland and Ireland: nine and Luxembourg: six. An equal number of alternate, or reserve, members were designated in the same proportion amongst the member states. This makes a total of 222 members and 222 alternates (until the next round of enlargements).

2.4.   *Selection of members*

Article 198a provided only that CoR members should be appointed for four years (with a renewable term of office) by the Council of Ministers, which was to act unanimously on proposals from the member states. Member states were given further autonomy in choosing their representatives in that members of the CoR were to be "completely independent in the performance of their duties, in the general interest of the Community". This means that member states were not constrained in their choice by having to consider any form of balance, although it was understood that they were expected to respect a certain political and geographical balance when choosing CoR members.

It was taken for granted, however that appointees would be *elected* representatives and in 1994, ten out of the original twelve states – Germany and the Netherlands were exceptions – did select only elected representatives at least for their full members (some alternates appointed were officials).

The UK too, appointed elected representatives in the end. Initially its government had wanted to appoint civil servants from the regional Government Offices which were due to be extended in 1994, arguing that since the new Committee was entitled "Committee of the *Regions*", it was inappropriate to appoint members of *local* government to it. This notion of non-elected representation was questioned by the EP and evoked some opposition throughout sub-national government within the EU. The main argument was that a CoR with a hybrid (elected /non-elected) membership would find it hard to co-ordinate actions of regional and local authorities [Scott *et al* p 63].

Unsurprisingly, the move caused political controversy in the UK as well. Opponents included leaders of the Conservative Groups from the three local authority associations who wrote to every Conservative MP in England and Wales asking them to support the local authority view. Labour moved a successful amendment during the committee stage of the

European Communities (Amendment) Bill 1992 to require total elected representation from local authorities. When the UK government ratified the TEU, paragraph 6 read:

> A person may be proposed as a member or alternate member of the United Kingdom of the Committee of the Regions constituted under Article 198a of the Treaty establishing the European Community only if, at the time of the proposal, he is an elected member of a local authority

[European Communities (Amendment) Act 1993].

This decision means that the UK is, ironically, the one member state in the EU that may appoint only elected members[4]. In fact, in the CoR's second term, all are elected members, except for some Dutch members (sub national government in the Netherlands is largely appointed by the national government of the day).

2.5.   *The basis of appointment of representatives*

The criteria on which members of the CoR are appointed varies:

- Tier of government

Belgium sends only regional representatives; Luxembourg and Greece have only local government representatives. Most other states attempt to spread their representation. Some (Austria, Germany, Spain) are constitutionally bound to do so. Fig 6.1 below shows the classification[5]:

- territorial balance

Belgian members must represent the four language zones; Austrian members need to represent the nine regions; each of the five largest German Länder has two representatives; the rest one each. The Irish contingent consists of one member from each of the newly-formed regions. Italy, Luxembourg and the UK attempt a territorial balance.

---

4   This irony is matched by a second, pointed out by Morris [1991 cited by Bache *et al* 1996 p 314] – that UK local authorities have a stronger constitutional role in the EU than they have in the UK.

5   these classifications are only approximate. In its first term, the CoR released information about its members' tier of origin. This time, it has not been thought helpful to do so. The table was therefore built up by referring to the sub-national governmental arrangements in each member state and the title of the authority to which the members belong.

Fig 6.1: CoR members 1998 by tier of government

State	Regional	Intermediate	Local	Total
Austria	9	-	3	12
Belgium	12	-	-	12
Denmark	4	-	5	9
Finland	5	-	4	9
France	14	5	5	24
Germany	21	1	2	24
Greece	-	-	12	12
Ireland	-	8	1	9
Italy	12	6	6	24
Luxembourg	-	-	6	6
Netherlands	-	6	6	12
Portugal	2	-	10	10
Spain	17	-	4	21
Sweden	-	5	7	12
UK	-	9	15	24
Total	**96**	**40**	**86**	**222**

- political balance

The Finnish and French representations reflect the spread of political forces at national level.   Italy, Luxembourg and the UK attempt a political balance.   The majority parties at regional and local level choose the Swedish representation. In the 1998 CoR, the two major parties (EPP and PES) ended up more or less in equilibrium, as shown in fig 6.2. below.

- views of sub-national government associations

German local government associations nominate persons for the three German local government seats; Danish representatives are appointed by the national local government associations. Consultation takes place with French sub-national government associations. Italian and UK sub-national government associations nominate candidates, but they need the approval of national government.

- selection of persons of status

Not all member states are concerned to select sub-national politicians of

Fig 6.2.: CoR membership 1998 by political affiliation

State / Party	EPP	PES	ELDR	EA	non-aligned	total
Austria	9	2	-	1	-	12
Belgium	6	4	1	1	-	12
Denmark	1	2	2	-	4	9
Finland	2	3	3	-	1	9
France	9	9	-	1	5	24
Germany	6	13	1	2	2	24
Greece	2	9	-	-	1	12
Ireland	2	1	1	3	2	9
Italy	9	5	-	-	10	24
Luxembourg	1	1	2	-	2	6
Netherlands	2	2	6	-	2	12
Portugal	4	5	-	-	3	10
Spain	13	3	1	-	4	21
Sweden	2	4	1	-	5	12
UK	4	13	3	2	2	24
Total	**72**	**76**	**21**	**10**	**43**	**222**

Key

EPP	European Peoples' Party
PES	Party of European Socialists
ELDR	Liberal Democrat and Reformers' Party
EA	European Alliance

(NB: Unaligned members do not belong to a pan-European political grouping, but this does not necessarily mean that they have no party affiliation within their own Member State.)

particular substance. Article 23 c of the Austrian constitution obliges the presidents of the nine regions to serve (although the local representatives do not have to be mayors). The Presidents of the Spanish autonomous communities are automatically members; French members will be presidents or vice-presidents of their region, president of a Département or Mayor of a Commune. Italian and Portuguese representatives are either presidents of their regions or provinces or mayors of major cities. Greek representatives are Mayors. Individuals of status from other countries may also be appointed, of course. For example, the 1998 CoR includes Oskar

Lafontaine, previously Minister of Finance, amongst the German delegation.

The net effect of the application of the different criteria is the creation of a heterogeneous body.

2.6.   *Organisation of the Committee of the Regions*

The CoR has five plenary meetings each year at which its Opinions[6] are considered. In its first term, about 200 opinions were adopted. Members are allocated seats alphabetically so as to encourage them to mix together. The main work is done in the "Commissions" or sub-committees that were set up at the CoR's third meeting, May 1994. Each member state has representatives in every Commission, and each member state contributes one Chairman.

The work of the CoR is overseen by its Bureau, which is elected for a two year term and which comprises a President, a first Vice President and 34 other members – three from each of the larger states and two from each of the smaller. The Bureau has responsibility for drafting the budget, overseeing the administration, referring items to the Commission and following up Opinions. It holds three meetings each year, with a meeting in March and one each in early June and December to coincide with the changes in Presidency of the Council of Ministers. The CoR has a Secretariat-General and cabinet.

3.   Challenges for the Committee of the Regions

For the CoR to become an instrument for participatory democracy, it needs to resolve its own inherent weaknesses and be aware of its status and role. Three objectives need to be achieved in pursuit of this aim:

First, the CoR needs to develop a corporate character. Members need to accept and respect the differing statuses of individual members and the status of their sub-national governments[7].

This objective is a prerequisite of the second: there is a need for the CoR to carve out for itself a meaningful role that does not significantly overlap

---

6   short documents which comment on and recommend changes to Commission proposals

7   In his inaugural address to the CoR, Jacques Delors [*European Access* 1994 No. 3, June] warned members against "failing to put the general interest above the internecine quarrels that may arise from the differences in your status and your own particular interests, let alone the inevitable confrontation of national interests".

with that of any other EU institution. The CoR needs to accomplish two other things to enable this objective to be achieved. First, it needs to be seen to be acting effectively within its existing remit [O'Neill 1995 p 16]. This would enable it to be taken seriously by institutions sympathetic towards the CoR and would foster its pursuit for increased powers. Second, the CoR needs to develop its relationships with those institutions that originally responded to it neutrally or even with hostility so that they may assist rather than obstruct it in the attainment of its goals.

Third, the CoR must keep this overall objective at the centre of its thoughts and activities. Gallacher, Assistant Director of the LGIB, stated that his view of the role of the CoR was not to act as regional advocate nor to supervise the allocation of regional funds, but rather to involve sub-national governments in policy-making[8]. Delors, in his address to the inaugural meeting of the CoR [*European Access* 1994 No. 3, June], offered some advice:

> For the task of the Committee of the Regions is nothing less than to enhance the democracy of the Union... The establishment of the Committee of the Regions was one of the provisions designed to draw every individual citizen into this great collective venture...

The danger is that an effective CoR seen to be *representative* of sub-national government at EU level could replace or supplant *participatory* sub-national government in relation to EU-wide issues. The CoR needs to remember that its aim is to become the "voice of sub-national government" within the EU – not its substitute.

This may be an overstated danger. In some member states – for example Germany, Spain and Belgium – sub-national government has a sufficiently high status to make its replacement by the CoR improbable. It is also unlikely that members of other EU institutions would be willing to allow the CoR to develop sufficiently in status so as to become a powerful rival to themselves.

4.   Meeting the challenges

4.1.   *The Corporate Character*

The key to any body developing a corporate nature is the belief that there is more that unites than divides it. However, there are signs that the CoR contains within it internal conflicts and contradictions which are still to be

---

8   Joseph Gallacher, Assistant Director, LGIB - presentation made at the Institute for German Studies, The University of Birmingham, Edgbaston, November 1995

resolved. Article 198a created a problem for appointed members in that their individual representative status is uncertain. In the absence of specific Treaty guidelines, there are many ways in which a member of the CoR could "represent" besides being a representative of party, country, region or type of council. S/he could also be a representative of[9]:

- a particular council
- local government in general (as opposed to regional government)
- regional government in general (as opposed to local government)
- sub-national government in general (as opposed to national/EU government)
- the member state of origin (eg UK)
- the type of member state (eg from Northern as opposed to Southern Europe).

These different roles lead to difficulties reconciling different interests held by individual members within the CoR and opposing interests held between groups of members. There are also problems with deciding which role members should play *vis-à-vis* national and supranational levels of governance.

- *The regional/local divide*

Although the two pan-European organisations, the CEMR and the AER, did not take the active part in the CoR that was anticipated [Gallacher 1995 p 18], in the early days there was evidence of a regional/local divide within the CoR. Albert Bore, a UK member, reported that initially it had been necessary to ask for the words "and local authorities" to be added to every document. Jordi Pujol, CoR member and President of Catalonia, argued for a formal split between the regions and localities on the Committee. However, members have evidently realised that this was a problem that needed to be addressed, and the threat of division has not materialised [Warleigh 1999 p 40].

- *Contrasts in sub-national government culture*

The CoR may be impeded in developing a corporate nature because of the different forms of sub-national government cultures that exist within the EU. Some of these differences are well documented, for example between centralising states like the UK and Luxembourg and federal states like Germany and between the continental European position of "general

---

9   This representative "schizophrenia" has particularly exercised Cllr Albert Bore, of the UK's delegation.

competence" and the *ultra vires* doctrine of the UK. However there are other differences of origin, remit and autonomy between the forms of sub-national government in more decentralised states which may affect the way of thinking and actions of their representatives on the CoR. Three of the founding member states of the EU: Germany, France and Italy, with Spain, – each of which has appointed at least fifty per cent of its membership from the regions – show very distinctive sub-national government characteristics and therefore demonstrate the different political backgrounds of their representatives on the CoR.

- *The nationality factor*

It is hard to estimate how significant the nationality factor is. McCarthy commented that the number of vice presidents (one from each member state) reflected the degree of importance that was attached to national delegations[10] - with every contingent demanding one representative among the vice presidents. Sir Ronald Watson, then recently appointed to the CoR, commented that[11]:

> ... it has become very obvious to me that at CoR there are very few members who are able to take a wider EU perspective and most of the discussions do relate to the effects that proposed EU directives will have on individual member states and regions.

Sir Ronald thought that this might be the result of briefings from home governments and regional associations. He added that even within political groupings, there was a tendency to break down into national factions.

- *Conflict among types of member states of origin*

A variation on the nationality factor is the potential conflict between different types of member states. The CoR has already indicated that it is interested in extending its financial support for national groupings to transnational groupings, eg the Mediterranean grouping[12]. Some members also fear that the principle of consensus between members of the CoR may be endangered by the development of north/south European and potential east/west European divides as new states line up for EU membership. This problem is not one experienced only by the CoR [Warleigh 1999 pp 40-

---

10 Elmarie McCarthy, LGIU, December 1995.

11 Letter to author 28 September 1998

12 Bore as previously cited

41], but the immaturity of the institution may render it more liable to fragment under this kind of pressure.

■   *Political factions*

Political factions were slow to appear within the CoR in the early years of its operations.   Duff noted that members seemed more at home with national rather than with European parties, where they exist.

Until 1994, the CoR failed to allocate resources to political groupings, although since then funds have been made available for pre-plenary political group meetings.   The majority of members now do belong to a political group (although a large minority do not) [see fig 6.2. above].   This may be because it enables the CoR to find ways of relating to the EP more effectively rather than because of the need to have political groupings *per se*.   Meetings before plenaries take place between leaders of political groups and leaders of EP political groups.

■   *Members' status*

The different statuses of representatives present something of a dilemma. The CoR needs persons of status to encourage other EU and national institutions to take it seriously.   Some of the member states – particularly those which were enthusiastic about the institution of the CoR – have taken care to appoint people of distinguished sub-national status as their representatives [see above].   In addition, some representatives have been chosen by their member states because of their high profile even though status was not a formal prerequisite.

Although this enhances the profile of the CoR as an institution, it stands in the way of its becoming a corporate body.   Anderson argues that the CoR is ineffective because of the difference in status of its members.   He says that the symbolic function of the CoR is undermined by its heterogeneity[13].   The leader of a German Land or Spanish autonomous community may effectively govern a region larger than a small country.   It is difficult for her/him to consider as a political equal – for example – a councillor from Norwich District Council or mayor of a Greek locality [see Duff 1993 p 22].   The latter may feel intimidated in such a presence.

On the other hand, Jacques Delors [*European Access 1994* No. 3, June] considered it to be an advantage, giving the CoR a unique flexibility:

> ... the leaders of large regions will sit alongside mayors from small towns, and mayors from major cities will mix with representatives of rural communities.

13   James Anderson, Department of Geography, the Open University, Paper presented at University of North London, December 1995

There is also the possibility that the "egalitarian" atmosphere, which has been generated by the CoR in its early days, may succeed in showing even members of the highest profile that their status outside the CoR is of more limited significance than they might have thought. Winnie Bang Petersen, spokesman for the *Direction des travaux consultatifs, Comité des Régions*, commented that some of the higher status members had suffered something of a rude awakening when they discovered that they were no more likely to be successful in having their demands met than their lower status colleagues[14].

4.2. *The meaningful role*

It is difficult to estimate the CoR's overall effectiveness within its organisational structure. CoR Opinions are adopted early in the EU legislative process so many issues considered by the CoR have yet to reach the final policy making stage, but a preliminary analysis highlighted a number of areas where comments had been taken on board by the Commission and the Council[15]. A study [CoR 1996], examining the CoR's impact during the first half of 1996, stated that:

> The points of view expressed in Committee of the Regions Opinions have had a significant impact on those of the other institutions and on EU policies

On the whole, though, an analysis of the Opinions that were endorsed or included in subsequent proposals are of the more innocuous variety. In any case, none of these give any evidence of effectiveness *per se*, since it cannot be ascertained whether CoR Opinions on these issues reflected rather than influenced Council and Commission thinking.

4.3. *The Committee of the Regions' relationships*

The CoR owes its existence in part to the EP and was originally welcomed by it. In the absence of a statutory relationship in its early days, the CoR tried to build up its own contacts with the EP. However, the first CoR had an indifferent relationship with the EP. For example, the "First

---

14 presentation made in Brussels, 07 November 1997 to delegation of Cheshire District Councils

15 These include the European Year of Lifelong Learning, the Commission's Anti-Drugs action plan, and the implementation of the URBAN programme (C 217/03: Opinion on draft notice from Commission re URBAN areas) [LGIB December 1995]

Conference" between the EP and members of regional and local authorities, held just before the CoR was set up, was attended by very few MEPs. This now seems to be changing as the CoR becomes less eclectic in its interests. Warleigh [1997 p 104] reported that the EP used the CoR's opinions as a basis for amendments to legislation, for example in the development of the LIFE programme. The problem also seems to have become less acute following the end of the term of office of the first President, Jacques Blanc, whose confrontational style alienated some MEPs [Warleigh 1999 p 26].

The EP is also worried about encroachment upon its representative role. Preston [1997] points out that "both are political as opposed to technocratic bodies...". This has roots in the equivocal nature of Article 198a [see above]. The CoR itself has been guilty of ambiguity in its promotional material, claiming to represent the people, rather than their sub-national governments[16]. This problem may resolve itself as the EP becomes more accustomed to the different form of representation incorporated in the CoR. There has already been some progress towards "closer and stronger relations". For example, a second major joint conference was held 2-3 October 1996. This conference's unanimously adopted final declaration stated that it was: "... essential to consolidate the CoR *inter alia* by ... extending its powers to include consultation by the EP" [http://europa.eu.int/comreg/pr/ 96107en.html]. The ToA achieved this ambition by specifying that in future the EP will also be able to consult the CoR [Art 198c]. By formalising the connection between the two institutions there is a prospect of improving the relationship.

Members of the CoR have a better relationship with the European Commission than with the EP. There are three discernible reasons for this. First, the Commission welcomed the establishment of the CoR. This was not, as with the EP, because of an expectation that this would improve democratic accountability but rather because the Commission hoped that the permanent establishment of a sub-national representative consultative body would assist in the decision-making process within the EU. So far as can be established, this optimism has been justified.

---

16   The CoR [1995] stated that:

> As elected representatives or heads of local and regional authorities, the 222 members of the Committee of the Regions serve the citizens in two ways; firstly, by ensuring that their direct interests are taken into account in the Union's policy-making process, and secondly, by keeping them informed about progress towards European union.

Second, there is no interinstitutional rivalry between the CoR and European Commission. Whilst the role of the CoR within the EU may be indeterminate at present, it is unlikely to encroach upon that of the EU's bureaucracy. Hence there is no reason for the Commission to feel threatened by the role or activities of the CoR.

Third, the Commission has indicated its willingness to co-operate with the CoR. The CoR member, Charles Grey, addressing the ADC in June 1994, commented that the Commission preferred to deal with regions rather than ministers on a consultative basis. Nicholls [1994 pp 201-202] notes that the Commission has a generally friendly attitude towards the CoR's membership, in particular in relation to the administration of structural funds. The Commission's co-operation has been demonstrated in a number of ways. It is not required to act upon CoR recommendations, but the former Regional Commissioner, Wulf-Mathies, undertook to report back on actions taken upon CoR's Opinions. In addition, she announced the Commission's intention to consult the CoR more widely than required by the treaty [Wulf-Mathies 1995, cited by Jeffery 1995]. The President of the Commission too reported regularly to the CoR and Santer set up a special unit in the Commission's Secretariat General to follow up its work [Preston 1997].

Future relations depend upon the CoR's ability to work with rather than apart from the newly-appointed Commission. McCarthy [1997 p 443] found that Wulf-Mathies had made it clear that the Commission did not expect the CoR to concern itself with high politics on the occasion of its ninth plenary in September 1995 when it considered adopting a resolution on the questions of Bosnia and nuclear testing.

4.4. *Committee of the Regions effectiveness*

Various commentators have warned about the threat posed by Article 198c to the effectiveness of the CoR. The Local Government Information Unit briefing [April 1994] commented "To be influential the CoR needs to be relevant. That means offering timely opinions which have a direct bearing on evolving legislation". Duff warned that there was a danger in permitting an unlimited range of opinions, since the CoR might be tempted to become too general in its approach, which he believed had been the case with ECOSOC[17]. Delors [*European Access* 1994 No. 3, June], too, in his address at the CoR's inaugural meeting, advised members to:

> ... avoid casting your nets too far... If you take too much on, if you try to be involved in everything, then you may fail to make a distinctive impression.

---

17 Duff, Andrew - lecture given at the Federal Trust Summer School, Hull, July 1994

His view was that the CoR should concentrate upon issues that affected regional and local authorities in particular. The CoR has not followed this advice comprehensively, although it has indicated that it is aware of the dangers. Whilst diversity may limit the CoR's effectiveness, there is also a corresponding danger that should the CoR confine itself to expressing Opinions only when asked to do so, it will have no opportunity to assist in setting an agenda for sub-national government within the member states.

The challenge for the CoR will be to act with sufficient discretion to satisfy, or at least not alienate, those bodies which have the power to enhance or retard its pursuit of additional competence. The CoR needs to steer the difficult path of fulfilling a variety of expectations and goals. Gallacher [1995] argues that:

> The creation of the Committee of the Regions was a political act, loaded with symbolic meaning and resulted from differing pressures from members states, the European Parliament and the Commission each with their own perception of what the regional body should be. As a result much of the discussion to date has been overlaid with the ambitions of various actors for a different kind of body.

It would be easy for the CoR to be effective in a limited way by restricting its input to the minimum required of it by those member states and organisations who want it to be either a vehicle for maintaining the *status quo* for sub-national government or an alternative to decentralising power within the EU. Striking the correct balance is more challenging for the CoR.

4.5.   *The future of the Committee of the Regions*

Only moderate proposals for increased powers are likely to be acceptable to centralised member states and hence to the European Council. The outcome of the 1996/7 IGC emphasises the point by the modesty of its proposals for extending the remit, autonomy and powers of the CoR. The ToA includes a restricted extension of the CoR's consultative remit to:

- general transport policy [Art 71 (1), Art 75]
- employment [Art 4 – guidelines and art 5 – incentive measures, also Art 128 (2), Art 129]
- combating social exclusion [Art 137 (2)]
- social directives [Art 125 – implementing Social Fund decisions; Art 137 (2)] – relating to art]
- vocational training [Art 150 (4)]
- environmental policy [Art 175 (1), (2) and (3)]
- cross border co-operation [Art 198c].

Source: http://ue.eu.int/Amsterdam/en/treaty/Partone/amst03.htm

The extension to the CoR's autonomy is restricted to:

- an amendment to Art 198b which empowers it to adopt its rules of procedure without submitting them to the Council for prior approval
- the repeal of protocol 16 of the TEU which means that the CoR will no longer share its organisational framework or administrative service with ECOSOC.

Nentwich and Falkner [1997 p 9] conclude:

> ... the Treaty of Amsterdam will not bring about a 'Europe of the regions'. It is not even a small step in that direction... [T]he CoR remains a purely consultative body and the issues of representativeness and legitimacy of its member are still unsettled. It is obvious that the formal decision-making structure gives the CoR only a very weak voice.

The effectiveness of the CoR is not only to be analysed in terms of formal powers, however. Although it is always difficult to estimate the assessment of the effectiveness of an institution (apparent incorporation of amendments and comments could have been intended anyway by the consulting institution), the inclusion of the CoR as an *à volunté* consultee concerning cross border consultation is significant. It may be argued that the CoR's previous "own initiative" contributions to this issue were considered of high enough value to warrant a more formalised role[18]. This may be an example of the potential of the CoR to extend its competence by demonstrating its expertise in areas outside its immediate remit.

In any case, although *ambitions* for an empowered CoR were high in the run up to the Amsterdam Treaty, *expectations* for an institution which was then less than three years old were not so optimistic.

The CoR needs more time to grow into its role. It may, if it avoids the more obvious pitfalls, become an effective pressure group for the tier of governance that is closest to the citizens. It may, given a degree of diffidence, also assist this tier of governance to grow in power and status.

---

18 The Commission's communication *on Cross-border Cooperation within the framework of the Tacis programme* [COM (97) 239 final, 27 May 1997] acknowledges the CoR's Opinions on *The Northern Dimension of the European Union and Cross-border Cooperation on the Border between the European Union and the Russian Federation and in the Barents Region* [COR 10/96, 12 June 1996] about the need to involve the border regions in the planning and implementation of cross-border cooperation measures. It also refers to the CoR's Opinion on *Current and future EU policy on the Baltic Sea region with specific reference to local and regional aspects* [CdR 141/96, 13 November 1996].

These prospects are fragile, not least because they are notions that may well be alien to elected politicians. The hope is that these particular elected politicians remain themselves sufficiently close to the citizenry to be aware of their limitations as representatives. The fear is that should they themselves hold or acquire personal status through their membership of the CoR they may also become more ambitious. Yet if members of the CoR try, however unsuccessfully, to ape the more familiar model of supranational or national politician, an opportunity for an alternative form of democratic enhancement will have been lost.

CHAPTER SEVEN

THE EUROPEAN UNION'S OPTIONS FOR PARTICIPATORY DEMOCRACY

1.   Options for participation

Chapter One outlined options for the extension of participatory democracy arguing that there was a positive correlation between active popular participation and beneficial democratic outcomes. These options were:

- public debate, referenda, media debate with electronic voting (enabling "all of the people" to take part)
- "people's parliaments", citizens' juries and opinion polling (enabling "representative samples of the people" to take part)
- local democracy, industrial democracy, demarchy and participation in voluntary organisations (enabling "only the people affected" to take part).

This Chapter looks at the options for "all of the people" and "some of the people", but focuses upon "only the people affected" in relation to interest groups and non-governmental bodies.

2.   Potential for participation

Some options may be excluded at the outset. Unless unforeseen and unlikely developments take place, the EU does not offer the potential to involve "all of the people" in *decision-making* by means of formal public debates (there is no forum large enough to accommodate 370,000,000 people!) nor media debates with electronic voting. Nevertheless, EU integration has generated public *interest*, which has occasionally had to be taken into account by the EU's decision-makers [see below 2.1.]. Referenda have also been held in several of the EU's member states in response to the speed and nature of EU integration [see below 2.2.].

   Looking at prospects for generally representative samples, there is no evidence that the EU intends to develop the concept of "people's parliaments" or "citizens' juries". Exhaustive opinion polling has taken place, but only for the purpose of informing decision-makers [see below 3.1].

Where participatory democracy generated by the EU does seem to have made an impact is in the field of "only the people affected", either at interest group, sub- or non-governmental levels. The EU has affected UK interest group activity [see below, 5]. There has been neither attempt nor intention to formalise citizen participation by means of employing anything like Burnheim's "demarchy", but the CoR offers some prospects for including sub-national government in the decision-making processes [see above, Chapter Six]. Whilst industrial democracy has been lightly touched by EU membership in practice, in theory the Social Chapter may offer some prospects for its enhancement at least by means of works' councils.

It may be objected that none of these opportunities for enhanced participatory democracy have been provided with the intention of achieving this end. The expression of public interest in the EU has often been other than that which the EU's decision-makers would have wished, and it has hardly been encouraged by them. Referenda have been called for various reasons, but by individual member states and not because the EU as a body is committed to them. Opinion polling has been commissioned by the European Commission in the regular *Eurobarometer* polls, generally for the purpose of gauging public reaction to the EU and its policies, rather than enabling representative samples of the public to take part in decision-making.

Involvement of "only the people affected" has usually been undertaken intentionally. The Commission in particular, but also the EP, has grasped the need to involve significant interests in the policy process for the purpose of effective and efficient policy-making and execution. This suggests that pragmatic considerations rather than a respect for democracy *per se* have led these two EU institutions towards greater involvement with sub- and non-governmental bodies.

Thus any involvement of "all" or "representative" samples of the people has been incidental, whilst involvement of "only the people affected" has taken place for other than democratic reasons.

This does not matter, however. The brief description of the emergence of representative democracy included in Chapter One showed that most developments in the field of democracy have taken place to fulfil essentially non-democratic purposes. Yet, as Arblaster [1991 p 38] notes, this did not prevent representative democracy from moving from the realm of "necessary evil" to that of the "universal honorific" [Sartori 1987 pp 3-4]. Developments in representative democracy occurred because of the actions and practices of individuals, and because of public response to them. It is argued then, that the practice, rather than the normative theory of participatory democracy, stands a fair chance of becoming equally acceptable and necessary in the EU.

3.   Involving all of the people

3.1.   *Public debate*

On one level only a minority of the EU's citizens are interested in the EU. That is to say, less than half of its citizens cast a vote in the 1999 European Elections. However, the issue of national sovereignty is one that raises interest within some of the EU's member states. A surprisingly high level of debate was aroused in the UK, Denmark, Ireland and France in relation to the ratification of the TEU, and this trend looks set to continue in all of the member states during the induction period of the single currency.

Much of this debate is ill-informed, and some of it has been generated by the media and member states' governments. However the issue of national sovereignty has a consequence beyond the barrage of misinformation and propaganda, since it relates not only to the power of a member state to determine its policies, but also to the ability of the citizens of that state to determine their own future. Fears that "Brussels" will dictate significant areas of citizens' lives are relevant in the democratic context.

This kind of debate could have arisen in the absence of EU membership. Several commentators have noted the reduced autonomy of national governments[1]. However, the EU has provided a scenario within which this debate can be conducted, and has supplied a framework within which it can take place.

It has also alerted national governments to the possibility of misinterpreting public opinion in the process of EU integration. Niedermayer [1995 pp 67-69] shows that support for this reached its highest level at the end of the 1980s but that it declined from autumn 1991. This was when doubts about the benefits of the single market and about the role of the EC after the collapse of communism in eastern Europe began to surface. The decline could be noted in all of the member states except Denmark (where it was low to begin with), but especially in the UK, Spain, Germany and France.

This is not to suggest that public opinion directly affected the provisions laid down in the TEU[2]. Although the TEU effected something of a compromise between supranationalists and intergovernmentalists [Coombs 1995 pp 162-163], it cannot be proved that public debate guided its makers. On the face of it, there appears to be a positive correlation between the

---

1 For example, Arblaster 1991 p 64; Zolo 1992 p vii; Hirst 1994 p 7; Archibugi and Held 1995 pp 5-6; Niedermayer and Sinnott 1995 p 1

2 Although the Danish and French responses appear to have influenced the pace of integration and have set their marks upon the ToA 1997.

attitude of the public and the attitude of decision-makers in the lead up to the TEU, but *post hoc ergo propter hoc* arguments are hard to sustain. Nugent [1994 p 424] bases his assertion upon empirical research when he says that "there certainly is no automatic relationship between what the people think about EU matters and what governments do".

Nevertheless, Laffan [1992 p 6] makes an uncontentious point when she comments that although there is no consensus about the relative importance of public opinion, there is an assumption that governmental actions should be seen to be legitimate. Ladrech [1993 p 69] argues more strongly that it may not be wise to ignore public opinion in the wider EU context, and he suggests that debates engendered in the progression towards the TEU may have the effect of making popular involvement an imperative in the integration process:

> If 1992-1993 marked a watershed in the history of European integration, the lesson that ought to have been learned is the significant political risk in ignoring public opinion and, consequently, the issue of a more participatory EC cannot be subsumed under the mantle of elitism, either national or supranational. Increased, yet structured, participation might allow for political integration to finally "determine by positive choice rather than inertial navigation the desirable destination of the European journey".

In this broader sense, public debate has its effect upon the EU's decision-making processes.

3.2. *Referenda*

The referendum or plebiscite is, strictly speaking, an illogical device to apply in decision-making in a polity based upon the premise that political decisions will be taken by representatives elected for that purpose. In some EU member states, however, the referendum is occasionally used in relation to constitutional issues[3].

The results of referenda have a more significant influence on leaders than any other expression of the views of "all of the people", although they are not always constitutionally binding. There have been various reasons for holding referenda on the subject of European membership and integration, although there is a question about whether these have significantly improved the democratic basis of the EU. They are held infrequently and they are not always genuine attempts to consult the people [Nugent 1994 pp 421-422][4].

---

3 For example, for such matters referenda must be held in Denmark and Ireland, and may be used in France and Italy [Gallagher *et al* 1992 p 147].

4 Hence, although the Danish gained some "opt-outs" from the TEU apparently as a result of their refusal to ratify it on the first attempt in June

However, the EU has been the means of extending democratic participation in the UK, if not in other member states, by means of the referenda on one occasion to date. Even here, the 1975 UK referendum was a means of enabling the Labour Prime Minister to keep the UK in the EEC despite the opposition of some of his Cabinet and propaganda in favour of a "yes" vote was heavily weighted. There have been no further referenda involving the whole of the UK since then[5]. There may be more in future, since the government has committed itself to holding a further referendum before economic and monetary union is ratified. If such a referendum does take place, it could be suggested that membership of the EU has been the instrument of introducing a hitherto unused participatory democratic device into what was previously a solidly representative system of government.

This is not to claim very much. Referenda, however frequent and regular, do not necessarily enable the informed decision-making that is a requirement of a fully democratic polity [Mather 1995 pp 179-180]. However, given a representative system that is as limited as the UK's, any opening of the decision-making processes to the citizenry may be welcomed on the grounds that such apertures once formed may be enlarged.

4.   Involving some of the people

The opportunity for "some", that is for representative samples, of the people as a whole to become involved with EU decision-making has been restricted to opinion polling. Both members of the Council (i.e., as national ministers) and the European Commission have authorised this form of distinguishing public reaction to the EU and towards its integration process[6].

The European Commission regularly conducts opinion polls amongst the populations of the member states to discern public views on a variety of

---

1992, the degree of propaganda to which the people were subjected between that time and the staging of the second referendum in 1993 may offer a better explanation for their subsequent reluctant approval.

5 Although separate ones have been held concerning the question of Scottish and Welsh devolution and the Good Friday agreement

6 In the UK, for example, both the previous Conservative and current Labour governments have carried out polls on attitudes towards economic and monetary union.

subjects concerning the EU. The *Eurobarometer* surveys include questions relating to the popular level of satisfaction with the EU and the member states; to the democratic practice in both; to the pace of EU integration and to specific EU policy areas such as transparency, foreign policy, immigration etc.

The Commission, therefore, is in a position to make a good assessment of popular views, but how far these views affect EU policies is more difficult to ascertain. It may be noted, however, that the Commission, as a non-executive body, appreciates the need for *consent* in relation to putting policies into practice.

5.   Involving only the people affected ("Associative Democracy")

The EU has a history of representing interests. The original Treaties of Paris and Rome, although they could be said to have formed a polity which was only weakly *democratic*, did devise one which could be termed strongly *representative* [eg see Andersen and Burns 1996 pp 227-229]. Thus the Council of Ministers represented the member states; the High Authority/European Commission represented the Communities as a whole and the indirectly elected European Assembly represented the people.

More significantly for the purpose of representing interests, ECOSOC was set up under the Treaty of Rome to represent employers, trade unionists and other significant actors. These are generally described as "the social partners". It has only advisory powers, and its members serve in an individual rather than a representative capacity. Its present membership of 222 persons is drawn from member states, in rough proportion to the size of the state, like those of the CoR (also a representative body). Of the "various interests" other than those of employer or worker, about half are drawn from agriculture, small or medium sized businesses and the professions, with the rest derived from public agencies and consumer groups. Members are proposed by national governments and are formally appointed by the Council of Ministers for renewable four year terms.

Unlike the European Assembly, ECOSOC has not developed its powers or its status, and the consensus is that it is a relatively insignificant body [Nugent 1994 p 241]. Later developments in the process of European integration do not appear to have assisted it[7]. Interest groups usually find it easier to approach more powerful levels of EU governance directly [Nugent 1994 p 241].

As the pace of integration intensified in the mid-1980s, the number of interest groups also increased. There are now about 3000 groups with links

---

7   For example, Duff [1994 p 33] suggests that, as a result of the TEU: "ECOSOC, which has languished, may be quickly surpassed [by the CoR]".

to EU institutions, 550 of which may be termed "Euro-groups"[8]. Half of these are from industry and commerce, a quarter represent agriculture and food with 20 per cent from the service sector, and 5 per cent from trade unions. Only the largest have fully-equipped and permanent offices in Brussels; others work through affiliates, consultants, temporary representatives or agencies, or depend upon national resources. Andersen and Eliassen [1996 p 45] argue that interests express themselves in direct action, particularly by means of lobbying, and that groups tend to be rather fragmented and specialised rather than corporatist. If this is so, and if such lobbying is effective, this would offer some prospects for the growth of direct participation of the EU's citizens in areas that most nearly concern them.

5.1. *Interest groups and the European Union's institutions*

- Interest groups and the Council

Although lobbying at European Council and Council of Ministers' level by national, regional and local interest groups is not encouraged [Nugent 1994 p 258], it does take place to some extent [Hayes-Renshaw 1996 p 149]. Individual members of the Council are also susceptible to the same kind of lobbying with which they are familiar at national level. Hayes-Renshaw [1996 p 149] has also discovered that the Council bureaucracy has become a target for lobbying by European-wide interest groups, which have sometimes been formed directly in response to the growth in EU policy areas, and sometimes as a result of national groups joining forces to concentrate their influence.

However, this does not prove that the people of the EU have a direct influence upon the members of the European Council or Council of Ministers. There are at least two reasons to be sceptical about such a claim. First, most issues are not debated at meetings of the Council itself[9]. Second, even if pan-European groups were effective partners in Council

---

8 Marks *et al* [1996b p 358] comment that the volume of interest group participation is now as great or even exceeds that of nation state capitals

9 It has been estimated that about 70 per cent of business is agreed at working group level and a further 15-20 per cent is agreed by Committee of Permanent Representatives [COREPER] senior officials. Recommendations from these bodies then appear as "A" points on Council agenda, and are generally accepted without discussion. Only the remaining 10-15 per cent are put forward as "B" items to be decided by ministers after debate [Hayes-Renshaw & Wallace p 1995 561]

decision-making, lobbying at supranational level requires substantial resources. Only the best resourced, therefore, are in a position to carry out such activities. This does not suggest that the involvement of a minority of pan-European groups would be an indication of popular involvement within Council policy fora.

- Interest groups and the Commission

The Commission is also susceptible to lobbying, to the extent that it has recently devised a register of lobbying groups [Preston 1996]. In addition, the Commission consults very widely of its own accord. Peterson [1995b p 75] notes that access to the crucial formulation stage of policy making is relatively open. These points together indicate that interest groups may take part in the policy-making process within the EU.

The Commission welcomes the involvement of groups for several reasons. First it has need of specialised knowledge. Second, the support of groups is persuasive when the Commission seeks the agreement of the Council to its proposals. Third, the Commission is used to seeking consensus, which is more easily obtained when groups provide broadly united positions. Fourth, some of its members, especially those from the UK, Denmark, the Netherlands and Germany, are also accustomed to consulting affected interests [Mazey & Richardson 1993 p 40]. Fifth, because the Commission has little power to implement decisions, it welcomes those groups who will later be involved in persuading their own members to carry out policies made at EU level. Sixth, it has been argued more recently, that the Commission is anxious to involve sectoral groups for the purpose of developing its integrationist approach in specific areas[10].

McLaughlin and Greenwood [1995 p 152] note, however, that the system involuntarily favours business interests as these are the more likely to have the financial resources to enable them to obtain access to documentation. Andersen and Eliassen [1996 p 47] argue that the Commission is in itself naturally sympathetic to business interests.

With the Commission, as with the Council, a great deal of policy making is carried out at lower levels in the Directorates General [DGs]. The question of how open the DGs are to interest groups therefore also needs to be considered. Peterson [1995a pp 481-487] found that the degree to which DGs consulted varied. Some DGs are seen to have been captured by their clienteles in integrated "policy communities" whilst others operated under relatively loose "issue networks". Yet each of the three case studies

---

10   Hooghe [1996 p 10] gives vocational training, research and development, large structural investments and land use as examples. All of these, as she notes, have long term effects upon policy development.

which Peterson [1995a] carried out supplies evidence of relative openness on the part of the DGs.

- Interest groups and the European Parliament

The EP is also heavily lobbied, and this has increased as the EP's powers have grown [Kohler-Koch 1997 p 9]. Like the Commission, the EP has established a public register and code of conduct for lobbying [McLaughlin & Greenwood 1994 p 144]. There are various methods and levels of approaching the EP, either by approaching individual members, committee chairmen or rapporteurs, the Petitions Committee, political groups or their secretariats. In addition, committees may hold "hearings" on issues [Nugent 1994 pp 261-262]. Like the Commission, the EP or its officials may approach appropriate interests when preparing reports.

Also, like the Commission, the EP may be seen to be particularly open to certain types of interest groups. Andersen and Eliassen [1996 p 47] found that the environmental and consumer lobbyists have been most welcomed by the European Parliament.

- Interest groups and the European Court of Justice

Mazey and Richardson [1993 p 42] point out that the ECJ is also an important target for lobbyists. They note that the ECJ has a role as protector and enhancer of individual rights, and that it has also been responsible for extending the EU's policy competences. Women's groups and environmentalists therefore have an incentive to lobby the ECJ. The ECJ is responsible for administering EU law that takes primacy over national legislation. Industrialists who find that their national governments' policies are contrary to the principles of the Single Market, also have good reason to approach the ECJ.

However, although the ECJ may be a target for lobbyists, it is not likely to seek out and consult with interest groups except in unusual circumstances. It may therefore be defined as an enabler, rather than a deliverer, of citizen participation in EU governance.

5.2.   *Interest groups and increased popular participation*

Most commentators agree that groups are significant in EU policy processes. For example, Mazey and Richardson [1993 p 46] acknowledge:

> Groups in many if not most policy sectors have certainly recognized that supranational decisions are now inevitable for many policy problems and that it is often in their interests to engage in anticipatory activity in order to influence the shape and direction of European-level policy solutions. Thus, increasingly, groups themselves have recognized the logic and momentum of greater Europeanization of solutions. They are, therefore, beginning to play a very significant role in the

process of European integration.

There are arguments for and against the involvement of interest groups in relation to democracy. On the one hand, following Burnheim's argument, it may be considered "democratic" that those who are most affected by a policy should take the lion's share in devising it. On the other, however, it is not easy to determine where material interests begin and end. The problem for democracy which interest groups pose is that their involvement with policy processes is rarely proportionate to the effects of the proposed policies upon a wider public which is not necessarily organised into a powerful interest group. Hence business interests, for example, may influence one aspect of Single Market legislation to their own advantage, but this advantage may not be similarly experienced by workers or consumers. Peterson [1995b p 88] comments:

> ...the idea that the EU has begun to resemble a Jeffersonian system of pluralism seems grossly simplistic. The vast resources and specialized expertise needed to wield influence often means that the power of groups which already control national policy agendas is simply reinforced and extended in EU policy networks.

With the EU, as with member states' governments, then, interest group involvement provides a pluralism that is skewed at best. Those with best access to information, most adequate resources and whose views coincide with those of policy makers' are likely to find themselves with "insider" status influencing policy at its formative stages and thereby demonstrating actual decision-making powers [Andersen & Eliassen 1993 p 45].

Peterson [1995b p 87] sounds an additional cautionary note in relation to the dangers to democracy posed by "insider" interest groups at EU level:

> ... the question of whether EU policy networks are able to insulate the early, crucial stages of policy-making from effective scrutiny by national governments or anyone else goes to the heart of debates about the EU's democratic deficit. When applied in other political settings, policy networks are often shown to be designed to shield from public scrutiny decisions made about the use of public power.

Peterson's point, however, is that although representative democracy may be marred in this manner by interest group activities, at the same time they may offer enhanced participatory democratic opportunities. He comments [ibid]:

> On the other hand, the relative youth of the EU as a system of governance provides fresh opportunities for interests that are weak or under-represented in national decision-making.

From this, it is arguable that the EU has not yet become a polity which is governed by multi-agencies, but that there is more formal involvement of "only the people affected" than is to be found within some of its member states.

5.3.   *UK interest group activity at European Union level*

The UK already has a culture of consultation with interest groups. The question arises then as to whether "fresh opportunities" to develop "associative democracy" are available within the UK in particular. Some evidence shows that environmental lobbyists at least have enjoyed an enhanced legitimacy when conducting their operations at the supranational level. The Commission uses groups, individuals and companies to assist in the implementation of environmental policies. It relies upon complaints from them in the absence of its own eco-police force. The EU has also placed the force of law behind groups' aims. "Green" groups have access to judicial review and can appeal to the ECJ. This adds power to their "watch dog" role. UK ministers and civil servants may not dismiss their concerns so easily, and their legitimacy is enhanced thereby. This in turn strengthens their position. The EU gives environmental groups additional outlets where they are more likely to receive a sympathetic hearing for their lobbying activities, such as the Commission and EP. The EP is sympathetic to the environmental lobby and as such has become an important focus for green activity.

If British environmental groups have enhanced status within the EU, it is partly because of their problems at UK level. Because Britain has lagged behind other EU countries in its environmental practices, enthusiasm within UK interest groups has increased. Because of the relatively closed policy community that they faced, groups in the UK have learned lobbying skills. Because of a shortage of direct parliamentary representation, British groups have large numbers of extra-parliamentary activists who find working within the EU to be a positive experience by comparison. UK pressure groups therefore see the EC as a progressive force, and are therefore co-operative with EU governance[11].

It is not clear, however, that the environmental movement's experience is reflected in general by the UK's interest groups. Some areas of UK policy making are unaffected, or relatively untouched, by the EU's policy competences. Even in areas, such as agriculture, where the EU is a primary player, the experience of the UK's agricultural lobby has been mixed.

---

11 It may be noted that EU environmental politics has not delivered the benefit of increased participation to the Germans, Dutch and Danes, who regard the EU's environmental credentials less favourably by comparison with their own. Green politics has successfully entered the party arena in Germany in particular, and this has undermined the significance of environmental pressure groups there to some extent.

6. Multi-sector or multi-level governance?

Interest groups do not have pretensions to govern; they are not accountable and can never be held to account. Their legitimacy depends upon their representativeness and the balance among competing groups which government can maintain. Elected sub-national government is accountable. The relationship between the EU and sub-national government suggests an alternative future for democratic practice – within a "multi-*level* governance"[12]. This model presupposes that various levels of government interact with various government agencies and non-governmental agencies, and that the outcome is a constantly shifting, but nonetheless inclusive, decision-making process that is able to be sufficiently flexible to take into account the needs and wants of all participants. It is a model rather than a reality, but as will be shown below [Chapter Eight], there is a persuasive case to be made for its applicability to the UK's situation within the EU.

---

12 See, eg, Marks 1993, cited by Newman 1996 p 119; Hooghe 1996; Marks *et al* 1996b

CHAPTER EIGHT

THE EUROPEAN UNION IN BRITAIN: TOWARDS MULTI-LEVEL GOVERNANCE

1.   Multi-level governance, local government and democracy

Multi-level governance, as outlined above [Chapter Seven], offers prospects for democracy which fit primarily into the category of "only the people affected" – in the sense that decision-making is conducted among enough levels to engage the participation of anyone who has an interest in a particular area.   Although it is not generally emphasised, a particular characteristic of multi-level governance that is pertinent to the centralised UK is the involvement of local government.   This, if it occurs, offers a departure in conventional practice within the British state.   In the UK, as shown in Chapter Two, local government is regarded as a servant rather than partner in government.

It may be objected at the outset that sub-national government does not conveniently fit into the category of "only the people affected", since sub-national government is itself a governing body, rather than a collection of interests.   The reason for making the claim is that sub-national government does have particular sets of interests to advance.   These interests are not specific in the social or economic sense[1].   However, in the senses that may be termed "territorial" and "political", every manifestation of sub-national government has a common identity of interests.

First, sub national government supports areas whose interests differ from those of the centre [see Newman 1996 p 110][2].   More particularly, the existence of sub-national government represents the possibility of diversity of needs and interests among areas of the same nation state.   Taking this

---

1 i.e., sub-national government is not formed from a particular gender or class, for example, nor is it a pressure group on behalf of an ethnic minority.

2 For example, in the UK it is claimed that central government furthers primarily the interests of the south east "stockbroker belt", as opposed to the more industrialised areas of the Midlands and northern England.   In Italy it is sometimes suggested that the aspirations of the industrialised north are taken into account in centralised decision-making more than are those of the poorer and rural south.

notion a stage further, sub-national governmental autonomy is necessary if such variations are to be accommodated within the political process. Unless or until nation states become homogeneous, sub-national government is one of the most certain means of ensuring that the interests of the (territorial) minorities may be furthered.

There is a second reason for advancing the claims of sub-national government that may be demonstrated by considering the example of Germany. The German state's Länder are now among the most independent within the EU, with an autonomy which, like that of the Belgian Regions, extends to taking part formally in some negotiations at EU level. Their independence is intentional. Following the Second World War, the West German state was divided into Länder specifically to avoid the concentration of power that had led to the rise of Hitler and the Third Reich [Jeffery 1995]. This reaction is reminiscent of liberal thinkers such as Mill, Locke and Popper who argue for the restraint, rather than the democratisation, of power. Sub-national government, here, represents the interests of all of those people who are not part of a central government, to fragment and limit the control which otherwise central government (even an elected one) could deploy. In this case, "the people affected" are those who are governed as *opposed* to those who govern them. They are, of course, a majority, but they are, or have the potential to be, a relatively impotent or oppressed majority.

This argument too can be taken a stage further in the UK where, whilst fulfilling the "interests" of sub-national government, there is a prospect for expanding the benefits of participatory democracy to "all of the people" rather than "only those affected". It is often claimed that those who occupy positions in sub-national government are no more interested in the devolution of power than those who make demands for its centralisation at nation state level[3]. However this position, if held by a majority of persons elected to sub-national government and their officials within the UK, is no longer so tenable in fact as it may be in theory.

This, paradoxically, is because of the degree to which governments of the last two decades have centralised power [see eg Taylor, 1995 pp 74-75]. If nothing else, this has forced UK sub-national governmental actors to find other friends. When Parliament proved to be an inadequate guardian of sub-national governmental liberties [see above, Chapter Two], extra-parliamentary associates were needed instead [Pycroft 1995 p 25]. Some of these associates are the EU's "social partners" – representatives of owners, workers and other interests – with whom sub-national government personnel work in devising strategies for their regions and areas; and some

---

3   This is epitomised in a comment made by a British civil servant that: "Everybody agrees that subsidiarity is desirable, providing it stops with themselves." [Rowsell 1995].

are the people within those areas themselves.

Thus, although the attitude of councillors and officers at sub-national levels towards power-sharing may have changed only marginally, sub-national actors have succeeded in applying the subsidiarity principle even if they instinctively feel revulsion for its fullest interpretation.

2.   The European Union and the status of sub-national government

The EU may prove to be the means for the employment of subsidiarity despite the limitations on its *de jure* interpretation agreed at the 1992 Edinburgh Summit. It has been argued that regional policy, of necessity co-ordinated at sub-national government level, could lead to a *de facto* devolution of political control to local and regional authorities.   For example, Jeffery [1996 p 254] argues that the EU integration process could have this effect because:

> Firstly [it] raises questions about the intrusive impact European integration can have from without on the established constitutional balance between central and sub-national institutions of government within the member states of the EU. Secondly, the responses of sub-national institutions to such external intrusions in turn raise questions about the potential scope and significance of the role of a "third level" – that of sub-national government – in the integration process.

Those commentators who take the broadest view argue that the nation state had a limited lifespan[4]. For example, Wallace [1994 p 55] suggests that states have lost most of their economic autonomy as a result of globalisation, whilst independent decision-making in relation to national defence and the maintenance of international boundaries has given way to multilateral bargaining. He adds that challenges to the legitimacy of national institutions have come from within existing states, making for fragmentation rather than integration. Such analysts slot the regional impact in the process of EU integration into the inexorable progression of the nation states' death-throes. Seen from their perspective, the development of the EU is a symptom rather than a cause of the demise of the nation state.

These critics, following neofunctionalist theory, believe that economic policies "spill over" into the political arena. Regional government, by courtesy of the EU's means of dealing with the allocation of Structural Funds[5], becomes more significant and gains in status and powers both by

---

4   Kaldor [1995 p 69] argues that "... the nation-state was and is a temporary phenomenon, even though there remains an extremely powerful attachment to the idea".

5 The EU, of course, needs the co-operation of sub-national tiers of government for effective co-ordination of EU funding and other decisions.

meeting the national level on more equal terms and by dealing directly with the EU – the supranational level.

Marquand [1991 p 37], although he is still doubtful about the final outcome, thinks that the economic role of the sub-national tier is set to be enhanced. He argues that this could lead to a more significant political role wherein sub-national governments are seen by their electors as important and also become more proactive in their direct dealings with the EU's institutions. Marquand's scepticism reflects his belief that it is unwise to write off the role of the nation state. He thinks that such activities would still lack the legitimacy of a *"de jure* regional structure"*, which would require a decision by a national government. Keating [1995 p 8] elaborates on this point. Employing the intergovernmentalist thesis, he argues that the EU came about by an act of will by the member states for reasons which were essentially nationally based, and therefore it is likely that member states will also determine the pace of its development. As he notes: "... the Community consists precisely of nation-states that have shown great reluctance to efface themselves in favour of a fully fledged European government." Whilst the Commission, in particular, needs the co-operation and support of sub-national government, this does not mean that the Commission can respond to its specific demands. Commission activities are limited by rules regarding the distribution of funds and the particular programmes that may be the recipients of those funds [Keating ibid p 14].

The validity of these positions needs to be tested. On the one hand, membership of the EU has had an impact, largely beneficial, on the status of sub-national government. Local government in the UK in particular, given the degree to which its status has been eroded, has been ready to seize upon the potential offered by the EU to reinvent and enhance its role [see Marks *et al* 1996a p168]. It has been equally prepared to seek the active co-operation of its electorate and the social partners. The development of cohesion policy post 1988 [see below] has inarguably increased the *number* of political actors including those at sub-national government level [Hooghe 1996 p 12]. At the same time, as Pycroft [1995 pp 21- 22] claims, further integration of the EU in the areas of the single market and common currency has led to a reduction in member states' influence over national economies. It has also led to an increase in the responsibilities of local government especially in the weaker and more vulnerable regions who derive limited benefits, sometimes disbenefits, from EU membership.

On the other hand, the UK is a centralised polity [see Chapter Two]. Although pressures from the European Commission, from the UK's Treasury (for effective use of EU money) and from UK business as the EU market expanded have made it almost essential to regionalise, this need not mean that regions become automatically autonomous or democratically governed. The way in which the UK's central government has acted on the EU imperative at least until the election of the Labour government in 1997 illustrates the Keating thesis about the significance of member state level decision-making in the development of the EU.

3. "The empire fights back" – the response of the UK government to regionalisation 1993-1997

In 1993, England was subdivided into ten regions, and amalgamated regional Government Offices were allocated to each, added to the existing Scottish, Welsh and Northern Irish Offices[6]. The resulting Government Offices cover the previously separate regional offices of the Departments of the Environment, Transport, Employment, and Trade and Industry, with the remit of managing programmes and fostering the development of policy areas. They speak as the voice of the government in the regions and at present deal directly with the EU in relation to the application of structural funds that are particularly aimed at areas of lower economic growth or areas that have particular economic problems.

Optimistic claims were made that the formation of these regional offices in the UK extended the principle of subsidiarity to sub-national government therein [cited by Taylor 1995 p 81]. At the time, the government heralded the development as "an important shift in power from Whitehall to the localities" [Taylor 1995, citing the *Local Government Chronicle*, 12 November 1993]. However, steps undertaken towards regionalisation in the UK were undertaken in a different way and in an apparently different spirit from that of the other member states.

The main point is that Government Offices are directed by senior civil servants, not by elected persons. The result has been a tighter grip by Whitehall. Central government gets better information, but not more accountability, and the localities have not achieved additional powers. The effect of integrating *government* offices regionally was to reduce the role of local authorities in regenerating their areas. Mawson argues that whilst this was intentional, any incoming government interested in decentralisation

---

6 As well as pressures that emanated from the EU, there was, in any case, a requirement to respond to changes in urban and inner city redevelopment programmes and to reorganisation in Whitehall. There was also a need to restructure the way in which regional government was organised within the UK. In particular, there was originally no financial integration of programmes in England, (unlike in Scotland, Wales and Northern Ireland) and this had been criticised by the Audit Commission [Marinnetto 1996 pp 72-73].

could build upon the existing structure. The next chapter [Nine] looks at the way in which the present government responded to regionalisation, and the extent to which the EU can hold itself responsible for its reaction.

4.   Sub-national government, funding and the European Union

Scott [1994 pp 65-66] notes that sub national government within the UK had begun to form alliances, as he thinks, to provoke a national debate about the role of local and regional government in the EU. He suggests that there is an opening for this in a polity with the two features of multi-tiered governance and democratic legitimacy. He suggests further that the UK's sub-national government had seized upon a resolution adopted by consensus by the Council of Ministers in 1991 on the meaning of subsidiarity as it applied to local government. This resolution urged that:

> Political and administrative decentralisation should be increased as a source of freedom, a means of involving citizens actively in public life and a way of adapting policies to local situations... responsibilities should normally be given to those authorities which are closest to the citizen and not to higher level authorities [Resolution 1 of EC Local Government Ministers, 9th session, May 1991, cited in Scott et al 1994 pp 65-66]

An apparent reason for the increased involvement for activities based upon the European dimension is the potential which the EU offers for distributing resources among regions by means of its cohesion policy.

The Commission intends to empower sub-national authorities [Hooghe 1996 pp 89-90]. The newly appointed Commissioner for Regional Policy, Michel Barnier, promised to maintain a dialogue with sub-national authorities, and explained at his hearing by the EP [September 1999]:

> ... the more local players share in the responsibility, the more they are committed and motivated, the more efficiently we will be able to use these appropriations

The Commission's end is not the enhancement of democratic practice *per se*. The intention is to reduced inequalities of wealth and development among the regions within the same member states [Klausen and Goldsmith 1997 pp 237-238]. The Commission sees the involvement of sub-state actors as a means towards eliminating inequality and hence removing an obstacle to EU integration[7].

---

7   Archer and Butler [1996 p 135] point out also to the danger of the marginalisation of the poorer regions that could otherwise have been expected to result from the creation of the Single Market. They suggest that the entrenchment and revision of the EU's regional policy in the SEA was intended by the Commission to reduce this danger.

To assist in this, the EU provides structural funds, which consist of the European Agricultural Guidance and Guarantee Fund [EAGGF], the European Social Fund [ESF] and the European Regional Development Fund [ERDF]. These are allocated in accordance with the needs of individual regions and sectors. National and regional authorities submit development plans and put together a Community Support Framework [CSF] based upon these. Operational Programmes based upon the CSF are drafted by national and regional authorities and then submitted to the Commission for approval.

In 1988, the EU's regional policy was developed further by the creation of specific "Objectives" to guide the allocation of structural funds. Of these Objectives, numbers 1 (promoting the development of regions lagging behind the EU average), 2 (concerning regions seriously affected by industrial decline and 5b (advancing the development of rural areas) had a strong regional basis. These three Objectives accounted for 96.5 per cent of the EU's financial commitments to regional policy in 1991. The delivery of the Objectives is outlined in a Single Programming Document [SPD] for the defined Objective area, which is based upon the region's CSF and drawn up by the Commission in consultation with the social partners.

At the same time, the 1988 regulations encouraged the involvement of local government with development agencies and business groups and with national government[8] (although *central* government is deemed the "competent authority" for organising this involvement). Marks *et al* [1996a] show that EU-based activities on the part of local authorities increased in the years following the SEA and argue that this was not solely because of the development of regional funding. They point out that there was also an unparalleled expansion in EU competencies in areas of concern to sub-national governments, for example, market competition, environment, social policy, and industrial as well as regional policy.

For the 1994-1999 programme, over one third of the EU's total budget was allocated to regional funding [Commission, DG XVI, 1996]. This totalled £87.7 billion in the whole EU and £5.7 billion in the UK. For the 2000-2006 programme, the total amount is €195 million – less than the

---

8 Bache *et al* [1996 pp 299-302 *passim*] summarise the range of lobbying activities open to and utilised by UK local government before 1988, showing that, although formal participation was not required, many joined European wide bodies in an attempt to influence the Commission. They accept, however, that "... the EU regional policy network in the UK before 1988 was heavily weighted towards central government control....[T]his decision making process... reflected a top-down view of implementation which the Commission sought to change in 1988".

figure of €240 million that the Commission requested from the Council. It represents a reduction in funding in real terms. The European Council, meeting in March 1999 in Berlin, agreed that for the UK, Objective One will cover Merseyside, West Wales and the valleys, South Yorkshire, Cornwall and Northern Ireland. Additional funding was secured for the Highlands and Islands.

The funding of these programmes presents a challenge and an opportunity to local government's powers of organisation and planning, given the restrictive framework within which they are required to work. The UK government has been anxious to maintain overall control over the EU's regional policy but the EU enables the participation of sub- and non-governmental agencies by means of the application of the structural funds [Pycroft 1995 p 25]. In practice, however, the extent to which local government takes advantage of the opportunities offered by Community initiatives depends only in part upon the ability and readiness of individual councils to participate. The structural funds are allocated within a tightly structured framework for allocating monies to designated areas and in the UK, the Government Offices are charged with the responsibility of approaching and organising suitable partners. To illustrate the way in which the process operates, this chapter draws upon the experience of the Objective Two programme as it applied to north west Cheshire. It shows that whilst the area in question may have benefited financially from its Objective Two status, any rewards accrued have only a limited connection with the aims and activities of its political activists and their partners.

5.   A study of Structural Funds and north west Cheshire

North west Cheshire, along with Greater Manchester and eastern Lancashire, [GMLC area], was awarded Objective Two status. The main reason for the inclusion of parts of Cheshire was that it is an Adjacent Area to the Merseyside Objective One area. The eligible population numbers 223,266, living primarily within the Ellesmere Port and Neston (Wirral and Chester Travel To Work Area [TTWA]) and Halton (Liverpool and Runcorn and Widnes TTWAs) Borough Council areas, with the north west tip of Vale Royal also included (Runcorn and Widnes TTWA). The prime industries of the area covered by Objective Two were chemical, engineering and vehicle manufacture, all of which were seen to be declining to the extent that there had been a loss of around 14,500 jobs between 1981 and 1991. Although the problems were regarded as substantial, they were not as severe as those afflicting Greater Manchester and Lancashire.

5.1.   *Allocation of European Union funds*

Structural Funds are allocated in accordance with primary objectives ("priorities"). For the GMLC area, these were identified as six Priorities:

- To encourage the growth of micro and small businesses
- To strengthen the competitiveness of the region's medium-sized companies
- To encourage the development of new growth sectors and business opportunities
- To attract increased inward investment and re-investment by existing major employers
- To further the development of tourism and cultural industries
- To focus attention on areas of greatest need

[Source: Commission, DG XVI 1993]

The means of achieving these Priorities were also laid down in the Measures that accompanied each Priority. For example, Priority One was to be achieved by:

- Measure 1: General support for micro and small businesses
- Measure 2: Improving access to capital
- Measure 3: Refurbishment and provision of workspace
- Measure 4: Training for micro and small business needs

[Source: Commission, DG XVI 1993]

In other words, the Commission laid down at the outset (albeit after consultation with interested local parties) the criteria which were to be met for any applications for funds. In addition, a bid for a project had to indicate the means by which it would achieve the quantifiable target for an individual measure. For example, training for those already in employment would be a 75 per cent achievement of a vocational qualification or a step towards one. Also laid down was the type of activity that would attract funds. For example, under Priority One, Measure One, activities would include business advice, diagnostic services, supply chain networks and training infrastructures [Commission, DG XVI 1993].   Other strictures included the scope of the Measure, its main beneficiaries and its cost (in all cases the grant would be the minimum necessary to enable a project to proceed).

The total sum of money available for the above projects was reduced because of the decision of the UK government to launch a "Regional Challenge" competition which would "cream off" 27.64 mecu from ERDF resources and 2.76 mecu of ESF resources in the GMLC area. Projects entered would have to meet additional yardsticks as well as the general Structural Fund criteria. This decision was of particular concern to the north west Cheshire area. Although projects submitted from Cheshire would be judged by the same Monitoring Committee responsible for overseeing the SPD (although the final decision was to be taken by the Minister), there was concern about the ability of the less industrialised sector on the edge of the GMLC area to work up a project which would be of strategic importance for the whole region.

5.2.   *Involvement of local elected persons*

The relative powers of the three participating levels – EU, UK central government through Government Offices, and the localities – are summarised in fig 8.1 below:

Fig 8.1: Allocation of powers for distribution of EU Structural Funds

The EU:

- Sets the ground rules – projects must adhere to rules relating to eligibility.
- Sets the "additionality" principle, so that EU funds made available must be matched at a lower level before projects can be implemented
- Sets the criteria within each Measure for projects
- Sets the parameters for the ERDF, to which any project must adhere

UK government, via Government Offices:

- Provides the Regional Plan upon which the CSF is based
- Carries out the scoring against each project (each must attain 150 points before it can be approved)
- "Top slices" 25 per cent funding on the total amount of EU funding available
- Allocates the total available among Measures
- Commits part of the funding within Measures to award to successful bidders under the Regional Challenge scheme
- Refers controversial projects to the Department of National Heritage, so that final decisions are taken by civil servants
- Allocates the division of funding within an Objective 2 area
- Needs to approve viring among Measures
- Appoints regional monitoring groups

Local level:

- County sub-groups submit projects for consideration
- County sub-groups approve projects under the authority delegated from regional sub groups

It can be seen from the above that central government, via the Government Offices, has a leading role to play. Bache *et al* [1996 pp 317-318] argue that "the controlling position of central government continues to be the dominant characteristic of the implementation of the structural funds in the UK". The implementation of a policy is the stage in the process at which it becomes a success or a failure. However, the initiation stage may be even more important. The study of north west Cheshire shows that the European Commission, which set the parameters for the programme through its SPD, was the most significant participant. The study indicates, that the local partners, albeit consulted and involved at most of the stages, were very much of tertiary importance.

In the SPD for the GMLC area, the Commission noted that: "Effective management and administration of the SPD is crucial to the achievement of its objectives" [Commission DG XVI 1994]. To achieve this, the Commission intended to involve as closely as possible those responsible for regenerating their areas. Hence Government Office North West had to bring together a Monitoring Committee, composed of a Regional Partnership. These were nominated by the organisations listed, but appointed by the Government office. The GMLC area Monitoring Committee consisted of representatives from:

- Government (one each from DTI, DETR & DfEE)
- Commission (one each from DG XVI & DGV)
- European Investment Bank [EIB]
- Local Authorities (five from Greater Manchester; two each from Cheshire and Lancashire)[9]
- Higher education (two)
- Further Education (two)
- the private sector (two)
- the voluntary sector (two)
- Training and Enterprise Councils [TECS] (four)

---

9 Government Offices decided the basis for local authority representation on the Monitoring Committee. Not all of them allowed elected persons [Bache *et al* 1996 p 307], but the North West Government Office did accept councillor nominees, and hence some, but not all, of the representatives were elected local councillors.

- Environment Agency (one)
- North West Tourist Board (one)
- English Partnerships (one)

It cannot be said that the Commission's hopes for working in close partnership with the lower tiers of government have been entirely fulfilled within north west Cheshire.

First, the North West Regional Plan, upon which the CSF for the period under consideration was based, was the not subject of wide or lengthy consultation.   Therefore, it was not particularly well-adjusted to the primary needs of the region [Pillinger 1992 p 29, cited by Bache *et al* 1996 p 304].   In any case, consultation does not necessarily imply that advice will be taken.   Six months before the SPD was finalised, Cheshire County Council, together with the relevant borough Councils, Halton and West Cheshire College, CEWTEC and NORMIDTEC and representatives of the voluntary sector and business community had drawn together its own "Operational Programme" for EU Objective Two Funding [Cheshire County Council 1994].   This was intended as a consultative document that could feed into the final SPD.   Cheshire's priorities were worked out in detail, with a "shopping list" of possible projects under the measures that it also laid down.   However, most of the work that was carried out on the "Operational Programme" proved to have been irrelevant.   When the SPD was published, its own Priorities were derived from more extensive consultation and although the Cheshire list was not entirely dissimilar to the Commission's list, some priorities were different from those which found their way into the final document.   In particular, the SPD priorities did not include the provision of land for development.   This was of particular concern to an area with a substantial amount of land previously used in the development of the chemical industry and now suffering the consequences in the form of land contamination and dereliction.

Second, north west Cheshire did not have the necessary resources to acquire skills and competencies necessary to act as equal partners.   The County Council and the relevant borough authorities did manage to fund a secondee to work at the Government Office, but the impact of one appointee was limited by comparison to that of the highly trained and experienced personnel of the Government Office[10].

Third, the heterogeneity of the Objective Two area created at the outset something of a stumbling block in relation to the close involvement of those most immediately concerned.   One issue highlighted immediately

---

10 Bache *et al* [1996 p 308] report that secondees from local government have, on the whole, enhanced understanding of the problems faced by the partners.

was that Cheshire, unlike the larger part of Greater Manchester, had not been afflicted evenly with declining industries. Cheshire, like many rural counties, suffers from patchy disadvantaged areas. It was an irony that, for example, the part of Vale Royal which could legitimately be included in the Objective Two area because of its incorporation within the Widnes and Runcorn TTWA was the wealthiest part of that borough. At the same time, the ward in Vale Royal which suffered the greatest amount of poverty was situated in the south of the borough – i.e., not within the TTWA, and therefore was not a potential recipient of Objective Two funding[11].

This is not to say that no economic benefits were gained. For example, funding was obtained for a major tourist attraction "The Blue Planet" aquarium in Ellesmere Port (albeit in the face of intense opposition from Chester Zoo). However, given the small part played by the actors closest to the projects [see fig 8.1 above], there is no indication that democratic practice has been greatly enhanced by their participation. Groups or individual organisations within the County sub-group have submitted projects. The sub-group had the delegated authority to assent to projects so long as they met the criteria of a specific Measure (according to the Government Office scoring) and so long as the total amount of money provided for that Measure had not been allocated already. In practice, this amounted to the power of veto, which is sufficiently draconian to be used only sparingly. In the case of the County sub-group, its members had to be aware that a veto used successfully against one of the partners' cherished projects, could prove to be a double-edged sword if the dissidents had projects for which they needed support.

Cheshire's experience also indicates that in practice the application of the EU's structural funds may be a blunt instrument by which to deliver local democratic participation in decision-making. The conclusion therefore is that the EU's regional policy does not open up substantial new vistas for participation for sub-state actors.

6.   Local government and the European Union

The relevance of the EU to UK local government has been the concern of academics since the Audit Commission reported in 1991 that UK councils demonstrated a general lack of awareness towards the EU [Goldsmith and Sperling 1997 p 95]. Various studies have since been undertaken[12] which

---

11 This problem is not uniquely experienced in north west Cheshire; ambiguity resulting from area designation has been a source of criticism of cohesion policy [Wishlade 1996 p 41]

12 For example, John 1994; Bennington 1994; Martin and Pearce 1992 and 1994 - cited by Goldsmith and Sperling 1997 p 95; Taylor 1995].

show that some councils have "'gone into Europe' in a big way". For example, they have appointed European officers, forged direct links with the EP and developed trans-European networks with local authorities elsewhere within the EU as well as opening their own Brussels offices [Taylor 1995 p 76]. A recent survey was conducted by Goldsmith and Sperling drawing upon the results of a Eurolog questionnaire substantiated also by case studies.

Goldsmith and Sperling's study noted the position of the UK's local authorities and the various changes to which it has been subjected from 1979-1997 [see also above, Chapter Two]. It concluded that this left UK local government "a pale shadow of itself" [Goldsmith and Sperling 1997 p 96]. It noted the significance of this in relation to seeking EU funding [*ibid* p 98], but also observed that not all local authorities had become very actively involved. The survey then considered the extent to which councils have developed their European strategies. It concluded that, although financial constraints had been a hindrance to as well as an incentive for local authority involvement, "few other barriers to participation seem[ed] to exist" [*ibid* p 106]. However, this did not mean the whole hearted embrace of the European ideal:

> The overall picture represented in these survey findings reveals that, whilst most British local authorities are now dealing with European matters in an organised fashion, most still operate in a reactive rather than a proactive way, with the result that there is still room for development of activity on this front.

Goldsmith and Sperling found that funding, particularly in relation to structural funds, is the main driving force encouraging councils to adopt a European strategy, and that as a result, it is the larger metropolitan councils which are the prime actors [*ibid* p 118]. In addition, if councils saw gaining access to funds as the only reason for dealing with the EU, some local councils might be deterred from further participation unless they achieved early success.

6.1.   *Is funding the only significant factor?*

However, in their study, Marks *et al* [1996a] found that bidding for funding was not a prime motivator in their study undertaken to discover what inspired sub-national government to take part in what they considered the most significant activity – an office based in Brussels. Starting from the premise that sub-national mobilisation was a deviation from a twenty-year trend towards state-centredness, Marks *et al* [1996a] considered five main hypotheses to explain the phenomenon:

- "resource pull" – the expectation that governments representing the poorest regions would be most likely to mobilise in Brussels
- "resource push" – that the richest sub-national governments would be most likely to be represented
- "associational culture" – that those regions most accustomed to forming partnerships with other agencies would be most likely to locate close to the EU's government
- "political autonomy" – that an office in Brussels would be attractive to sub national governments with greatest political autonomy since they would be more directly affected by decisions made there
- "regional distinctiveness" – that where regional cultural or linguistic distinction could be identified as a source of friction between that region and its central government, sub-national mobilisation would lead to the establishment of an office near to supranational government

They found that neither "resource pull" nor "resource push" factors accounted for the establishment of sub-national government offices in Brussels. Marks *et al* noted that the EU did not have a great deal of money to distribute, and that the primary factors in deciding how funds were to be allocated were interactions between national governments. They did not find either that poverty on the part of sub-national government itself was a reason for failing to locate in Brussels, pointing out [1996a p 188] that low cost options for locating there were available.

Marks *et al* found indirect evidence that regions with a strong "associational culture" were likely to seek representation in Brussels, and they found more solid evidence [1996a p 186] to suggest that the more autonomous sub-national governments were likely to be established there. The strongest factor of all, however, was that of "regional distinctiveness". Almost all regions with distinctive ethnic, cultural or linguistic identities had an office in Brussels. Marks *et al* [1996a] see a circle of autonomy evolving – strong regional identity increases demand for regional government; strongly entrenched regional governments intensify regional identity.

The conclusions which Marks *et al* [1996a p 188] presented suggest first that the greater number of areas in which a particular unit of local government has competence or interest, the more likely that unit is to invest in establishing an office in Brussels. Second, they suggested that a unit of sub-national government which sees itself in conflict with the centre state is more likely to move literally as well as metaphorically towards EU-centred governance. Third, and most surprising, they argue that their research shows that sub-national government is not primarily interested in the EU because it hopes to obtain funding.

These conclusions were not applied exclusively to the UK. Also Marks *et al*'s [1996a] findings do not fully explain later developments in the mobilisation of EU-orientated policy formation within UK sub-national government. They do, however, provide a framework for examining the way in which the UK's sub-national government has evolved its relationship with the EU.

6.2.   *How has sub-national government reacted?*

- The regional level

At the regional level, efforts have been concentrated in two directions. First all of the UK's English regions have formed regional associations (see Chapter Nine). Second, some self-styled regions have established offices in Brussels, from which they act as lobbying organisations. Between 1984 and 1994, 23 sub-national offices from the UK had been established in Brussels [John 1995]. Those set up in the 1980s[13] tended to be single local authorities, set up for the purpose of lobbying the EC for funding. Most of them (except for Lancashire) were based upon the elected councils. From 1988 however, the more structured allocation of funding via the setting up of Objectives made the advantages of being on the spot less significant. Since that time, authorities with offices in Brussels have tended to be more concerned with policy related matters [*ibid*]. From 1990 more regionally based offices, usually in partnership with local businesses or other interests, were established. These include Northern Ireland [1991], Wales [1992], Yorkshire and Humberside [1992], East Midlands [1992], North of England [1992], and Scottish Local Authorities [1993] [John 1995 p 2].

At the same time, county and some borough councils have also set up their own offices. Cheshire County Council, for example, established itself in Brussels in 1996. In other cases, county councils have launched joint ventures with other council and non-council partners[14].

There appears to be two results from this type of activity. First, there is a net effect of a general stimulation of interest among practitioners at sub-national levels of government. Having an office in Brussels brings home to regional and local levels the significance of the EU as well as the less calculable benefits derived from lobbying processes. The second effect is of a drawing together of UK sub-national government as a "community". Approaches are varied, of course, and the goals of the different authorities also differ. However, as John [1995 p 12] notes:

---

13 Birmingham, Strathclyde, South of Scotland and Lancashire

14 For example, Kent joined forces with the University of Kent and one district council [John 1995 p 7]

Because there is cooperation between [*sic*] the offices and all the representatives know each other, other bodies start to regard them as a coherent group. Whilst the UK government would appear to be cool toward sub-national interests, symbolised by their resistance to appointing elected representatives on the Committee of the Regions, the UK Permanent Representation in Brussels (UKREP} welcomes and is in regular contact with the representatives... This link was symbolised by the UKREP's invitation of all the sub-national representatives to a regional policy reception in March 1993. UKREP now formally recognises the local offices and holds regular meetings with them.

This is a pertinent example of the application of the incrementalist aspect of neofunctionalist theory. Both UKREP and UK sub-national offices inhabit Brussels. It is natural (as well as intentional on the part of the sub-national offices) that there should be some informal contact among the compatriot participants. If UKREP finds such contact beneficial, it is unsurprising that it would want to extend it. If responses to such invitations are welcomed, the further incremental step of formalising and regularising contacts is a logical one to take. At this point, sub-national authorities, provided that they retain a sense of common purpose, have achieved a legitimate albeit informal status in the decision-making processes at EU level.

▪ **The local level**

However, the establishment of Brussels offices is mainly limited to metropolitan authorities and regional agencies. Pycroft [1995 pp 22-23] looked at evidence provided by the 1991 Audit Commission survey into local authorities' preparedness for the Single Market and the Liverpool Institute of Public Administration and Management [LIPAM]. He showed that it is the county councils and metropolitan authorities that have pursued EU activities with the greatest enthusiasm. Initially this was tied to prospects for gaining access to funds. The LIPAM study showed that for 85 per cent of county councils and 93 per cent of metropolitan authorities, European funding was significant to their activities, whilst this was true only for 62 per cent of district authorities. Pycroft also noted that district authorities that qualify for structural funds find EU funding significant.

However, as shown above, when a survey was carried out on a wider scale, funding ("resource pull") was not shown to be a prime motivator of sub-national governments' EU activities at least in encouraging them to site an office in Brussels. "Associational culture", "political autonomy" and especially "regional distinctiveness" were of more importance [Marks *et al* 1996a].

The studies carried out by Marks *et al* [1996a], Pycroft and Goldsmith and Sperling all have limited foci. Marks *et al* selected a particular activity - siting an office in Brussels – as a measure of local/regional authorities' EU involvement. On the other hand, Pycroft's LIPAM study, whilst considering a wider variety of sub-national government activities within the EU context, appears to have taken it as read that access to EU funding would be of primary importance to instigating such involvement. Whilst Goldsmith and Sperling's study was more comprehensive, it had a heavier emphasis upon larger councils with more extensive policy competences. Their survey was sent to all metropolitan districts and half of the counties but to only a third of shire districts. 47.6 per cent responded [1997 p 98], but Goldsmith and Sperling do not indicate how many of these were shire districts, and the analysis of the results which follows is not broken down into local authority type.

Although the studies shed light upon the relationship of sub-national government with the EU, they exclude UK non-metropolitan borough authorities with low access to the EU's structural funds, with limited "associational culture" and with only restricted "regional distinctiveness". If such councils exhibit sufficient awareness of the EU to warrant the development of EU-centred policies and activities, it may be argued that the EU has had an impact upon the UK's sub-national government, which in turn implies a *de facto* devolution of competence.

The non-metropolitan borough authorities chosen are two Cheshire councils: Vale Royal Borough Council and Congleton Borough Council. These Councils were selected because both had been the subjects of "European Audits" by Euro Information Centre North West [EICNW] in association with LIPAM (Congleton in 1995 and Vale Royal in 1996/7). This offered the opportunity to draw from this research and to examine the extent to which the two Councils were affected by the studies themselves. In addition, the two Councils have sufficient similarities (size, status, statutory responsibilities, economic base, social mix and geographical location) for valid comparisons to be made. They also have enough differences (political composition, organisation, methods of operating and relationships with outside bodies) to enable factors affecting the extent of their "Europeanisation" to be identified.

6.3.   A Study of two councils[15]

▪   **Characteristics**

---

15 Additional information for this study was obtained from:

David Owen – Corporate policy manager, Vale Royal Borough Council

Ian Paton – European/economic strategy officer, Vale Royal Borough Council

Robert Birchenough, Economic and European development Officer, Congleton Borough Council

Officers of Vale Royal and Congleton Borough Councils

Members of Vale Royal and Congleton Borough Councils

The characteristics of the two authorities examined do not indicate that there is a high likelihood of developing a significant European identity. Fig 8.2 below shows that their political autonomy is very low and their local distinctiveness is limited. However, of the two, Vale Royal exhibits a higher degree of "associational culture".

Marks *et al*'s [1996a] analysis, when applied to the two Councils, indicates that there it is unlikely that they would acquire a very strong European identity. Nevertheless, as will be seen below, by examining both actions and attitudes, both Councils and their members have begun to consider their position in Europe.

Fig 8.2: Characteristics of the two Councils

Borough Council ——————— Factor	Congleton Borough Council	Vale Royal Borough Council
Resource pull	Ineligible for structural funds	Restricted "Objective 2 status" (north west tip only)
Resource push	area classed as "semi-urban" not regarded as disadvantaged	area classed as "semi rural" not regarded as disadvantaged
"Associational culture" (links with outside bodies)	limited [source: EICNW 1995 survey]. However, SRB success led the Council towards forming more outside links	High degree. EICNW 1996/7 survey reports that its partnerships are "an excellent preparation for EU activity"
Political autonomy	non-metropolitan borough political status: *ultra vires* financial status. Largely dependent upon central funding/ spending assessments from government	non-metropolitan borough political status: *ultra vires* financial status. Largely dependent upon central funding/ spending assessments from government
local distinctiveness	"hybrid borough" with four towns and a large rural area	"hybrid borough" with two towns, one large village, but predominantly rural
	no conflict with upper tier of local government (Cheshire County Council)	conflict with Cheshire County Council concerning unitary status 1996 - led to poor relationships
	prepared to work with Cons. or Labour government despite Liberal political control	prepared to work with Cons. government despite Labour political control

■   Attitudes

Officers were asked how important European issues were to the Council.
The results are shown below [Fig 8.3]:

Fig 8.3.: Significance of European issues to Council officers

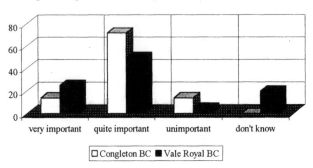

[Source: Survey of officers of Congleton and Vale Royal Borough Councils conducted by
author]

Fig 8.3. shows that the majority of officers from both Councils rated the
EU as being either "very" or "quite" important to their Council.

Members' attitudes were ascertained by enquiring about the level of
importance they attributed to the Council adopting a coherent European
strategy. Fig 8.4. shows the results:

**Fig 8.4.: Overall importance of European strategy to Council
members**

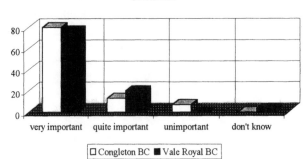

[Source: Survey of members of Congleton and Vale Royal Borough Councils conducted by
author]

This shows that members of both Councils were at least prepared to pay lip-service to the significance of the EU. They were also asked to say why they thought it was important – what did they hope to gain from it. The results showed that what members expected and what they wanted from EU involvement were not quite the same. Figs 8.5. and 8.6. [below] give the details:

Fig 8.5: Members' preferences for EU benefits

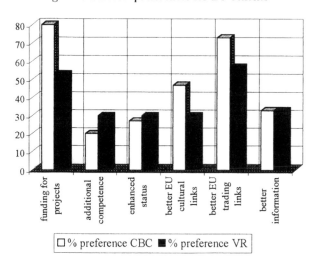

[Source: Survey of members of Congleton and Vale Royal Borough Councils conducted by author]

Fig 8.5. shows that Congleton members mainly wanted funding (which they were aware they were unlikely to achieve), whereas Vale Royal members' greatest preference was for improved trading links (possibly reflecting the level of "associational culture" with the manifold economic partnerships built up by the borough Council). In both cases, additional competences and enhanced status were lower priorities, although a higher percentage of Congleton members wanted better EU cultural links (many Vale Royal councillors are already involved with "twinning" arrangements through their town and parish councils).

Vale Royal members mainly expected an increase in trading links with other EU countries. This was probably because the Council has been involved with a Trade Fair in Brussels [March 1998] which was organised through the Council's European and Economic Strategy Officer. There

Fig 8.6: Members' expectations of EU benefits

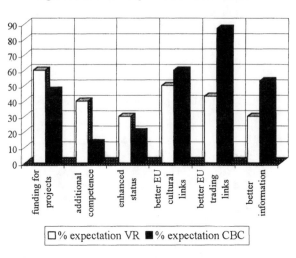

[Source: Survey of members of Congleton and Vale Royal Borough Councils conducted by author]

were also relatively high expectations of enhanced cultural links and better information. Despite their non-eligibility for Structural Funds, a higher percentage of Congleton members expected funding opportunities (but by no means as high a percentage as that which wanted them), although members' expectations in general were lower than those of Vale Royal members.

- **European Union actions and activities**

Fig 8.7. [below] summarises the actions and achievements to date of the two Councils. Neither has based itself in Brussels, so far, although Congleton has used the Cheshire County Council office there. Both have appointed appropriately titled officers, in each case within the Council's policy unit (implying a corporate approach to EU issues). Vale Royal has recently adopted new arrangements for member involvement with the Council, based upon suggestions in the government's White Paper (*Modern Local Government: In Touch with the People*). The Council's European strategy will need to be restructured to fit in with the new system, but a Lead Councillor for European activities has already been designated.

Fig 8.7: Summary of actions and activities of the two Councils

Activity	Congleton Borough Council	Vale Royal Borough Council
Office in Brussels	no	no
Appointment of designated officer	"European and Economic Development Officer" within Council's policy unit	"European and Economic Strategy Officer" within Council's policy unit
Designated budget	none	£29,700 for year 1998/9
Officer level EU group	none	in hand
Member level EU group	yes. Meets infrequently, concerned only with EU funding	one being formed in 1999 by "lead Councillor"
Member familiarisation	trips to Brussels by groups of Councillors and officers have been undertaken	trips to Brussels by groups of Councillors and officers have been undertaken
Strategy	based upon funding prospects "no evidence of detailed understanding of potential EU opportunities" [EICNW survey 1995]	lobbying for funds; improving information to local businesses and the public; developing action plans in partnership with interested parties; applying a corporate approach to European activities

- **Congleton Borough Council**

According to the EICNW study [1995], there was a "growing awareness" amongst certain officers and members that the Borough needed to seek economic development opportunities. The Borough was said to lack a "coherent long term vision for development", but the researchers thought that this perception might be changing.

Congleton members had not previously seen the EU as a priority as a means of enabling economic development. However, they were conscious of cutbacks in local government funding and expenditure, and this had encouraged them to look towards the EU instead. The EICNW researchers [1995] thought that greater political commitment towards EU activity was needed.

The EICNW study was completed in 1995, and although it was evident from talking to individual members and officers that some individuals were well aware of the potential from and desirability of an active European strategy, the conclusions which the EICNW auditors drew are still pertinent. The received impression was one of frustration on the part of those interviewed. The responses from both officers' and members' surveys indicate the source of this disappointment. Congleton's European strategy is based mainly upon the economic benefits which the Council hopes (but does not really expect) to derive from the EU. It is not fully persuaded of the other potential benefits of enhanced autonomy and status obtainable from extensive EU activities and from a coherent EU strategy.

As noted above [Fig 8.2], Congleton has had a difficulty in carving out an identity for itself. In line with Marks *et al*'s [1996a] conclusions, this provides an explanation for its inchoate response to European issues. It is, however, surprising that a Council that is controlled by the Liberal Democrats should not indicate the same kind of fervour for the wider Europe that is demonstrated by the national party[16].

Nevertheless, Congleton has not wanted to ignore developments on the wider continent of Europe. It has a notion of co-operation with the EU and with the EU's partnership-based approach. It has a concept of at least the economic benefits to be derived from such a strategy, even if its strategy is embryonic. Most importantly, the Council has appointed an E/EDO, although the appointee's budget is indeterminate, and the remit is restricted. Some members and officers indicated in their responses that they were depending upon the appointee to develop a coherent European strategy. This suggests that the appointment is a decisive step, indicative of changing attitudes towards the EU. However, members and officers interviewed were also aware that there is a need for these changes to penetrate more deeply, so as to provoke an active and receptive response to the new appointee's initiatives.

- **Vale Royal Borough Council**

According to the EICNW survey [1996/7], Vale Royal had a "shopping list" of ambitions with regard to Europe. These were:

- to make sure that Vale Royal's voice is heard in Brussels
- to assist local companies to do more business with the rest of Europe
- to secure EU funding
- to develop tourism to attract more visitors from Europe
- to develop a "European flavour" to life in the Borough

---

16   This may be explained by the decentralised nature of the Liberal Democrats who tend not to enforce national views upon local parties.

- to learn from experience of other authorities in Europe in areas like environmental planning and community development.

The responses from members and officers indicate that at least some of them are appreciative of these aims. More enthusiasm about European issues could be detected from Vale Royal respondents, and greater familiarity with the prospects that the EU could offer was demonstrated. Like Congleton, there is so far no coherent European strategy, but there is a better appreciation amongst members and officers of the need for one. The budget and remit afforded to the new E/EDO is an indication of the higher priority which is given to European issues, although these still, like Congleton, concentrate most heavily upon perceived economic rather than political benefits to be derived from the EU.

Vale Royal has had similar problems to Congleton in carving out an identity for itself [see fig 8.2. above]. As a Council, it still suffers from territorial heterogeneity. There is, however, a synthesis of attitudes amongst members. Labour, Conservative and Liberal Democrat members have backed the Council's European strategies and taken part in familiarisation visits.

Marks *et al* [1996a] argue that "resource pull" is not a prime factor in influencing sub-national authorities in their attitudes towards Europe. Nevertheless, it has had some effect upon Vale Royal, where the Council's partial Objective 2 status has attracted the attention of both members and officers who have no specified responsibilities for European activities. The other main difference is the Council's "associational culture", which was commented favourably upon in the EICNW study [1996/7]. Vale Royal has a better-developed partnership approach than Congleton, although its poor relationship with the County Council [see fig 8.2.] detracts from this.

6.4.   *Significant factors for Councils*

This chapter set out to test the hypotheses advanced by Marks *et al* [1996a] regarding factors that influenced sub-national government in relation to the EU. The findings do not entirely bear out their conclusions. The two factors which Marks *et al* [1996a] thought were most important – "political autonomy" and "regional distinctiveness" – could not be applied satisfactorily to UK authorities of the size and status of the Councils under consideration.

However, Marks *et al* [1996a] used the location of an office in Brussels as the benchmark of "Europeanisation". They suggested that lack of resources did not prevent this, but in fact, Vale Royal has costed a modest project of this kind, and has found it well beyond the means of a Council whose total annual budget is only £10,175,000.

The more limited approach to "Europeanisation" which Vale Royal and Congleton have adopted has been influenced by "resource pull", or, more precisely, by the perception of potential resources. This was a factor that Marks *et al* [1996a] thought to be relatively insignificant because the EU has not much money to distribute. However, a relatively small amount of money can seem a great deal to a local authority that has, in EU terms, a minute budget. In the case of both Councils, it has meant that they have become aware of the need to develop European policies. Superficially both Councils have taken the same decisions – to send members and officers on familiarisation trips; to apply for European funds; to engage in some form of "partnerships for Europe"; and to appoint an E/EDO. These all represent an expansion in the thinking of UK non-metropolitan Councils that was not evident ten years ago.

In the case of Vale Royal, the thinking has developed more substantially towards greater awareness and increased European activity. The difference between the two Councils could be explained in terms of personalities – that proactive responses are forthcoming from proactive individuals. There is, however, a more concrete difference, and this is what Marks *et al* [1996a] described as "associational culture" which is much stronger in Vale Royal than in Congleton. Vale Royal has pursued an active partnership strategy.

This leads to the conclusion that, on the findings of these studies, even relatively insignificant UK local authorities have become aware of the EU, and this awareness has led to the development of policies to govern their European activities. This indicates that the EU has had an impact upon the UK's sub-national government. The motivating factor, despite Marks *et al* [1996a], has been "resource pull", but even where the reality has not measured up to the expectation, the UK's non-metropolitan councils have continued with and have developed their European strategies. Whilst all councils have reached this point, some have taken a more proactive stance, and the reason for this can be identified as the pre-existence of an "associational culture".

7.   Conclusion

This Chapter has been concerned with factors that have influenced the attitudes and behaviour of sub-national elected persons in relation to decision-making within the EU. The intention was to establish whether there were prospects that the EU was responsible for encouraging the development of multi-level governance. If this were the case, there would be an indication that active popular participation in government was increasing because of the UK's membership of the EU.

The conclusion is that the EU has generated additional activity at both regional and local levels. This has also, as indicated in the case studies of the two non-metropolitan councils, penetrated into even the lower tiers that have no direct links with the EU. If sub-national government is to be revived in the UK, the EU will have had some responsibility for this. British sub-national government has discovered a new role for itself because of the UK's membership of the EU.

However, membership of the EU is not the only significant factor influencing the UK's constitutional and institutional progress. Of immediate interest is the way in which the incoming Labour government of 1997 is affected by and interacts with EU initiatives, leading towards a "converged democracy". Chapter Nine examines the latest developments.

CONVERGING DEMOCRACY: BLAIR'S BRITAIN AND THE EUROPEAN UNION

1.   The 1997 Labour government, constitutional reform and the European Union

This chapter shifts the focus from the *ad hoc* manner in which the UK's democracy has been affected by the country's membership of the EU to the proactive development of the UK's constitutional practices carried out by the 1997 Labour government. It examines the way in which its reforms relate to a democratically integrating EU.

No-one could claim that the 1997 Labour government led by Tony Blair owed its principles or the bulk of its policy initiatives to the EU. Blair, like his predecessors, believes in integration for practical rather than ideological reasons [see Chapter Six]. However, as government spokespersons have been keen to emphasise, it was a "new" Labour party, committed to "modern" government, which was elected. The implication was that the Blair government had a clear set of objectives, based upon a thorough appreciation of the position of a small but economically, socially and politically advanced country in a globalised world, which could take on and integrate with supranational governance. As Blair said, Britain was to be "at the heart of Europe".

Even without a statement on modernity, it follows that a government with ambitions to become a major player on the supranational stage needs to do more than pay lip service to the supranational level's economic principles, political culture and constitutional ethos. On the economic front, the Labour government has adopted a strategy that may lead to economic and monetary union with the majority of the EU's states – "Euroland". There is some ambiguity within the strategy, but its aim is reasonably clear. On the other hand, the 1997 UK government has generally been unreceptive to the European version of social democracy – the implication here is that it is the rest of the EU that needs to modernise. The UK government's constitutional agenda has been understated in relation to the EU, but in the long term it may have more significance for integration. Its main legislative constituents are summarised thus:

Fig 9.1: Labour's constitutional initiatives 1997-1999

Individual rights and freedoms	Human Rights Act 1998; draft Freedom of Information bill 1999; White Paper: *Quangos: Opening the Doors* 1998
National institutional reform	White Paper: *Modernising Parliament: Reforming the House of Lords* (cm 4183) 1999; House of Lords Act 1999
Regional devolution	Scotland Act 1998; Government of Wales Act 1998; Northern Ireland Assembly (Elections) Act 1998; Regional Development Agencies Act 1998; Greater London Authority Act 1999
Local government reform	Local Government Act 1999; White Paper: *Modern Local Government: In touch with the People* (cm 4014) 1998; White paper: *Local Leadership, Local Choice* (cm 4298) 1999; Local Government (Organisation and Standards) Bill 1999
Electoral reform	Referendum Act powers (Scotland and Wales) 1997; Greater London Authority (Referendum) Act 1998; Scotland Act 1998; Government of Wales Act 1998; European Parliamentary Elections Act 1999

The EU is not necessarily the motivating force behind all of these developments (although it has had an impact in some). However, as shown below, the changes tend to bring the UK in line with other member states of the EU, and they have the potential to implant the country more firmly as a leading light in a modernised and progressive Europe. The implication of the reforms is that they also become part of *democratic* renewal within the UK state.

2.   Individual rights and powers

2.1.   *Human Rights (Act 1998)*

The Human Rights Act 1998 finally incorporated the Convention for the Protection of Human Rights and Fundamental Freedoms, agreed by the Council of Europe in Rome, 4 November 1950, into the UK's domestic politics. It will come into force 2 October 2000. As the Home Secretary, Jack Straw, [*The Guardian*, 02 January 1999] wrote:

> The Human Rights Act marks a transfer of power from government to the governed by making it much more difficult for the state to act in an arbitrary or unreasonable way. No longer will British people have to go to Strasbourg to enforce their fundamental rights. Instead, citizens will be able to have those rights upheld by courts here in the UK.

The Convention includes various protections:

- the individual's right to life [Article 2]

- freedom from torture [Article 3]
- freedom from enforced labour [Article 4]
- the right to liberty and security [Article 5]
- the right to a fair trial [Article 6]
- the rule of law (in that no-one may be punished unless a law has been broken) [Article 7]
- the right to respect for personal and family life [Article 8]
- freedom of thought, conscience and religion [Article 9], with the freedom to express those thoughts and beliefs [Article 10] and the right to foregather peacefully with others who share them [Article 11].

Article 14 ensures that everyone may exercise these rights, irrespective of "sex, race, colour, language, religion, political or other opinion, national or social origin, association with a national minority, property, birth or other status". However, restrictions on the political activities of "aliens" are permitted under Article 16, and rights under the Convention may not be abused [Article 17]. The First Protocol [1952] endowed additional rights such as protection of property, the right to education and the right to free elections. The Sixth Protocol abolished the death penalty except in times of war.

The enactment of the Human Rights Bill has more symbolic than substantial significance, but it does affect the balance of powers of the UK's institutions to some extent. For example, it limits the powers of Parliament. Legislators now must frame pertinent primary and secondary legislation in a way that is compatible with the human rights convention [Human Rights Act 1998, Clause 3(1)]. This must be affirmed in writing by the promoter of any future parliamentary legislation [*ibid*, Clause 19 (1) and (2)]. It also constrains the powers of any public authority other than Parliament in that it may not act nor fail to act in a manner incompatible with the Convention [*ibid*, Clause 6(1), (3) and (6)].

The Act both extends the powers and limits the freedom of the British judiciary. UK courts now have the capacity to enforce fundamental rights [Human Rights Act 1998, Clause 4(2)], as Straw noted. However, they must also take into consideration relevant previous decisions or opinions of the European Court of Human Rights or of the European Commission of Human Rights when making a judgement [*ibid*, Clause 2(1)].

Finally, the rights of the individual are enhanced. A person has an absolute right to appeal for judgement to the UK's courts in the case of an apparent breach of the Convention which injures her/him personally [*ibid*, Clause 7(1) and (3)]. If the appeal is granted, the court is empowered to award redress or remedy [*ibid*, Clause 8(1)].

Nevertheless, governmental autonomy is respected within the wording of the Act. The government has exercised its right under Article 15(1) of the Convention to exclude the UK from its clause 5(3) which restricts the time a suspect may be held in captivity in respect of terrorist activities [*ibid*, Schedule 3]. The government also continues to embrace a reservation, first expressed by the UK's representative in 1952, about the Convention's First Protocol, Article 2. A parent's right to have a child educated in accordance with her/his religious and philosophical convictions is accepted by the UK but "only so far as it is compatible with the provision of efficient instruction and training, and the avoidance of unreasonable public expenditure" [*ibid* Schedule 3, Part 2].

The government did not really take a major step despite the fundamental nature of the Convention's rights and freedoms. All of these were available *de facto* to UK citizens before the enactment of the Human Rights bill. Nevertheless, the UK government's promotion of the bill delivered three messages. First, it informed the rest of Europe, including its fellow EU-members, that it wished to be associated formally with its political culture. By passing the Act, the UK government indicated that it sanctions the rights of supranational authorities to secure a form of constitutional conformity as well as political and economic integration. Second, it gave notice that it was prepared to do this, even where it had an impact upon the UK's admittedly flexible constitution. Third, it told UK citizens that their rights were sufficiently respected to be enshrined, almost irrevocably, in law.

It should be noted though, that under the UK's constitutional conventions, just as parliament passed the Act, a subsequent parliament could revoke it.

2.2. Draft Freedom of Information Bill, 1999

The enactment of a freedom of information bill is another legislative measure that would bring the UK into line with the majority of its fellow EU states. It would build upon a body of EC legislation about access to certain kinds of information (eg on the environment) which have been incorporated into UK statute. Its progress also reflects the EU's own attempts to make its decision-making processes more transparent[1]. The

---

1 All of the EU's institutions have now incorporated measures to ensure public access to documentation into their rules of procedure, for example: **Council**, General Secretariat: *Council's rules of procedure*: EC, 1997; ISBN: 92-824-1496-5; EC No.BX-01-96-454-EN-C; **Commission**: *Access to Commission documents. A citizen's guide*, 2nd ed.: EC, 1997; ISBN: 92 827-8315-4: EC No.CM-96-96-764-EN-C; **Parliament**: *97/632/ECSC, EC, Euratom: EP Decision of 10.7.97 on public access to European Parliament documents*: OJ L263, 25.9.97, p27-9; **Economic and Social Committee**: *Decision on public access to ESC documents*: OJ L339, 10.12.97, p18 **Committee of the Regions**: *Decision of the Committee of the Regions of*

concept of a freedom of information act also has implications for democratic empowerment.
Freedom of information is not a new idea, even in the UK. A directive was issued in 1977 by the then head of the Civil Service, which promised the release of government information. The Labour Party has been committed to freedom of information since 1974, and a Green Paper proposing a non-statutory code on open government was issued in 1979. It was, however, a Conservative government that finally introduced a code in 1994, and revised it before leaving office in 1997 [Select Committee on Public Administration Third Report, 28 July 1999].

The Labour government elected in 1997 was headed by a leader who was committed to the principle of freedom of information. Speaking in 1996, Tony Blair [cited in *The Guardian*, 22 June 1999] stated the Labour party's intentions:

> Our commitment to a freedom of information act is clear... We want to end the obsessive and unnecessary secrecy which surrounds government activity and make government information available to the public unless there are good reasons not to do so. So the presumption is that information should be, rather than should not be, released.

The draft Freedom of Information Bill follows the publication of a White Paper: *Your Right to Know* [HMSO December 1997], which promised to provide "a general statutory right of access to the information held by public authorities". It also implied an enhancement of democracy, pledging the government to bring about a "fundamental and vital change in the relationship between government and governed".

However, the draft Freedom of Information Bill, likely to be introduced in the 1999-2000 parliamentary session, has proved to be something of a disappointment. It has attracted adverse comment from critics within and

---

17.9.97 concerning public access to documents of the Committee of the
17.9.98 *Regions: OJ* L351, 23.12.97, p 70-71; **European Investment Bank**: *Rules on public access to documents: OJ* C243, 9.8.97,p13-15; **European Environment Agency**: *Decision of 21.3.97 on public access to European Environment Agency documents: OJ* C282, 18.9.97, p5-7; **European Training Foundation**: *Decision of the Governing Board on public access to European Training* - Foundation documents: *OJ* C369, 6.12.97, p10-11. In addition, the Treaty of Amsterdam has replaced Article A's second paragraph with the words "This Treaty marks a new stage in the process of creating an ever closer union among the people of Europe, in which decisions are taken *as openly as possible* and as closely as possible to the citizen"

outside government.

The House of Commons Select Committee criticised the draft Bill on the grounds that it was not sufficiently predisposed towards the disclosure of information, and that the powers ascribed to the Parliamentary Commissioner were not strong enough. It also thought that exemptions were too widely delineated (there are twenty one different categories of exclusions), and that too much emphasis was placed upon voluntary rather than statutory disclosure by public authorities. It recommended that "good international practice should be followed unless the Government can demonstrate that it has caused problems" [Select Committee on Public Administration – Third Report 28 July 1999].

The Campaign for Freedom of Information was explicit in its displeasure at the contents of the draft Bill. It issued a detailed critique of the Bill on a number of aspects, pointing out that exclusions could cover information relating to public safety, and that the Bill provided for new exemptions to be created at short notice. Like the Select Committee, the Campaign for Freedom of Information was critical about the emphasis upon discretionary rather than statutory disclosure [Clause 14]. It also pointed out that significant parts of the Act need not be implemented until five years after its enactment – which seemed an excessive amount of preparation time. The Campaign's director, Maurice Frankel [Press release: 24 May 1999] did not think that the draft Bill represented an advance upon the existing code. He commented that it:

> ... achieves the remarkable feat of making the code, introduced by a government opposed in principle to FoI, appear a more positive measure than legislation drawn up by a government committed to the issue for 25 years.

Charter 88 was also "deeply disappointed", commenting [*Charter 88 response to the Freedom of Information Bill*] that it was:

> ... particularly concerned about the 21 exemptions from the Bill, which will put the most important government information beyond reach. The emphasis remains strongly in favour of secrecy and means that large amounts of information will remain unavailable.

The promise of the Bill, and hence the empowerment of the people to which freedom of information should lead, has not been fulfilled to date. However, the bill at present in draft form, may be revised in response to some of the criticism before it reaches the statute book.

2.3.   *Quangos (White Paper "Quangos: Opening the Doors" 1998)*

The notion of non-elected and often unfamiliar persons who are unaccountable to the public taking decisions that affect people's lives is an uneasy one for democrats. Governments tend to protest that they are essential for efficiency, and that they are accountable to them through parliament or another statutory body. What makes governments uneasy is the fear of over-proliferation and consequent *in*efficiency. Hence action on non-governmental organisations has not been limited to the 1997 Labour government – it was also undertaken by the Conservative government of 1979, when Sir Leo Pliatzky was invited to carry out a study on *ad hoc* agencies. The outcome of this was the abolition of almost 500 quangos by 1983. However, the Conservative governments of the 1980s and 1990s were also committed to "hiving off" public sector responsibilities. This meant a rise in *ad hoc* agencies managing health authorities, training and enterprise councils and grant maintained schools etc. In 1996, Sir Leonard Peach, commissioner for public appointments, issued a code of practice on quango appointments.

The 1997 Labour government was concerned about the efficiency and transparency of non-elected public bodies. Its 1998 White Paper: *Quangos: Opening the Doors* followed a consultation document: *Opening up Quangos* in 1997. The prescriptions in the White Paper include:

- greater openness, with annual public meetings and formalised public consultation (the draft Freedom of Information bill is intended to cover quangos)
- more accountability, using parliamentary Select Committees and requiring board members to register their interests
- increased information, with publicly available documentation; fewer non-departmental public bodies - new ones are only to be established following an efficiency test
- opening up of public appointments, working towards a more representation for ethnic minorities and women.

No bill followed the White Paper's publication, but most of its recommendations could be put into practice without one. There have been no radical changes following the White Paper either, however. New quangos have been created, notably nine Regional Development Agencies [see below] and a new Countryside Agency, to be headed by the previous chairman of the Countryside Landowners Association. No existing quangos have been abolished.

There have been no significant changes relating to appointments. The Lord Chancellor has asked Sir Leonard Peach to undertake a review of the system of appointing judges and senior legal figures, but ruled out the establishment of an independent commission. This has been a matter of concern because it has been shown that despite the government's proposal to get a better balance of public appointments, judges appointed since May 1997 have similar characteristics to those nominated under preceding governments. In July 1999, Sir Leonard Peach also issued a report showing that the majority of quango appointees in the Health Service were Labour activists. He recognised, however, that this was a reflection of the balance of councillors who were most likely to be appointed and who were also more likely to be Labour members. The same report showed, however, that the proportion of women appointed had increased.

Successive governments have taken up the issue of quangos. Whilst the 1997 government has undertaken some action, it does not appear that its initiatives will transform the relationship between non-governmental bodies and the public.

3. National institutional reform: The House of Lords

The 1997 Labour manifesto expressed Labour's intention to reform the House of Lords by abolishing the rights of hereditary peers to sit in it and by deciding upon the means by which it should be constituted in future. This may be seen as part of the government's modernisation agenda – the terms of reference for the Royal Commission that will make recommendations upon the new constitution take this into account:

> Having regard to the need to maintain the position of the House of Commons as the pre-eminent chamber of Parliament and taking particular account of the present nature of the constitutional settlement, including the newly devolved institutions, the impact of the Human Rights Act and developing relations with the European Union...

The UK was the only EU member state that had a second chamber based primarily upon inheritance. It is also seen as a political act, since the majority of hereditary peers are supporters of the Conservative party, although the notion of permanently endowing one political party with an inbuilt majority in a second chamber is itself an anachronism.

The Bill had a stormy passage, facing opposition from the government's own MPs in the Commons as well as in the Lords. In an effort to avoid undue conflict, the government agreed a compromise that would reprieve a number of hereditary peers in December 1998. Since this agreement was made without the apparent knowledge or agreement of William Hague, the leader of the Opposition, Viscount Cranborne, Conservative leader in the Lords, was dismissed, although the compromise itself, retitled the "Weatherill amendment", stood.

The Bill received its first reading in the Commons in January 1999 just before the issue of the White Paper: *Modernising Parliament – Reforming the House of Lords* [Cm 4183]. Its second reading was carried through with the opposition of 34 Labour MPs who wanted to end the Prime Minister's powers of patronage over life peerages in February. In March the Lords defeated the government by 192 votes to 126 in support of an amendment that objected to the abolition of hereditary peers before settling upon a future composition. During this second reading, Conservatives claimed that peers do not sit in the Lords because they have inherited that right. They argued that it is the 'writ of summons' from the monarch, received by most of the peers, that gives them the right to sit until the end of a parliament. Ironically, the Conservatives pointed out that to deprive peers of this title could enable them to invoke the Human Rights Act. Nevertheless, in May, a cross-party alliance of peers endorsed the compromise reprieving 92 members, and it appeared that the Lords would accept the Bill. However, in July, a well-attended session of the Lords voted by 353 to 203 to investigate the legality of the wide-scale "expulsion" of hereditary peers. This was only a delaying tactic. The Bill received a third reading in the Lords, 26 October 1999, during which a series of amendments to increase the number reprieved and introduce elections for life peers were tabled and rejected. The Lords supported the bill by 221 votes to 81. Those hereditary lords who wished to benefit from the reprieve began their campaign for the support of their peers. Elections were held in early November. A final appearance in the Lords on 11 November 1999 resulted in the Lords accepting that "*la reine veult*" their removal.

The bill that aimed to reform the Lords was a very short one. Before the inclusion of the "reprieve" compromise, it had only five clauses. Its purpose was to:

> Restrict membership of the House of Lords by virtue of a hereditary peerage; to make related provision about disqualifications for voting at elections to, and for membership of, the House of Commons; to establish an Appointments Commission with functions in relation to the conferment of life peerages under the Life Peerages Act 1958; and for connected purposes.

The first clause stated that "No-one shall be a member of the House of Lords by virtue of a hereditary peerage", but the second [House of Lords Bill 1999 Clause 2 (2)] enables "not more than 90 people" to be excepted from it. Clause 3 deals with the appointment of life peers, which is to be carried out by an "Appointments Commission", comprising eight members of the Privy Council [*ibid* Clause 3(8)]. Three of these would be the nominees of the three main political parties [*ibid* Clause 3(9)]; one was to be the nominee of the Cross Bench peers [*ibid* Clause 3(9)]. The other four would be appointed by special Commission of the Prime Minister, the Speaker of the House of Commons, and the Lord Chairman of Committees of the House of Lords [*ibid* Clause 3(8)]. The Commission would recommend non-party appointees [*ibid* Clause 3(2)], whose names the Prime Minister must submit to the monarch [*ibid* Clause 3(5)], and it would scrutinise all nominees in accordance with recommendations of the Committee on Standards in Public Life [*ibid* Clause 3(2)]. Criteria were laid down for the subsequent composition of the Lords. It must have a reasonable political balance and the ratio of non-partisan to political appointees must be stable [*ibid* Clause 3(7)]. In future, hereditary peers will have the same rights to vote or become members of the Commons as commoners [*ibid* Clause 4(1)]. The Bill did not affect Church of England representatives who sit in the Lords.

It was to be expected that the Lords would be obstructive when countenancing their elimination. However, there has been criticism from those less personally affected about the system that will replace the hereditary element. Charter 88 [January 1999] commented in a press release: "Whilst the Government's commitment to Lords' reform is welcome, their proposed reforms do not enhance British democracy." There were three areas of concern: *what* function the revised second chamber should serve; *who* should constitute the members and *how* members should be selected.

A Royal Commission under Lord Wakeham was appointed to make recommendations on the "second stage" of Lords reform to a Joint Committee of both Houses of Parliament in December 1999. Its report fit within the context of the government's White Paper that was explicit about current government thinking. On the question of the Lords' role, the White Paper stated unambiguously that "the Royal Commission's proposals for the reformed second chamber must make it clear that it remains the subordinate chamber". It therefore envisaged little change in its existing role, although enhanced powers of scrutiny for EU legislation rated a mention [White Paper, Chapter 7 (17)]. The White Paper also wants representation to be as wide as possible, interestingly adding that regional representation, possibly by means of giving MEPs a role, could be a way forward. It comments that this is "a very common role for second chambers overseas."

On the question of *how* membership of the Lords should be acquired the White Paper makes it plain that the government favours "a part nominated, part elected structure", arguing that this would best combine legitimacy with representativeness. This has been criticised on the grounds that it secures too much power for the leaders of political parties. Charter 88's press release [January 1999] commented: "[Appointments] contribute to the democratic deficit, particularly if appointment rests with one individual, the Prime Minister, who already arguably wields too much political power". The government suggested that an "independent" panel should supervise nominations.

A second chamber with its hereditary element removed (eventually); which contains a wide spread of virtual [see Chapter One] and elected representatives offers the potential for enhanced democracy in the UK, particularly if regional representation is featured. However, it is clear that no second chamber, however constituted, is to be allowed to detract from the essential sovereignty of the first. It will be rendered unable to try to do so if a high proportion of its members owe their position to political or executive patronage. This would be the case whether such patronage were exercised directly or indirectly.

4.   **Regional devolution** (Scotland Act 1998, Government of Wales Act 1998, Northern Ireland Assembly (Elections) Act 1998; Regional Development Agencies Act 1998, Greater London Authority Bill 1999)

Wales has been formally a region of the UK since 1536; Scotland has been integrated into it since 1707 (although its legal and educational systems have always been separate). The United Kingdom of Great Britain and Ireland became an entity in 1801 (although only Northern Ireland remained part of the UK after 1921). Separation from the UK did not become an issue in Scotland and Wales until the late 1970s, although a Scottish Nationalist Party was created in 1934 and Plaid Cymru was formed in 1925. The Callaghan-led Labour government (1976-1979) held referenda on devolution, but in March 1979 it was rejected by both Scottish and Welsh voters. This effectively killed devolutionary prospects for the next decades, although the Labour party researched the issue from the early 1980s onwards. In its 1997 manifesto, the Labour party pronounced that "Subsidiarity is as sound a principle in Britain as it is in Europe", and promised "devolution", although not "federation". All such proposals would be subject to referenda.

Devolution was to take different forms. For Scotland, the manifesto proposed:

> ... the creation of a parliament with law-making powers, firmly based on the agreement reached in the Scottish Constitutional Convention, including defined and limited financial powers to vary revenue and elected by an additional member system.

An assembly, not a parliament, was intended for Wales. It was to control existing Welsh Office functions, but was to have only secondary legislative powers, and no tax raising powers. The main issue for Northern Ireland was the completion of the peace process, which already included the formation of a devolved legislative body. London was promised a directly strategic authority and a mayor. The remaining regions of England were to have appointed regional chambers, which, in accordance with popular demand, could evolve into elected regional government.

All but one of these commitments has been fulfilled, or is already included in enabling legislation. Elections to the new Scottish and Welsh bodies were held in May 1999. The turnouts for both were relatively low, however, with 58.7 per cent in Scotland and 40 per cent in Wales. The elections followed Acts for instituting referenda, the referenda themselves [see below] and subsequent Acts devolving the requisite powers. As promised in the Labour manifesto, the Scotland Act 1998 enables the Parliament to enact primary legislation within its legislative competences [Scotland Act 1998, Clauses 24-31] and provides for limited tax raising powers for the Parliament [*ibid* Clauses 73-79]. The Government of Wales Act 1998 gives the Welsh Assembly authority over the Welsh Health Authority [The Government of Wales Act 1998, Clause 27] and enables it to implement secondary legislation from the UK [*ibid* Clause 28] or EU [*ibid* Clause 29]. Other powers are largely consultative.

The Northern Ireland (Elections) Act came into force in 1998, enabling initial elections to be held for participants to prepare the implementation of the Northern Ireland Agreement [Northern Ireland (Elections) Act 1988 Clause 1(1)]. However, regular elections will not be held until after the successful conclusion of the peace talks, also to be approved by a referendum [*ibid* Clause 8(3)]. The Act provides for each constituency to have six members [*ibid* Clause 1(5)], elected by single transferable votes [*ibid* Clause 2(3)].

A referendum has been held to authorise the establishment of a mayor and assembly for London [see below] and a Greater London Authority Bill was presented in the Commons in December 1998.

The missing commitment is devolution to regional elected bodies in the rest of England. "An Act to make provision for regional development agencies in England; to make provision about the Development Commission and the Urban Regeneration Agency; and for connected purposes" received Royal Assent in November 1998. This meant that England has Regional Development Agencies [RDAs], intended to bring about economic regeneration of the English Regions, based upon existing regional Government Office areas (with the exception of the amalgamation of Merseyside and the North West regions). They work with (non-elected) Regional Assemblies, also provided for within the RDA Act, some of which have been formally designated as such. However, despite the almost instantaneous response from within England's regions, all of which formed shadow regional assemblies before the Bill was enacted, it appears unlikely that elected regional bodies will appear in England.

There has never been elected regional *government* in England, although various Labour governments have made attempts during this century to devolve regional *administration*. The most notable of these was the 1964-1966 Wilson government's creation of Regional Planning Boards staffed by civil servants, but overseen by appointed Regional Economic Planning Councils. Initially there was some thought of these becoming the forerunners of elected bodies, but this idea was dropped after their main promoter, the Deputy Prime Minister, George Brown, left the Department of Economic affairs. The regional economic scheme collapsed effectively within two years.

A similar prospect seems in line for the 1997 government. The Deputy

Prime Minister and Secretary of State for the Environment, Transport and the Regions, John Prescott, has always indicated his enthusiasm for elected regional bodies and his junior minister, Richard Caborn shared this sentiment. However, following the 1999 governmental reorganisation, Caborn was moved from the DETR, and Prescott was required to concentrate his attention on the transport part of his brief. The cabinet, as in the 1960s, is divided upon the issue of elected regional bodies, and the government is unconvinced that there is a great public demand for elected regional government.

Despite this, the 1997 government's devolution agenda is a radical one, which has been implemented quickly. How far it will lead to a UK of the regions, composed of bodies resembling Germany's Länder or, more likely, Spain's autonomous communities (which vary in powers according to the degree of regional identity and popular support), is hard to determine. In Scotland, it seems that the popular appetite for full independence has been whetted; but this is not the case in Wales, and the issues surrounding Northern Ireland's politics are too complex to be resolved by constitutional measures alone. The outcome for the English regions may depend more upon the economic success and popular awareness of the success of the RDAs and Regional Assemblies than upon governmental intentions.

Issues such as the "West Lothian question" (which asks why Scottish MPs should be allowed to help determine English policies when similar Scottish issues would be resolved within the Scottish Parliament alone) remain. The Labour party has shown itself ambivalent about political, as opposed to constitutional, devolution. It has demonstrated a wish to control both the nomination and behaviour of its representatives in devolved bodies, particularly noticeable in regard to the leader of the Welsh Assembly and the candidate for the mayoralty of London. This has led to questions about the effectiveness of regional government – if a Labour London mayor, for example, is to "fight" for the capital, how likely is it that this can be achieved within the parameters of Labour party policy? The immediate results of devolution are unlikely to encourage more of it. The outcome of both the Scottish and Welsh elections were poor for the Labour party, and this may weaken the 1997 government's ardour for devolution. The autonomy of the Scottish Parliament led almost immediately to prospects of different provisions from the rest of the UK in Scotland for Freedom of Information [see above] and for higher education fees.

The future of regional devolution is uncertain. Nevertheless, the 1997 government will be able to take some credit if devolved government becomes part of the UK's constitutional character.

5.   Local government reform (Local Government Act 1999; White paper: *Modern local government: In touch with the People* 1998; White paper: *Local Leadership, Local Choice* [Cm 4298] 1999, Draft Local Government (Organisation and Standards) Bill 1999)

It is in this area which the government has the best opportunity to demonstrate liberal and decentralising characteristics, enabling democratic enhancement from local government's closeness to the people and putting the UK's sub-national government in a similar position *vis-à-vis* national government to other EU member states.

Chapter Two showed that the actions undertaken by both the Thatcher (1979-1990) and Major (1990-1997) Conservative governments limited both the functions of sub-national government and its opportunities for enhancement. They also resisted any underlying trends towards devolution in the UK [John and Whitehead 1997 p 11]. The tendency was in the opposite direction, as fig 9.2. [below] illustrates:

Fig 9.2: Shifts in public spending 1993-1994

	£ million
unelected state spending	54422
transfer of spending from local authorities to quangos and central government	31142

[Source: The Labour Party (1995): "A Choice for England" - consultation paper on Labour's plans for English regional government [London, the Labour Party]]

Like its predecessors, the 1997 Labour government has been fairly proactive in the field of local government reform. Substantial consultation has taken place, the funding structure of local government has been examined; the financial regime reconstructed. No wide scale restructuring of the system of local government has been undertaken to date, although it has been suggested that elected *regional* government would have to be accompanied by single-tiered local government.

In legislative terms, there has been one significant Local Government Act – that of 1999. This Act has had the effect of revising rather than eliminating constraints upon local government's autonomy. Hence, the concept of "best value" replaces compulsory competitive tendering [Local Government Act 1999, clauses 1-22], although councils still need to prove that their services are competitive and there will be a Best Value Inspectorate to monitor the delivery of all local services. The Act replaces the Conservative government's "capping" regime with regulation of Council Tax and precepts [*ibid* Clauses 23 and 24], but still enables the

Secretary of State to penalise "high spending" councils financially.

There have been few other indications that the government values the autonomy of local authorities as they exist at present.   The complex formula for working out a Standard Spending Assessment (upon which the government grant is based) remains unchanged and with it the assumption that all councils should deliver about the same level of services within areas of comparable need. The three "big spenders" – Education (45.4% of total), Personal Social Services (18.3% of total) and Environmental, Protective and Community Services (18.2% of total) – continue to be highly regulated.   For example, the Department for Employment and Education has been prescriptive about the way in which a substantial part of local government expenditure is applied, with a variety of education initiatives whose delivery is overseen by the Office for Standards in Education [Ofsted].   The Department of Environment, Transport and the Regions has encouraged housing authorities to transfer their housing stocks by refusing to allow councils to fund housing investment on deteriorating properties, and by financing directly the housing benefits of tenants of non-local government social landlords only[2].

The general tenor of the government's attitude towards local government was set in its detailed White Paper: *Modern local government: In touch with the People* [1998].   Local government's existing practices are *not* considered to be modern. The White Paper [Forward and Introduction] states that:

> ... councils need to break free from old fashioned practices and attitudes. There is a long and proud tradition of councils serving their communities. But the world and how we live today is very different from when our current systems of local government were established. There is no future in the old model of councils trying to plan and run most services. It does not provide the services which people want, and *cannot do so in today's world.* [author's emphasis]

The White Paper also points out that local government is poorly supported by the electorate with an average electoral turnout of only 40 per cent – the lowest in the EU – ("Too often local people are indifferent about local democracy..."). It ascribes this to councils' "culture of inwardness", which is not only outdated, but which can "open the door to corruption and wrongdoing" [*ibid*, Chapter 1 (11) and (12)]. Councils are also said to be unrepresentative in a virtual sense (not enough women, employed persons or ethnic minorities) [*ibid*, Chapter 1 (13)].

The White Paper acknowledges that central decrees and controls have reduced popular interest in local democracy: "Compulsory Competitive Tendering (CCT) and universal capping... [have] weakened public interest and confidence in local government, and reduced councils' capacity to

---

2 In most cases, it is the Council's Housing Revenue Account (mainly rents) that finances housing benefits for council tenants

serve their communities" [*ibid*, Chapter 1 (14)]. According to the White Paper, however, the main problem is councils' committee structure. It is "opaque"; it takes up too much of councillors' time and it prevents individual members from exerting influence over council decisions. The main answer to these problems is a reshaping of the internal structure of local councils. The White Paper urged councils to revise their existing methods of operating and choose from three main options. These were: a directly elected mayor with a cabinet; a cabinet with a leader; or a directly elected mayor and council manager [*ibid* Chapter 3 (17)], with remaining councillors adopting strong "scrutiny" roles [*ibid* Chapter 3 (41)]. Councils, once reconstituted in this format, could win further autonomy by applying for "beacon" status – either for the whole authority or for particular services [*ibid* Chapter 2 (20)]. Beacon councils would get wider organisational and financial freedom, so long as their service delivery met governmental targets [*ibid* Chapter 2 (23) and (24)]. The White Paper also prescribed a "new ethical framework" for local government, building upon Nolan Committee recommendations [*ibid* Chapter 6 (3)] and announced its intention to introduce legislation requiring every council to adopt an obligatory Code of Conduct [*ibid* Chapter 6 (4)].

The White Paper urged councils to "act now" without awaiting legislation. It was, however, followed by a further White Paper: "Local Leadership, Local Choice" [Cm 4298] 1999, which repeated in essence the prescriptions of the first White Paper, and which formed the basis of the draft Local Government (Organisations and Standards) Bill 1999. This bill makes provision for local authority executives [Local Government (Organisations and Standards) Bill 1999, Clause 2] and assigns their functions. It also provides for public referenda before pursuing the most radical option of an elected mayor [*ibid* Clause 11] and enables referenda on a local authority's internal structure to be conducted. A referendum may be held where it is requested by a petition of at least five per cent of the electorate [*ibid* Clause 14] or where the Secretary of State requires one [*ibid* Clause 15]. The second part of the draft bill sets up the Code of Conduct referred to in the White Paper, providing for internal standards committees [*ibid* Clause 29] and external Standards Boards for England and Wales [*ibid* Clause 31]. The function of the latter is to investigate cases where it appears that a councillor or council has failed to comply with its code of conduct [*ibid* Clause 32]. The draft bill was included in the 1999 Queen's speech and is likely to be enacted during 2000.

The 1997 government, then, has undertaken a number of initiatives concerning elected local government. The outcome for sub-national autonomy is uncertain. Local government income, expenditure and both the level and form of service delivery will still be largely dependent upon central governmental decisions. Changes that could have been made to enhance councils' independence have not been undertaken. These could have included a revision of the national curriculum to give more powers to local education authorities; devolved spending powers to schools could have been reversed; housing authorities could have been enabled to borrow on the open market to invest in their properties, and so on. Concentrating upon structures and codes of conduct implies that the government sees the UK's electoral apathy about local government (curiously extended under Labour, when the average turnout for the council reduced to 29 per cent in 1999) as a matter for the councils, rather than for central government, to address. But this reaction ignores limited amount of autonomy that British local government possesses, when compared with the more "popular" local authorities of France (average electoral turnout 68 per cent) and Germany (average electoral turnout 72 per cent). This is a question concerning powers, not structures. The local authorities of most other EU countries have "general competence" – they can act except where legislation forbids it. The UK government has not adopted this principle – local government can only act when central government permits, and the 1997 government's initiatives have extended this by telling councils *how* they may act.

6.   Electoral reform

6.1.   *Referenda* (Referendum Act powers: (Scotland and Wales) 1997; Greater London Authority (Referendum) Act 1998)

As noted above [Chapter Seven], referenda are required in some EU states and are sometimes used in others when determining constitutional issues. The 1997 Labour government has adopted this practice, doubling the number of referenda previously held in the UK within two years. Four have been conducted:

- to approve the institution of the Scottish Parliament and the Welsh Assembly (enabled by the Referendum Act (Scotland and Wales) 1997)
- to endorse the Good Friday Agreement and subsequent Northern Ireland Assembly (the provision of an Assembly is legitimated by the Northern Ireland Assembly Act 1973, and hence did not need enabling legislation)
- to approve the establishment of the Greater London Authority (enabled by the Greater London Authority (Referendum) Act 1998).

They were all conducted only among residents of the areas.

On the whole, public participation in these events has been encouraging, although it tended to reflect the degree of concern felt about the underlying issues rather than the principle of referenda. Hence 81 per cent turned out in May 1998 to give their views on the Good Friday Agreement – a matter of crucial importance to Northern Ireland. 60.4 per cent participated in the Scottish referendum held in September 1997 – demonstrating the enthusiasm of the Scottish for a devolved *parliament* (which was supported by almost three-quarters of the voters). By contrast, the Welsh referendum, held a week after the Scottish one, only attracted a 50.1 per cent turnout, with voters almost equally divided for and against the notion of a Welsh *assembly*. The turnout in London was low – only 32 per cent of the London electorate participated in the referendum establishing a London authority with an elected Mayor.

It appears that despite these diverse results, the plebiscite is likely to remain a feature of the UK's political life. Future referenda are intended for local government electors whose councils will need to seek the approval of modernisation proposals [Local Government (Organisation and Standards Bill) 1999, Clauses 11; 14 and 15 – see above]. At least one nation wide referendum is planned since Blair has announced that he will seek endorsement of a decision to join the EU's single currency.

6.2.   *Proportional representation* (Scotland Act 1998, Government of Wales Act 1998, European Parliamentary Elections Act 1999)

As noted above [Chapter Six], the UK has moved only reluctantly towards proportional representation, despite the requirement in the Treaty of Rome for "a uniform procedure" for electing MEPs. The 1997 Labour government expressed an early interest in electoral reform, however, establishing the Jenkins Commission to look into the issue. It also put forward a series of bills in 1998 that established different voting systems for the new Scottish Parliament and Welsh Assembly and also for the EP elections.

For the Scottish Parliament and Welsh Assembly, electors have two votes, one for the constituency and one for the electoral region, for which political parties are to submit closed lists. Seats are allocated from the electoral regions as "top ups" for the parties, in accordance with proportional representation [Scotland Act 1998, Clause 1(2) and (3); Government of Wales Act 1998 Clause 4(1), (2) and (3), Clause 6(1)]. The *issue* of devolution was a controversial topic in the UK [see above], but comparatively little discussion took place upon the method of electing the new bodies. Although the voting procedures used in Scotland and Wales were departures from previous electoral practice, they had a less radical impact than the notion of having elected bodies at all. However, this was not the case for the EP Elections.

For the EP elections, the system chosen divided England into nine electoral regions (based upon existing Government Offices), with a varying number of MEPs to be elected by PR for each depending upon size of population [European Parliamentary Elections Act 1999]. Scotland, Wales and Northern Ireland comprised single electoral regions. The problems that the government faced in getting the bill enacted, however, stemmed more from the proposed practice than from the bill's principles. Schedule 3(2) of the Bill stated that "A vote may be cast for a registered party, or an individual candidate, named on the ballot paper". This, known as the "closed list" system, meant that voters could no longer give their expressed support to individuals, unless they were standing as independent candidates. Despite protests from the government that this system was the one adopted by the majority of the other EU states (not strictly true – see fig 5.3., above), the House of Lords, itself facing the onslaught of the government's modernisation programme [see above], raised strenuous objections, rejecting the Bill five times. Surprisingly to some, the Lords emerged as defenders of electoral rights.   For example, the Labour (Eurosceptic) peer, Lord Shore of Stepney [*Official Report* 12 November 1998, Column 851] commented:

> The issue is about the open list against the closed list. It is about an open democratic list against a closed party management list. It is about accountability to the electorate, to the voters, against accountability to a party committee...

Time ran out on the Lords' ability to delay bills under the Parliament Acts [see above], however.   Following a Speaker's ruling, and amid some confusion about "deals" extracted from government to permit the survival of a limited number of hereditary peers [see above], the European Parliamentary Elections Bill was finally enacted in January 1999. It was only the second occasion since 1949 in which the Lords exercised the powers granted under the Parliament Acts.

Electoral reform has not been comprehensive under the 1997 government.   Local councils and (most importantly) the House of Commons itself, are still elected under the "single member simple majority system". The turnouts under proportional representation and variations on PR have been disheartening for the government and the results have been discouraging for a Labour party that won such a large majority in the 1997 General Election. There is a "hung" Scottish Parliament, in which Labour won only 56 of the total 129 seats (turnout: 58.7 per cent); and Welsh Assembly where Labour won 28 of the 60 seats (turnout: 40 per cent)[3]. The results of the European Elections were also disappointing for Labour, which won only 29 out of 87 seats, with a depressingly low turnout of 24 per cent. This may mean dampened governmental enthusiasm for further experiments in proportional representation.

---

3 In both cases Labour did well in the "first past the post" allocation of seats, but the way in which the votes were distributed meant that the majority of "top up" seats were allocated to other parties.

7.   Conclusion

The 1997 Labour government has fulfilled the majority of commitments towards reforming the UK's political institutions in terms of legislation. In doing so, it has brought about a legal constitutional culture that is more attuned to that of its fellow EU members. Individual rights are embodied in legislation as in every other EU state; an anachronistic legislative body will have a reformed membership that makes it more akin to second chambers elsewhere in the EU. More legal powers and practical functions have been devolved, which may lead to the kinds of reforms carried out in Germany, France, Spain and Italy earlier this century. Changes in electoral arrangements have been undertaken, although proportional representation remains the exception rather than the norm, unlike the rest of the EU. All this has been achieved in a remarkably short time.

The UK, however, remains a centralised state in which the rights of individuals and non-governmental institutions depend upon the will of Parliament. This Parliament will have a reformed second chamber, but it is unlikely that the new chamber's legitimacy will be entirely derived from popular mandate, and it is equally unlikely that its powers will be substantial. A commitment to human rights may be a permanent feature of the UK in the new millennium, but freedom to the kind of information that may be necessary to exercise them fully remains elusive. It is not included in the draft Freedom of Information bill. There will be devolution in form, but not necessarily in content. The Labour party's internal ambivalence shown over the selection of its representatives implies that its leadership in government is reluctant to relinquish central control over policy. There is less ambivalence about local government. Despite the rhetoric on subsidiarity in Labour's 1997 manifesto, there is little in the White Paper on local government that suggests that the government intends to bring decision making down to the lowest level. During Thatcher years, Jones and Stewart [1983 p 73] argued that giving local government additional *responsibilities* was not enhancing their independence:

> Local authorities' discretion is about to do what central government does not like. Any central government will give local authorities the freedom to do what central government likes; it is the freedom to do otherwise which counts.

The government does not propose giving sub-national government "the freedom to do otherwise", and it has not suggested any constitutional changes that would give it autonomous status within the UK constitution.

The 1997 government has taken steps that may lead to the creation of a more open and European political culture within the UK. However, the outcome will depend upon the impact of the UK's new arrangements upon its citizens (see Chapter Seven) and the way in which the new and reformed bodies interact with the EU's institutions (see Chapter Eight).

Conclusion: snapshots and photographs

The subject of this book was democracy. The aim was to examine ways in which the EU's citizens, in this case those living in the UK, may become empowered by means of the UK's membership of the European Union. Within a complex system of governance, like the EU's, such an examination needed to be conducted in terms of looking at how the EU's citizens could extend their participation in government at supranational, national, non-governmental and sub-national tiers.

It was pointed out at the beginning that the supranational quality of the EU means that its inhabitants automatically have more control over the "top" tier, if only through the EP, than they have within intergovernmental groupings of nations. It was acknowledged that this is unappreciated by the EU's *demos*. It is certainly insufficient to legitimise the EU in the Weberian sense of the word. The EP, as indicated in Chapters Four and Five, is not likely to accomplish the feat despite its growing powers.

There are other ideas. For example, the EU might, as the highest point of the governmental pyramid, force or persuade national governments to deconcentrate their powers. However, supranational governance, despite the views of Eurosceptics, is not synonymous with supranational sovereignty. Representatives of national governments decide in which areas and to what extent EU laws will apply, and they have resolved that the internal constitutions of member states are *ultra vires* of the EU. Neither is there much evidence that any form of neo-functionalist spillover will result in making subsidiarity a legal and binding principle to be applied by the EU *within* its member states.

However, because the EU is not sovereign, it requires national and sub-national co-operation for its policies to be implemented effectively. Although it has not been a key theme of this book, it was implied from time to time that national co-operation has its price. The EU consists of sovereign states whose representatives can say "no", and on some occasions can make their refusal substantial (for example when the UK government refused to sign the TEU without concessions). EU institutions need to take account of this. One explicit objective of this book was to demonstrate that sub-national and non-governmental co-operation also has its price and that the price in practice is the meaningful involvement of widening groups of individuals. Democratic enhancement can follow involvement, and there is enough evidence presented herein to demonstrate that this is happening within the EU's member states. This has particular significance, of course, for a centralised state like the UK.

Another theme of the book was the consideration of the significance for public life of further integration. The EU, as Forsyth [1994 p 57] has pointed out, is itself a federalised state. The practice of federalism could demonstrate that it is feasible and therefore applicable to other systems of governance. It is improbable, however, that a Eurosceptic UK public will learn to appreciate sufficiently the EU's devolutionary nature to want to emulate it in the short term. What is more likely is that other member states' examples of decentralisation and enhancement of democratic rights could form the basis of popular demands. Organisations such as Charter 88, for example, are encouraged and empowered by the mainland west European commitment to freedom of information.

A second possibility is that member states' governments, whose representatives sit regularly and sometimes informally in the Council of Ministers, may have their doubts about constitutional changes assuaged by their colleagues. They may come to understand that devolution, for example, is not to be feared when other national governments, otherwise remaining in overall control, succeed in decentralising their decision-making processes. Then there are pressures to conform. To be a full part of, or to "lead", the European project, a state needs to be part of the inner circle. The Blair government, as demonstrated in Chapter Nine, has dipped more than a toe in the water of constitutional modernisation as its leader tries to fulfil his ambition to place Britain "at the heart of Europe". Laffan [1999 pp 175-176] now claims that "the devolution process in the United Kingdom is transforming the last centralized state in western Europe into a multi-levelled system of governance". It has not achieved this yet. Devolution itself needs to be transformed into a meaningful redistribution of powers between the centre and the localities before the UK's population can experience direct democracy. Bache [1999] points out that multi-level *participation* is not the same as multi-level *governance*. It is easy to confuse the two activities, but, as Bache implies, it is important not to do this, because democracy, like government legitimacy, needs to be appreciated by the *demos* before it has a true function. Any declaration of the existence of participatory democracy without a popular perception of power will impede rather than accelerate the institution of multi-level governance.

Bache thinks that it is the national governments', rather than the EU's, attitudes that will determine whether popular participation will become popular governance. Nevertheless, the EU can affect national governments' attitudes. Apart from motivating leaders of centralised states to develop a more participatory constitution, devolution specifically is encouraged by some of the EU's policies, in particular its approach to the distribution of Structural Funds. Decentralised decision-making has had relative success within the programmes for regionally-based regeneration. Involvement of sub- and non-governmental groups has had a beneficial impact, and, so far, has not been obtained at the price of a noticeable loss of central powers.

By these means, a number of the EU's processes and practices coalesce. Political and bureaucratic pressures, developing separately and for different reasons, lead towards more opportunities for popular participation. It should be pointed out, of course, that neither politicians nor bureaucrats have the achievement of increased democracy as their primary objective. Politicians want to be effective governors, preferably international leaders. Bureaucrats need extensive and successful administration.

As Chapter Seven pointed out, their motives do not really matter. Democracy in both the ancient and modern worlds did not develop because powerful leaders or bureaucrats wanted it. Combinations of circumstances and necessities led to Athenian participatory democracy and to modern liberal democracy. The point in both cases was that, once established, each form of democracy became pervasive and enduring. Over the last one and a half centuries, it has been taken for granted that the only feasible democratic form was liberal/representative.   Both the difficulties of governing a supranational entity by this means and the practical necessity of devolving decision-making in these circumstances open up other options.

However, this book provides a snapshot, not a photograph of contemporary democratisation.   It is a blurred picture, reflecting the difficulty of pinning down the subject long enough to be able to represent it accurately.   Democratic evolution is a messy affair, involving many processes and many groups of players.   Many commentators have remarked that the EU is a new kind of governance. What is exciting to the student of the EU is that new forms of interactions among governors and governed appear to be arising as the integration develops and as shortcomings of liberal democratic controls over it become apparent. It is possible that this will lead to a new and more meaningful form of democracy in the long run. The EU may yet prove inaccurate Michel's [1962 p 371] prognosis that the ebbing and flowing of democratic currents will never lead to a net gain for democracy.

BIBLIOGRAPHY

Adonis, A (1993): *Parliament Today* (Manchester, Manchester University Press)

Aquinas, St Thomas (c 1256-1274) (1959): *Selected Political Writings* (Oxford, Blackwell)

Andersen, S S & Burns, T (1996): "The European Union and the Erosion of Parliamentary Democracy: a study of post-Parliamentary Governance" in Andersen, S S & Eliassen, K A (eds): *The European Union – How Democratic is it?* (London, Sage)

Arblaster, A (1991): *Democracy* (Oxford, OUP)

Archer, C & Butler, F (1996): *The European Union: Structure and Process* 2nd Edition (London, Pinter)

Archibugi, D and Held, D (1995): *Cosmopolitan Democracy* (Cambridge, Polity Press)

Aristotle (c 353 BC) (1961): *Politics and the Athenian Constitution* (London, Dent & Sons)

Armstrong, H (1997): Speech delivered to the Local Government Association annual conference, 25 July

Attina, F (1990): "The voting behaviour of the European Parliament Members and the problem of the Euro-parties" (*European Journal of Political Research*, 18)

Bache, I (1999): "The extended gatekeeper: central government and the implementation of EC regional policy in the UK" (*Journal of European Public Policy* 6 (1))

Bache, I; George, S and Rhodes, R A W (1996): "The European Union, Cohesion Policy and Subnational Authorities in the United Kingdom" in Hooghe L (ed): *Cohesion Policy and European Integration* (Clarendon Press, Oxford)

Bagehot, W (1864) (1964): *The English Constitution* (London, C A Watts & Co Ltd)

Bains, M A (1972): *The New Local Authorities: Management and Structure* (London, HMSO)

Banchoff, T and Smith, M P (1999) (eds): *Legitimacy and the European Union* (London and New York, Routledge)

Barnett, A (1994): "The Empire State" in Barnett, Anthony (ed): *Power and the Throne* (London, Vintage, in association with Charter 88)

Barber, B (1990): *Strong Democracy* (Berkeley, University of California Press)

Batley, R (1991): "Comparisons and Lessons" in Batley, R & Stoker, G (eds): *Local Government in Europe – Trends and Developments* (Basingstoke, Macmillan)

Beetham, D (1993): "In defence of legitimacy" (*Political Studies* 41 (3))

Beetham, D (1992): "Liberal Democracy and the Limits of Democratization" in Held, David (ed): *Prospects for Democracy* (Cambridge, Polity Press)

Beetham, D (1975): "From Socialism to Fascism: the relation between theory and practice in the work of Robert Michels" (*Political Studies*, 25)

Beetham, D and Lord, C (1998): *Legitimacy and the European Union* (Harlow, Longman)

Birch, A H (1967): *The British System of Government* (London, Allen & Unwin Ltd)

Birch, A H (1964): *Representative and Responsible Government* (London, Allen & Unwin)

Blunkett, D & Jackson, K (1987): *Democracy in Crisis – the Town Halls Respond* (London, Hogarth)

Bogdanor, V (1996): "The European Union, the Political Class, and the People" in Hayward, J (ed): *Élitism, Populism, and European Politics* (Oxford, Clarendon Press)

Bogdanor, V (1995): *The Monarch and the Constitution* (Oxford, Clarendon Press)

Bogdanor, V (1994): *Observer* 20 March

Bongers, P & Chatfield, J (1993): "Europe of the Regions: Regions and Local Authorities in the Governance of Europe" in Duff, Andrew (ed): *Subsidiarity within the European Community* (Federal Trust for Education and Research, PSI Publishing)

Bosanquet, B (1882) (1965): *The Philosophical Theory of the State* (London, Macmillan & Co Ltd)

Bowler, S & Farrell, D M (1995): "The Organising of the European Parliament: Committees, Specialization and Co-ordination" (*British Journal of Political Science* 25 (2), pp 219-243)

Boyce, B (1995): "The June 1994 Elections and the Politics of the European Parliament" (*Parliamentary Affairs*, 48 (1) pp 141-156)

Boyce, B (1993): "The Democratic Deficit of the European Community" (*Parliamentary Affairs* 46 (3))

Brittan, S (1989): "The economic contradictions of democracy"(*Political Quarterly*, 60 (2))

Budge, I & McKay D (1988): *The Changing British Political System: Into the 1990s* (Harlow, Longman)

Burch, M & Wood, B (1990): *Public Policy in Britain* (Oxford, Blackwell)

Burke, E (1775) (1964): "Speech on conciliation with America, 22 March 1775" in Burke, E: *Speeches and Letters on American Affairs* (London, Everyman)

Burke, E (1774) (1964): "Speech to the Electors of Bristol, 3 November 1774" in Burke, E: *Speeches and Letters on American Affairs* (London, Everyman)

Burnheim, J (1986): "Democracy, Nation States and the World System" in Held, David & Pollitt, Christopher (eds): *New Forms of Democracy* (London, Sage)

Burnheim, J (1985): *Is Democracy Possible?* (Cambridge, Cambridge, Polity Press)

Burns, D: Hambleton, R & Hoggett, P (1994): *The Politics of Decentralisation: Revitalising Local Democracy* (Basingstoke, Macmillan)

Butcher, H; Law, I G; Leach, R & Mullard, M (1990): *Local Government and Thatcherism* (London & New York, Routledge)

Cabinet Office (1999): *Modernising Parliament – Reforming the House of Lords* (White Paper: Cm 4183) (London, The Stationery Office)

Carvel, J (1994): *(Guardian* 23 May)

Chandler, J A (1996): *Local government today* (Manchester and New York, Manchester University Press)

Cheshire County Council (1994): *Operational Programme for European Union Objective 2 Funding 1994-1996* (Cheshire County Council Environment Planning Services)

Cochrane, A (1986): "Community Politics and Democracy" in Held, David & Pollitt, Christopher (eds) *New Forms of Democracy* (London, Sage)

Commission, DG XVI (1996): *Structural Funds and Cohesion Fund 1994 99.Regulations and commentary. January 1996* EC, ISBN: 92-827-4350 0;EC No.CX-88-95-121-EN-C

Commission, DG XVI (1993): *UK: Greater Manchester, Lancashire and Cheshire – Single Programming Document 1994-1996, Objective 2* (No ERDF: 94.09.13.022; No ARINCO: 9A4.uk.16.011)

Committee of Independent Experts (1999): "First report on allegations regarding fraud, mismanagement and nepotism in the European Commission" (Brussels, European Union, 15 March)

Constant, B (1815) (1957): *Principes de Politique* (Oeuvres, Paris; Editions Gallimard, – cited by Spicker, P (1996): "Concepts of Subsidiarity in the European Community" *(Current Politics and Economics in Europe*, V, 2/3 pp 163-175

Coombs, D (1994): "Problems of Governance in the Union" in Duff, A; Pinder, J & Pryce, R (eds): *Maastricht and Beyond* (London & New York, Routledge)

CoR (1996): *Impact and follow up of CoR's Opinions January to July 1996* (Brussels, The Committee of the Regions, Office for Official Publications of the European Communities, October)

CoR (1995): CoR publication (Office for Official Publications of the European Communities)

Corbett, R (1999): "The European Parliament and the Idea of European Representative Government" in Pinder, J: *Foundations of Democracy in the European Union: from the Genesis of Parliamentary Democracy to the European Parliament* (Basingstoke, Macmillan)

Corbett, R (1994): "Representing the People" in Duff, Andrew, Pinder, John and Pryce, Roy: *Maastricht and Beyond* (London & New York, Routledge)

Crewe, I (1993): "Voting and the Electorate" in Dunleavy, P; Gamble, G; Holliday, I & Peele, G (eds): *Developments in British Politics 4* (Basingstoke, Macmillan)

Cross, C & Bailey, S (1986): *Cross on Local Government Law* (London, Sweet & Maxwell)

Dahl, R (1989): *Democracy and its critics* (Newhaven and London, Yale University Press)

Dahl, R (1967): *A Preface to Democratic Theory* (Chicago, University of Michegan)

Dahl, R A & Tufte, E R (1974): *Size and Democracy* (Oxford, Oxford University Press)

Dankert, P (1997): "Pressure from the European Parliament" in Edwards, G and Pijpers, A (eds): *The Politics of European Treaty Reform: The 1996 Intergovernmental Conference and Beyond* (London, Pinter)

Davies, D (1995): speaking on BBC2 *Newsnight*, 1 April

Davis, H and Stewart, J (1993): "The Growth of Government by Appointment" (*Local Government Management Board*)

Dearlove, J & Saunders, P (1991): *Introduction to British Politics* (Cambridge, Polity Press)

Department of the Environment, Transport and the Regions (1999): *Local Leadership, Local Choice* – Command Paper Cm 4298 (London, The Stationery Office Limited)

Department of the Environment, Transport and the Regions (1998): *Modern Local Government: In Touch with the People* – White Paper Cm 4014 (London, The Stationery Office Limited)

Department of the Environment, Transport and the Regions (1997): *Building Partnerships for Prosperity* – Command Paper Cm 3814 (London, The Stationery Office Limited)

Dicey, A V (1982): *An Introduction to the Study of the Law of the Constitution* (Basingstoke, Macmillan)

Dinan, D (1997): "The Commission and the Reform Process" in Edwards, G and Pijpers, A (eds): *The Politics of European Treaty Reform: The 1996 Intergovernmental Conference and Beyond* (London, Pinter)

Duchy of Lancaster (1998): *Quangos: Opening the Doors* – White Paper (London, the Stationery Office Limited)

Duff, A (1994): "The Main Reforms" in Duff, A; Pinder, J and Pryce, R (eds): *Maastricht and Beyond* (London & New York, Routledge)

Duff, A (1994): "Ratification" in Duff, A, Pinder, J and Pryce, R (eds): *Maastricht and Beyond* (London & New York, Routledge)

Dunleavy, P & Rhodes R A W (1983): "Beyond Whitehall" in Drucker, H et al: *Developments in British Politics* (Basingstoke, Macmillan)

Dunn, J (1984): *John Locke* (London & New York, Routledge)

Earnshaw, D & Judge, D (1995): "Parliament, co-decision and the EU legislative process" (*Journal of European Public Policy* 2 (4) pp 624-649)

Eliassen, D (1996): "Swedish Working Document concerning access to documents in the European Institutions" (*European Access*, No 4, August)

Elliot, M (1983): "Constitutional Continuity and the Position of Local Government" in Young, K (ed): *National Interests and Local Government* (Heinemann, London)

European Council (1997): *Treaty of Amsterdam*

European Council (1997): *Treaty on European Union* (1992)

European Parliament (1995): *Resolution on the finalising of the Treaty on European Union* (17 May)

European Parliament (1984): *Draft constitution of the European Union*, 9, 2, the "Herman Report"

Ezard (1993): *Guardian* 15 December

Farrar, C (1993): "Ancient Greek political theory and democracy" in Dunn, J (ed) *Democracy, The Unfinished Journey – 50BC to AD1993* (Oxford, OUP)

Featherstone, K (1994): "Jean Monnet and the 'Democratic Deficit' in the European Union" (*Journal of Common Market Studies* 32 (2) pp 149-165)

Featherstone, K & Yannopoulos, G N (1995): "The European Community and Greece: Integration and the Challenge to Centralism" in Jones, B & Keating, M (eds): *The European Union and the Regions* (Oxford, Clarendon Press)

Fernia, J (1993): "Elites, participation and the democratic creed" in Dunn, John (ed): *Democracy, The Unfinished Journey – 50BC to AD1993* (Oxford, OUP)

Financial Times (1995) 11 March

Finer, S E (1988): *Man on Horseback* (Colorado, Westview Press)

Fishkin, J S (1994): *Democracy and Deliberation*

Ford, G (1993): *The Evolution of a European* (Nottingham, Spokesman)

Forsyth, M (1994): "Federalism and confederalism" in Brown, C (ed): *Political Restructuring in Europe* (London and New York, Routledge)

Frankland, M (1994): *Observer* 5 June

Gallacher, J (1995): "Committee of the Regions – An Opportunity for Influence" (*Local Government International Bureau*, Special Report No 3)

Gallagher, M; Laver, M; Mair, P (1992): *Representative Government in Western Europe* (New York, etc, McGraw-Hill)
George, S (1994): "Supranational Actors and Domestic Politics: Integration Theory Reconsidered in the Light of the Single European Act and Maastricht" (Sheffield, University of Sheffield)
George, S (1991): *Britain and European Integration since 1945* (Oxford, Blackwell)
George, S (1990): *An Awkward Partner* (Oxford, Oxford University Press)
George, S (1985): *Politics and Policy in the European Community* (Oxford, Clarendon Press)
Gerth, H & Mills, C W (1967): *From Max Weber* (London, Routledge and Keegan Paul Ltd)
Gibbons, J (2000): "Spain" in Lodge, J (ed): *The 1999 Elections to the European Parliament* (Basingstoke, Macmillan) (in preparation for publication)
Goldsmith, M & Sperling, I (1997): "Local Governments and the EU: The British Experience" in Goldsmith, M J F and Klausen, K K (eds): *European Integration and Local Government* (Cheltenham, Edward Elgar)
Goodman, J (1997): "The EU: Reconstituting democracy beyond the Nation State" (Contemporary European Studies Association of Australia, *Newsletter*, May)
Gough, J W (1957): *The Social Contract* (Oxford, Clarendon Press)
Government Office, North West (1997): "Regional Development Agencies" (Consultation Paper, Summer)
Green, P (1994): "Subsidiarity and European Union: Beyond the Ideological Impasse" (*Policy and Politics*, 22 (4))
Green, P (MEP) (1994): *Guardian* 25 January
Greenwood, S (1992): *Britain and European Co-operation since 1945* (Oxford, Blackwell)
Gyford, J (1984): *Local Politics in Britain* (London, Croom Helm)
Hague, R; Harrop, M & Breslin, S (1992): *Comparative Government and Politics* – 3rd Edition (Basingstoke, Macmillan)
Hailsham, Lord (1978): *Dilemma of Democracy* (London, Collins)
Hancock, M D; Conradt, D P; Peters, B G; Safran, W and Zariski, R (1993): *Politics in Western Europe* (Basingstoke, Macmillan)
Harden, I (1992): *The Contracting State* (Buckingham – Philadelphia, Open University Press)
Haseler, S (1994): "Monarchy is feudal" in Barnett, A (ed): *Power and the Throne* (London, Vintage, in association with Charter 88)
Hanson, A H & Walles, M (1990): *Governing Britain* (Glasgow, Fontana)
Hayes-Renshaw, F (1996): "The Role of the Council" in Andersen, S S & Eliassen, K A (eds): *The European Union, how democratic is it?* (London, Sage)

Hayes-Renshaw, F and Wallace, H (1995): "Executive power in the European Union: the functions and limits of the Council of Ministers" (*Journal of European Public Policy* 2 (4) pp 559-582)

Held, D (1993): "Democracy and the New International Order" (IPPR, Premier Printers, October)

Held, D (1987): *Models of Democracy* (Cambridge, Polity Press)

Heseltine, M (1991): Association of District Councils' conference, 28.6.91 (*Municipal Journal* 5-11 July)

Hirst, P (1994): *Associative Democracy* (Cambridge, Polity Press)

Hobbes, T (1651) (1988): *Leviathan* (London, Penguin)

Hornblower, S (1993): "Creation and Development of Democratic Institutions in Ancient Greece" Dunn, J (ed): *Democracy, The Unfinished Journey – 50BC to AD1993* (Oxford, OUP)

Hooghe, L (1996): "Building a Europe with the Regions" in Hooghe L (ed): *Cohesion Policy and European Integration* (Clarendon Press, Oxford)

Hutton, W (1995): *The State we're in* (London, Jonathan Cape)

Institute for Public Policy Research (1993): *A Written Constitution for the United Kingdom* (London, Mansell)

Jacobs, F; Corbett, R & Shackleton, M (1992): *The European Parliament –* 2nd Edition (Harlow, Longman)

James, P S (1989): *Introduction to English Law –* 12th Edition (London, Butterworths)

Jeffery, C (1996): "Towards a "Third Level" in Europe? The German Länder in the European Union" (*Political Studies* 44 (2) pp 253-266)

Jeffery, C (1995): "Whither the Committee of the Regions? Reflections on the Committee's 'Opinion on the Revision of the Treaty on European Union'" (Documentary Survey, *Regional and Federal Studies*, 5 (2))

Jeffery, C (1995) (Institute for German Studies, University of Birmingham): *The German Länder* (presentation given at a conference held at the University of North London, December)

Johansen, R C (1992): "Military policies and the State system as impediments to democracy" in Held, David (ed): *Prospects for Democracy* (Cambridge, Cambridge, Polity Press)

John, P (1995): "A base in Brussels: A good investment for local authorities?" (*Local Government Information Bureau*)

Jones, B (1995): Conclusion in Jones, B & Keating, M (eds): *The European Union and the Regions* (Oxford, Clarendon Press)

Jones, G & Stewart, J (1983): *The Case for Local Government* (Local Government Briefings, London, Allen and Unwin)

Jones, P (1988): "Intense preferences, strong beliefs and democratic decision-making" (*Political Studies*, 36 (1))

Kaldor, M (1995): "European Institutions, Nation States and Nationalism" in Archibugi, D and Held, D: *Cosmopolitan Democracy* (Cambridge, Polity Press)

Keane, J (1988): *Democracy and Civil Society* (London, Verso)

Keane, J (1992): "Democracy and the Media – without foundations" in Held, David (ed): *Prospects for Democracy* (Cambridge, Polity Press)

Keating, M (1995): "Europeanism and Regionalism" in Jones, B & Keating, M (eds): *The European Union and the Regions* (Oxford, Clarendon Press)

Keating, M & Harnsworth, P (1986): *Decentralisation and Change in Contemporary France* (London, Gower)

Keating, M & Jones, B (1995): "Nations, Regions, and Europe: the UK Experience" in Jones, B & Keating, M (eds): *The European Union and the Regions* (Oxford, Clarendon Press)

Keersmaeker, de (Executive Director of the Helsinki Citizens' Assembly) (1994) *(hCa* (Helsinki Citizens' Assembly) Quarterly 9 (1))

Kennedy, H: *Preface* from Barnett, A (ed) (1994): *Power and the Throne* (London, Vintage, in association with Charter 88)

Kettle, M (1994): *Guardian* 10 December

King, D (1993): "Government beyond Whitehall" in Dunleavy, P; Gamble, G; Holliday, I & Peele, G (eds): *Developments in British Politics 4* (Basingstoke , Macmillan)

Klausen, K and Goldsmith, M (1997): "Local government and the European Union" in Klausen, K and Goldsmith, M (eds): *European Integration and Local Government* (Cheltenham, Edward Elgar)

Knipping, F (1996): "Subsidiarity, Role of the Regions, Committee of the Regions", report submitted to conference "Internal Equilibrium of the enlarged Union"

Kohler-Koch, B (1997): "Organized Interests in the EC and the European Parliament" (*European Integration online Papers*, Vol 1, No 009; http://eiop.or.at/eiop/texte/1997-009a.htm)

Ladrech, R (1993): "Parliamentary Democracy and Political Discourse in EC Institutional Change" (*Journal of European Integration*, 17 (1) pp 53-70)

Laffan, B (1999): "Developments in the Member States" (*Journal of Common Market Studies*, 37, Annual Review 1998/1999)

Laffan, B (1992): *Integration and Co-operation in Europe* (London, Routledge)

Layfield, F (1976): *Local Government Finance: Report of the Committee of Enquiry* (HMSO)

Leonardi, R (1995): *Convergence, Cohesion and Integration in the European Union* (Houndsmills and London, St Martin's Press)

Lessnoff, M (1986): *Social Contract* (Basingstoke, Macmillan)

Lively, J (1981): *Democracy* (Oxford, Blackwell)

Locke, J (1690) (1986): *Two Treatises of Govenrment* (London, Everyman)

Lodge, J (1996): "The European Parliament" in Anderson, S S and Eliassen, K A (eds): *The European Union – How Democratic is it?* (London, Sage)

Lodge, J (1994): "Transparency and Democratic Legitimacy" (*Journal of Common Market Studies*, 32 (3) pp 343-368)

Lodge, J (1993): "EC policy making: institutional dynamics" in Lodge, J (ed): *The European Community and the Challenge of the Future* (London, Pinter Publishers)

Lodge, J (1991): "The Democratic Deficit and the European Parliament" (London, Fabian Society Discussion Paper no 4, the Fabian Society)

Lodge, J (1991): "The European Parliament" (Fabian pamphlet)

Lodge, J (1989): "EC Policy-making: institutional considerations" in Lodge, J (ed): *The European Community and the Challenge of the Future* (London, Pinter Publishers)

Lodge, J (1989): "Environment: towards a clean blue-green EC?" in Lodge, J (ed): *The European Community and the Challenge of the Future* (London, Pinter Publishers)

Lodge, J (1986): "Institutional provisions: Towards a Parliamentary democracy" in Lodge, J (ed): *European Union: The EC in Search of a Future* (London, Macmillan)

Lukes, S (1980): *Power, a Radical View* (London, Macmillan)

Lukes, S (1979): "On the Relativity of Power" in Brown, S C (ed): *Philosophical Disputes in the Social Sciences* (Sussex, Harvester Press)

McCarthy, R E (1997): "The Committee of the Regions: an advisory body's tortuous path to influence" (*Journal of European Public Policy* 4 (3) pp 439-454)

Machiavelli, N (1514) (1981): *The Prince* (London, Penguin)

McKay, D (1989): *American Politics and Society* – 2nd Edition (Oxford, Blackwell)

MacKenzie, W J M (1975): *Explorations in Government, Collected Papers 1951-1968* (Basingstoke, Macmillan)

McKie, D (1994): *Guardian* 11 July

McKie, D (1994): *Guardian* 27 February

McLaughlin, A M & Greenwood, J (1995): "The Management of Interest Representation in the European Union" (*Journal of Common Market Studies*, 33 (1) March pp 143-156)

McLean, I (1989): *Democracy and New Technology* (Cambridge, Polity Press)

McLean, I (1986): "Mechanisms for Democracy" in Held, D & Pollitt, C (eds): *New Forms of Democracy* (London, Sage)

MacShane, D (1995): "Europe's next challenge to British Politics" (*Political Quarterly* 66 (1) pp 23-35)

Madison, J (1787) (1965): "The Union as a Safeguard continued" from "*The New York Packet*, Friday, November 23, 1787," in Hamilton, A: *The Federalist* (London, Everyman)

Marinetto, M (1996): "New Developments in the Regional Structure of Government Departments: the New Government Offices for the Regions, with Specific Reference to the Government Office for London" (*Public Policy and Administration* 11 (4))

Marks, G; Nielson, F; Ray, L & Salk J (1996a): "Competences, Cracks, and Conflicts: Regional Mobilization in the European Union (*Comparative Political Studies*, 29 (2) pp 164-192)

Marks, G; Hooghe, L & Blank, K (1996b): "European Integration from the 1980s: State-Centric *v*. Multi-level Governance" (*Journal of Common Market Studies* 34 (3) pp 341-378)

Marquand, D (1994): *Guardian*, 4 November

Marquand, D (1991), in Crick, B (ed): *National Identities* (Oxford, Blackwell)

Martin, D (1993): "European Union – the Shattered Dream" (John Wheatley Centre 1993)

Martin, D (1993): *Europe: an ever closer Union* (Nottingham, Spokesman)

Martin, D (1989): "Power to the People – a Federal Britain in a Democratic Europe" (text of the Eleventh John P Mackintosh Memorial Lecture, University of Edinburgh)

Martin, D (1988): "Bringing common sense to the Common Market: a left agenda for Europe" (Fabian Society pamphlet no 525, London & Worthing, College Hill Press Limited (TU))

Marx, K (1867) (1967): *Das Kapital* (Chicago, Henry Regnery Co)

Mather, J (1997): "Transparency in the European Union – an Open and Shut Case?" (*European Access* (1))

Mather, J (1995): "Democratic Impediments to Participatory Democracy" (*Politics* 15 (3) pp 175-182)

Mawson, J (Head of the School of Town and Regional Planning, University of Dundee) (1995): *The UK and the regions* (presentation given at conference organised by the University of Birmingham, November)

Michels, R (1915) (1962): *Political Parties* (London, Collier-Macmillan)

Mill, J S (1859, 1861) (1988): *Utilitarianism, On Liberty and Considerations on Representative Government* (London, Everyman)

Miller, D (1992): "Deliberative Democracy and Social Choice" in Held, David (ed): *Prospects for Democracy* (Cambridge, Polity Press)

Milward, A (1992): *The European Rescue of the Nation-State* (Berkeley: University of California Press)

Moravcsik, A (1993): "Preferences and Power in the European Community: A Liberal Intergovernmental Approach" (*Journal of Common Market Studies* (31) pp 473-524)

Moravcsik, A (1991): "Negotiating the Single European Act: National Interests and Conventional Statecraft in the European Community" (*International Organization* (45) pp 651-658)

Morgan, R (ed) (1994): *The Times Guide to the European Parliament* (London, Harper Collins)

Mosca G (1923) (1939): *The Ruling Class* (New York, McGraw-Hill)

Mount, F (1993): *The British Constitution Now* (London, Mandarin 1993)

Mulgan, G (1994): "How the jury's verdict can help revive democracy" (*Guardian* 18 August)

Mutimer, D (1989): "1992 and the political integration of Europe: neofunctionalism reconsidered" (*Journal of European Integration*, 13 (1) pp 75-101)

Nentwich, M and Falkner, G (1997): "The Treaty of Amsterdam: Towards a new Institutional Balance" (European Integration online Papers, Vol 1 No 015: http://eiop.or.at/eiop/texte/1997-0115a.htm)

Newton, K & Valles, J (1991): "Political Science in Western Europe 1960-1990" (*European Journal of Political Research*, 19)

Newman, M (1996): *Democracy, Sovereignty and the European Union* (London, Hurst & Company)

Nicholl, W (1994): "Representing the States" in Duff, A; Pinder, J & Pryce, R (eds): *Maastricht and Beyond* (London & New York, Routledge)

Niedermayer. O (1995): "Trends and Contrasts" in Niedermayer, O and Sinnott, R (eds): *Public Opinion and Internationalized Governance* (Oxford, OUP)

Niedermayer, O and Sinnott, R (1995): introduction to Niedermayer, O and Sinnott, R (eds): *Public Opinion and Internationalized Governance* (Oxford, OUP)

Nugent, N (1995): "The leadership capacity of the European Commission" (*Journal of European Public Policy* 2 (4) December pp 603-623)

Nugent, N (1994): *The Government and Politics of the European Union* (Basingstoke, Macmillan)

Nye, R A (1977): *The Anti-Democratic Sources of Elite Theory* (London, Sage)

Olson, M (1971): *The Logic of Collective Action* (Boston, Harvard University Press)

O'Neill, N (1995): "Crisis or Opportunity: Regional and Local Government" (Discussion paper of the Jean Monnet Group of Experts, published by the Centre for European Union Studies, University of Hull, England, in conjunction with the Representation of the European Commission in the United Kingdom)

Page, E C & Wouters, L (1994): "Bureaucratic Politics and Political Leadership in Brussels" (*Public Administration* 72 (3) pp 445-459)

Pareto, V (1923) (1976): *Sociological Writings* (Oxford, Blackwell)

Parliamentary Monitoring Service (1996): PMS *Parliamentary Companion* (London, PMS Publications Ltd in association with Parliamentary Monitoring Service Ltd and Parliamentary and EU News Service Issue Number 26, January)

Parry, G; Moyser, G & Day, N (1992): *Political Participation and Democracy in Britain* (Cambridge, Cambridge University Press)

Pateman, C (1972): *Participation and Democratic Theory* (Cambridge, Cambridge University Press)

Pearce, C (1980): *The Machinery of Change in Local Government 1888-1974* (London, Allen & Unwin

Peterson, J (1995a): "Playing the Transparency Game: Consultation and Policy-making in the European Commission" (*Public Administration* 73 (3) pp 473-493)

Peterson, J (1995b): "Decision-making in the European Union: towards a framework for analysis" (*Journal of European Public Policy* (2) (1))

Peterson, J (1994): "Subsidiarity: A Definition to Suit Any Vision?" (*Parliamentary Affairs*, 47 (1) pp 116-132)

Peterson, J (1991): "Technology Policy in Europe: Explaining the Framework Programme and Eureka in Theory and Practice" (*Journal of Common Market Policies* (29) PP 269-290)

Petite, M (1998): "The Treaty of Amsterdam" (Harvard University on-line papers http://www.law.harvard.edu/Programs/JeanMonnet/papers/98/98-2-05.htm:

Philip, A B (1994): "Old Policies and New Competences" in Duff, A; Pinder, J & Pryce, R (eds): *Maastricht and Beyond* (London & New York, Routledge)

Phillips, A (1992): "Must feminists give up on democracy?" in Held, D (ed): *Prospects for Democracy* (Cambridge, Polity Press)

Pinder, J (1994): "Building the Union: Policy, Reform, Constitution" in Duff, Andrew, Pinder, John and Pryce, Roy (eds): *Maastricht and Beyond* (London & New York, Routledge)

Plamenatz, J (1973): *Democracy and Illusion* (Harlow, Longman)

Plant, R (1994): (*Guardian* 7 December)

Plato (c 375 BC) (1948): *The Republic* (London, Everyman)

Pollitt, C (1986): "Democracy and Bureaucracy" in Held, D & Pollitt, C (eds): *New Forms of Democracy* (London, Sage)

Popper, K (1991): *The Open Society and its Enemies – Vol I: The Spell of Plato* (London & New York, Routledge)

Popper, K (1974): *The Open Society and its Enemies – Vol II: The High Tide of Prophecy: Hegel and Marx* (London, Routledge & Kegan Paul, 1974)

Preston, J (1997): "Sub-National Mobilization and the Committee of the Regions: Implications for National/Sub-National Government" (Paper presented at the Second UACES Research Conference, Loughborough University, 10/12 September 1997, cited by permission of the author)

Preston, M (1996): "Openness and the European Union Institutions" (*European Access* (4))

Prior, D (1995): "Citizen's Charters" in Stewart, J and Stoker, G: *Local Government in the 1990s* (Basingstoke, Macmillan)

Pryce, R (1994): "The Treaty Negotiations" in Duff, A; Pinder, J & Pryce, R (eds): *Maastricht and Beyond* (London & New York, Routledge)

Puddephatt, A (1996): addressing PAC Conference, Northumbria University, 4 September

Pycroft, C (1995): "The Organisation of Local Authorities' European Activities" (*Journal of Public Policy and Administration* 10 (4) pp 20-33)

Redcliffe-Maud (1969): *Royal Commission on Local Government in England 1966-1969* (HMSO)

Reif, K & Niedermayer, O (1993): "The European Parliament and Political Parties" (*Journal of European Integration* 10 (2-2) pp 157-172)

Rhodes, R A W; Bache, I and George, S (1996): "Policy Networks and Policy-Making in the European Union: A Critical Appraisal" in Hooghe, L ed: *Cohesion Policy and European Integration* (Clarendon Press, Oxford)

Richie, M (1995): (*European Voice*, 23-29 November)

Rousseau, J-J (1762, 1750, 1755) (1990): *The Social Contract* and *Discourse* (London, Everyman)

Rowsell, P (Assistant Secretary, Local Government Division II, Department of the Environment, London) (1995): "The UK Government and the CoR" (presentation given at a conference held at the University of Birmingham, November)

Sabine G (1963): *A History of Political Theory* – 3rd edition (London, Harrap)

Sartori, G (1987): *The Theory of Democracy Revisited* (London, Chatham House)

Scharpf, F W (1994): "Community and autonomy: multi-level policy-making in the European Union" (*Journal of European Public Policy* 1 (2) pp 219-242)

Schumpeter, J (1976): *Capitalism, Socialism and Democracy* (London, Allen and Unwin Ltd)

Scott, P (1994): "Education Policy" in Kavanagh, D & Seldon, A (eds): *The Major Effect* (Basingstoke, Macmillan)

Scott, A, Peterson, J & Millar, D (1994): "Subsidiarity: A "European of the Regions" v. the British Constitution?" (*Journal of Common Market Studies*, 32 (1))

Shklar, J (1969): *Men and Citizens* (Cambridge, Cambridge University Press)

Sinn, H-W (1994): "How much Europe? Subsidiarity, Centralization and Fiscal Competition (*Scottish Journal of Political Economy*, 41 (1) pp 85-107)

Smith, B C (1985): *Decentralisation: the Territorial Dimension of the State* (London, Allen & Unwin)

Smith, S (1986): "Reasons of State" in Held, D & Pollitt, C (eds): *New Forms of Democracy* (London, Sage)

Spicker, P (1996): "Concepts of Subsidiarity in the European Community" (*Current Politics and Economics in Europe*, V, 2/3 pp 163-175

Spinelli, A (1966): *The Eurocrats* (Baltimore, John Hopkins Press, 1966)

Stedman Jones, G (1983): *Languages of Class* (Cambridge, Cambridge University Press)

Steppat, S (1988): "Execution of functions by the European Parliament in its first electoral period" (*Journal of European Integration* 12 (1) pp 5-35)

Stevens, C (1995): "Decentralization: a meaningless concept?" (*Public Policy and Administration* 10 (4))

Stewart, J, Kendall, E; Coote, A (1994): *Citizens' Juries* (IPPR)

Stewart, J & Stoker, G (1995): "Fifteen Years of Local Government Restructuring 1979-1994: An Evaluation" in Stewart, J and Stoker, G: *Local Government in the 1990s* (Basingstoke, Macmillan)

Stewart, J & Stoker, G (1989): *The Future of Local Government* (Basingstoke, Macmillan)

Stoker, G (1990): "Government beyond Whitehall" in Dunleavy P *et al* (eds): *Developments in British Politics III* (Basingstoke, Macmillan)

Stoker, G (1988): *The Politics of Local Government* (Basingstoke, Macmillan Education)

Straw, J (1994): "Abolish the Royal Prerogative" in Barnett, Anthony (ed): *Power and the Throne* (London, Vintage, in association with Charter 88)

Taylor, K (1995): "European Union: The Challenge for Local and Regional Government" (*Political Quarterly* 66 (1) pp 74-83)

The Stationery Office (1999): *European Parliamentary Elections Act 1999* (London, The Stationery Office Limited ISBN 0 10 540199 4) Crown copyright 1999 with the permission of the Controller of Her Majesty's Stationery Office

The Stationery Office (1999): *Local Government Act 1999* (London, The Stationery Office Limited, ISBN 0 10 542799 3) Crown copyright 1999 with the permission of the Controller of Her Majesty's Stationery Office

The Stationery Office (1999): *Greater London Authority Bill* (London, the Stationery Office Limited)

The Stationery Office (1999): *House of Lords Bill* (London, the Stationery Office Limited)

The Stationery Office (1999): draft *Freedom of Information Bill* (London, the Stationery Office Limited)

The Stationery Office (1999): draft *Local Government (Organisation and Standards) Bill* (London, the Stationery Office Limited)

The Stationery Office (1998) *Government of Wales Act 1998* (London, The Stationery Office Limited ISBN 0 10 543898 7) Crown copyright 1998 with the permission of the Controller of Her Majesty's Stationery Office

The Stationery Office (1998): *the Greater London Authority (Referendum) Act 1998* (London, The Stationery Office Limited, ISBN 0 10 540398 9) Crown copyright 1998 with the permission of the Controller of Her Majesty's Stationery Office

The Stationery Office (1998): *the Human Rights Act 1998* (London, The Stationery Office Limited ISBN 0 10 544298 4) Crown copyright 1998 with the permission of the Controller of Her Majesty's Stationery Office

The Stationery Office (1998): *the Northern Ireland (Elections) Act 1998* (London, The Stationery Office Limited, ISBN 0 10 541298 8) Crown copyright 1998 with the permission of the Controller of Her Majesty's Stationery Office

The Stationery Office (1998): *the Regional Development Agencies Act 1998* (London, The Stationery Office Limited, ISBN 0 10 544598 3) Crown copyright 1998 with the permission of the Controller of Her Majesty's Stationery Office

The Stationery Office (1998): *the Scotland Act 1998* (London, The Stationery Office Limited, ISBN 0 10 544698 X) Crown copyright 1998 with the permission of the Controller of Her Majesty's Stationery Office

The Stationery Office (1997): *the Referendums (Scotland and Wales) Act 1997* (London, The Stationery Office Limited, ISBN 0 10 546197 0) Crown copyright 1997 with the permission of the Controller of Her Majesty's Stationery Office

Thompson, I & Mather, J (1999): "Guide to EU documentation" (*Journal of Common Market Studies, Annual Review of Activities*)

Thucydides (c 420-404 BC) (1972): *History of the Peloponnesian War* (London, Penguin)

Tocqueville, A de (1850) (1980): *On Democracy, Revolution and Society* (eds: Stone, J & Mennell, S) (Chicago, University of Michegan)

Ullman, W (1975): *Medieval Political Thought* (Harmondsworth, Penguin)

Urwin, D (1982): "Territorial Structure and Political Developments in the United Kingdom" in Rokkan, S & Urwin, D W (eds): *The Politics of Territorial Identity – Studies in European Regionalism* (London, Sage)

Van Caenegem, R C (1999): "Medieval Flanders and the Seeds of Modern Democracy in Pinder, J: *Foundations of Democracy in the European Union: from the Genesis of Parliamentary Democracy to the European Parliament* (Basingstoke, Macmillan)

Van Kersbergen, K & Verbeek, B (1994): "The Politics of Subsidiarity in the European Union" (*Journal of Common Market Studies*, 32 (2) pp 215-236)

Verney, S and Featherstone, K (1996): "Greece" in Lodge, J (ed): *The 1994 Elections to the European Parliament* (London, Pinter)

Wallace, W (1994): "Rescue or Retreat? The Nation State in Western Europe, 1945-1993" (*Political Studies*, 42 – Special issue pp 52-76)

Walzer, M (1983): *Spheres of Justice* (Oxford, Blackwell)

Ware, A (1992): "Liberal democracy: One form or many?" in Held, D (ed): *Prospects for Democracy* (Cambridge, Polity Press)

Ware, A (1986): "Political Parties" in Held, D & Pollitt, C (eds): *New Forms of Democracy* (London, Sage)

Warleigh, A (1999): *The Committee of the Regions: institutionalising multi-level governance?* (London, Kogan Page)

Warleigh, A (1997): "A Committee of No Importance?" (*Politics* 17 (2) pp 101-107)

Weale, A (1997): "Democratic Theory and the Constitutional Politics of the European Union" (*Journal of European Public Policy* 4 (4) pp 665-669)

Weiler, J H H (1992): "After Maastricht: Community Legitimacy in Post-1992 Europe" in Adams, W J (ed): *Singular Europe – Economy and Polity of the European Community after 1992* (Chicago, University of Michegan Press)

Westlake, M (1995): "The European parliament, the national parliaments and the 1996 Intergovernmental Conference" (*Political Quarterly* 66 (1) pp 59-73)

Westlake, M (1994): *The Commission and the Parliament* (London, Butterworths)

Widdicombe, D (1986): *The Conduct of Local Authority Business: Report of the Committee of Enquiry into the Conduct of Local Authority Business* (HMSO)

Williams, S (1994): "A Citizen Monarchy" Barnett, A (ed): *Power and the Throne* (London, Vintage, in association with Charter 88)

Willis, M (1995): "Community Care and Social Services" in Stewart, J and Stoker, G: *Local Government in the 1990s* (Basingstoke, Macmillan)

Wishlade, F (1996): "EU Cohesion Policy: Facts, Figures and Issues" in Hooghe, L ed: *Cohesion Policy and European Integration* (Clarendon Press, Oxford)

Wistrich, E (1994): *The United States of Europe* (London, Routledge)

Wood, A (ed) (1989): *The Times Guide to the European Parliament 1989* (London, Harper Collins)

Wright, T (1994): *Citizens and Subjects* (London, Routledge)

Young, K (1994): "Local Government" in Kavanagh, D & Seldon, A (eds): *The Major Effect* (Basingstoke, Macmillan)

Young, K (1983): "Beyond Centralism" in Young, K (ed): *National Interests and Local Government* (London, Heinemann)

Zander, M (1989): *The Law-making process* – 3rd Edition (London, Weidenfeld and Nicolson)

Zolo, D (1992): *Democracy and Complexity* (Cambridge, Polity Press)

INDEX